The Candle and the Guillotine

BERGHAHN MONOGRAPHS IN FRENCH STUDIES

Editor: **Michael Scott Christofferson**, Associate Professor and Chair of Department of History, Adelphi University

France has played a central role in the emergence of the modern world. The Great French Revolution of 1789 contributed decisively to political modernity, and the Paris of Baudelaire did the same for culture. Because of its rich intellectual and cultural traditions, republican democracy, imperial past and post-colonial present, twentieth-century experience of decline and renewal, and unique role in world affairs, France and its history remain important today. This series publishes monographs that offer significant methodological and empirical contributions to our understanding of the French experience and its broader role in the making of the modern world.

Recent volumes:

Volume 17
The Candle and the Guillotine:
Revolution and Justice in Lyon, 1789–1793
Julie Patricia Johnson

Volume 16
A Human Garden: French Policy and the Transatlantic Legacies of Eugenic Experimentation
Paul-André Rosental

Volume 15
National Policy, Global Memory: The Commemoration of the "Righteous" from Jerusalem to Paris, 1942–2007
Sarah Gensburger

Volume 14
At Home in Postwar France: Modern Mass Housing and the Right to Comfort
Nicole C. Rudolph

Volume 13
General de Gaulle's Cold War:
Challenging American Hegemony, 1963–1968
Garret Joseph Martin

Volume 12
Building a European Identity: France, the United States, and the Oil Shock 1973–1974
Aurélie Élisa Gfeller

Volume 11
France in the Age of Organization: Factory, Home and Nation from the 1920s to Vichy
Jackie Clarke

Volume 10
Collective Terms: Race, Culture, and Community in a State-Planned City in France
Beth S. Epstein

Volume 9
Mitterrand, the End of the Cold War, and German Unification
Frédéric Bozo

Volume 8
Shades of Indignation: Political Scandals in France, Past and Present
Paul Jankowski

For a full volume listing, please see the series page on our website:
https://berghahnbooks.com/series/monographs-in-french-studies

THE CANDLE AND THE GUILLOTINE
Revolution and Justice in Lyon, 1789–1793

Julie Patricia Johnson

NEW YORK • OXFORD
www.berghahnbooks.com

First published in 2020 by
Berghahn Books
www.berghahnbooks.com

© 2020, 2026 Julie Patricia Johnson
First paperback edition published in 2026

All rights reserved.
Except for the quotation of short passages
for the purposes of criticism and review, no part of this book
may be reproduced in any form or by any means, electronic or
mechanical, including photocopying, recording, or any information
storage and retrieval system now known or to be invented,
without written permission of the publisher.

Library of Congress Cataloging-in-Publication Data
Names: Johnson, Julie Patricia, author.
Title: The candle and the guillotine : revolution and justice in Lyon, 1789-93 / Julie Patricia Johnson.
Other titles: Revolution and justice in Lyon, 1789-93
Description: New York : Berghahn, 2020. | Includes bibliographical references and index.
Identifiers: LCCN 2020006136 (print) | LCCN 2020006137 (ebook) | ISBN 9781789206760 (hardback) | ISBN 9781789206777 (ebook)
Subjects: LCSH: Lyon (France)--History--18th century. | France--History--Reign of Terror, 1793-1794. | France--History--Revolution, 1789-1799. | Criminal justice, Administration of--France--History--18th century.
Classification: LCC DC195.L9 J64 2020 (print) | LCC DC195.L9 (ebook) | DDC 944/.5823041--dc23
LC record available at https://lccn.loc.gov/2020006136
LC ebook record available at https://lccn.loc.gov/2020006137

British Library Cataloguing in Publication Data
A catalogue record for this book is available from the British Library.

EU GPSR Authorized Representative
LOGOS EUROPE, 9 rue Nicolas Poussin, 17000, LA ROCHELLE, France
Email: Contact@logoseurope.eu

ISBN 978-1-78920-676-0 hardback
ISBN 978-1-83695-374-6 paperback
ISBN 978-1-83695-375-3 epub
ISBN 978-1-78920-677-7 web pdf

https://doi.org/10.3167/9781789206760

Pour Luca, mon petit fils Lyonnais

Contents

List of Illustrations	ix
Acknowledgements	xi
Introduction	1

Part I. Inspirations

Chapter 1
The Most Polished Town — 11

Chapter 2
Life in the Country — 24

Chapter 3
Crises and Revolution — 37

Chapter 4
The Candle Flares — 47

Part II. Aspirations

Chapter 5
Patriots and Traitors — 65

Chapter 6
'A Lively Political Milieu' in Lyon — 83

Chapter 7
New Judges — 100

Chapter 8
The First Republic — 114

Part III. Retributions

Chapter 9
Trials and Emotions … 129

Chapter 10
Prison Wars … 145

Chapter 11
Ousting of the Jacobins … 158

Chapter 12
Bastille Day, 1793 … 175

Chapter 13
Terror in Lyon … 188

Conclusion … 198

Glossary of Terms … 203

Glossary of Names … 206

Bibliography … 209

Index … 219

Illustrations

Figure 0.1 *Destruction des édifices de Lyon* (Destruction of the Facades of Lyon). — 4

Figure 1.1 *Plan géometral de Lyon*, 1789 (Map of Lyon). — 12

Figure 2.1 *Maison d'Ampère* (Ampère home – now the Musée d'Ampère). — 27

Figure 2.2 *La Gruerie Poleymieux* (The Forestry Court). — 29

Figure 4.1 *Jean-Marie Roland de la Platière*. — 51

Figure 4.2 The route to the local church. — 56

Figure 5.1 Castle tower remains, Poleymieux. — 72

Figure 5.2 *Seigneur Guillin Dumontet*. — 74

Figure 5.3 Judicial systems in the departments of France; flow chart, 1791–93. — 77

Figure 6.1 Théâtre des Célestins (constructed in 1792). — 86

Figure 6.2 Detail of map of Lyon. — 89

Figure 7.1 *La prison de Roanne* (The Prison of Roanne). — 101

Figure 7.2 Joseph Chalier, leading magistrate in the Tribunal de District and member of the Jacobin Club. — 104

Figure 9.1 *Le pont Morand du quai de Retz et les Brotteaux* (The Morand Bridge from the Rhône River). 138

Figure 11.1 *La Liberté et l'Egalité* (Liberty and Equality), 1793. 167

Figure 13.1 *Carte Siege de Lyon* (Map of Siege of Lyon). 189

Figure 13.2 *Tribunal révolutionnaire de Lyon* (Revolutionary Tribunal of Lyon). 194

Figure 13.3 *Mitraillade des Lyonnais aux Brotteaux* (Massacre of Lyonnais at Brotteaux). 195

Figure 14.1 *Chalier partant de sa prison* (Chalier leaving his prison). 201

Acknowledgements

Lyon is a wonderfully historic city. Wandering its crooked streets, climbing its slopes and gazing at its beautiful buildings have all been a great pleasure. Imagining the people who actually lived and worked behind the facades over the ages has been fascinating. But piecing together the emotions and the conflicts of a period as dynamic as that of the French Revolution has been especially rewarding. The Lyonnais rioted and discussed, suffered and triumphed in their own inimitable way through this time, and I hope this book gives the reader some sense of the four tumultuous years it deals with. I have been very lucky to have studied at Melbourne University under the supervision of Peter McPhee, who helped me understand how people of different backgrounds, classes and genders experienced this most transformative of times. Through him, I have been introduced to some of the foremost French historians from around the world, including Marisa Linton, Timothy Tackett and Michel Biard, all of whom helped inform my thinking about the Revolution. I am also appreciative of the advice and help from Robert Aldrich, Malcolm Crook, Paul Hanson, Steven Clay and Julie Fedor during my thesis project and afterwards from Greg Burgess. I wish I had had the privilege of meeting Bill Edmonds, who wrote about Lyon before I did. I am sure we would have had some fascinating discussions.

A travel scholarship from the University of Melbourne helped fund my preliminary trip to Lyon and a further scholarship, provided by Helen Davies, enabled a subsequent productive trip to the archives. I am grateful to the friendly and supportive staff of the golden Archives départementales du Rhône and to those at the Bibliothèque municipal de Lyon. Both institutions went beyond their remit in helping me find relevant documents and welcomed me back enthusiastically whenever I managed to visit Lyon. I am grateful to staff and friends of the Musée d'Ampère, Poleymieux, including M. Dûrr and M. Bernard Pallandre, who have helped me understand Ampère *père*. Staff of the Musée Gadagne in Lyon provided important material and information from their collections in an expeditious and helpful way as did the Musée de Beaux-Arts. I want also to thank Chris Chappell and the series editor at Berghahn for their advice and help in ensuring the book was the best possible version, and I accept that any remaining errors are my own.

My inspiring family helped me survive the ups and downs of the research and study behind this book. I am grateful to Gemma and Fred, who gave me a room of my own in Lyon and set me off each day in the right direction; to Kate and Adrian, who helped me tease out historical conundrums and questions; to Tess and Chris and Amelia for their never flagging encouragement, help and positivity; and to Vic for encouraging and supporting me along the way.

Introduction

On 22 January 1794, a Prussian, Frédéric-Christian Laukhard, arrived in Lyon with a small group of *sans-culottes* he had befriended. He wanted to join the 'good cause' of revolution and had heard there were other Germans there who had formed a battalion. On the way, he noticed the 'terrified' inhabitants they passed. They 'hardly dared open their mouths, afraid that a word would slip out that the *sans-culottes* could interpret as being counter-revolutionary or favourable to aristocrats and which would mean an order of death'.[1] Once in the city, and left to his own devices, Laukhard was confronted with 'misery and destruction':

> Entire rows of houses, always the most beautiful had been burnt, churches, convents ruined. When I reached the guillotine the blood of those executed several hours earlier was still running in the square.

The Prussian gradually became 'filled with horror' and asked those living nearby whether it would not be the decent thing to clean up human blood. 'Why should we?', someone replied, 'It is the blood of aristocrats and rebels. It is the dogs who should lick it up.'[2] Those he met continued to talk of the guillotine as a *joujou* (toy) and suggested he come the next day or the following day to see it in action.

The fortunes of the city had shifted enormously from the earliest years of the French Revolution when one resident, Jean-Jacques Ampere and his brilliant son André-Marie, had watched 'candle in hand' as the new democratic institutions began to operate.[3] Jean-Jacques had soon after left his son in the company of the seventeen volumes of the Encyclopédie of the Enlightenment era that had inspired the family while he took up a post as an elected magistrate. He would gradually become embroiled in political events leading to the guillotine being set up in the central square of the city. The 'candle' and the 'guillotine' bookend the changing experience of the French Revolution, as it touched the lives of the people of Lyon. From the enthusiasms of 1789 to the horrors of the guillotine that

Laukhard described, little more than four years had elapsed. It is these fraught years that this book examines.

Lyon was a city that had engaged passionately with the revolutionary changes of 1789. It had lively entrepreneurs like Joseph Chalier, who was bursting with ideas for how the city should grow. It had 'enlightened' bourgeois, like one Jean-Jacques Ampère, anxious to guide their own education and the education of their children by frequenting the libraries, the bookshops and the theatre. Both Chalier and Ampère were among the conscientious and capable men elected to judicial office with a new vision for society and who would go on to apply the new revolutionary laws. They became citizen magistrates when elected to the innovative role of the *juge de paix* (justice of the peace) from 1791. This position of functionary was responsible for the crucial changes in the delivery of justice. Although inspired by the English system of magistrates, the powers of the position went much further. The incumbents were elected and paid by the state and expected to provide direct justice for citizens at all levels of the new legal edifice. My book has a particular focus on these judges because their election was widely seen as one of the most important of the democratic changes then instituted, as authors like Melvyn Edelstein and Malcolm Crook have highlighted.[4] But the position also invited new and important questions about the rule of law that had been envisaged at the time of the French Revolution.

Municipal and judicial officers elected at the end of 1791 had every reason to hope that their hard work and enthusiasm in setting up a new judicial regime would be successful and would obviate the need for 'popular' violence that had erupted at various points of the Revolution. However, confusion between legal procedure and real justice emerged during the turbulent years of 1792 and 1793 and would lead eventually to grave consequences for the city. The judges themselves became divided along political lines. The need to uncover fanaticism and conspiracies among rival factions in the day-to-day interpretation and implementation of their work gradually overtook the belief in an innate justice that many of those elected had originally expected. This book will attempt to understand how the enthusiasm for justice of the Lyonnais magistrates turned into an obsession with 'conspiracies' and 'fanaticisms' that then led to civil war and the 'terror' that threatened the citizens of Lyon.

While in hindsight we can see the problems inherent in contradictory interpretations of the 'rule of law', no such problem was anticipated by those who championed and helped enact the new changes. By following the trajectories of those Lyonnais elected as judges, we can see how the passions and enthusiasms of early revolutionary 'choosers' gradually deepened into bitter divisions as political rivalries grew in the city. The more radical Jacobin leaders elected at the end of 1792 suspected hidden 'aristocratic' agendas. They asked whether new insidious crimes that threatened the state itself were being dealt with too leniently by judges disguising their own vested interests. The more conservative judges however saw the danger of a total collapse of law and order if procedures and rules were not followed.

These questions about how the new 'rule of law' would operate in a revolutionary state are critically important to any understanding of the 'Terror' that has often been seen as a deliberate and inflexible policy of the radical Jacobins applied as law in 1793–94. The city of Lyon was believed at the time to be a leader in the 'federalist' revolt against the nation and thus deserving of the most extreme condemnation. Although the charge of 'federalism' has been contested recently, Lyon is still viewed as one of the most tragic examples of what has been called the 'Terror'.[5] Georges Couthon, a member of the powerful 'Committee of Twelve' in Paris, came to Lyon in October 1793. His instructions were to oversee the subjugation of the city after its capitulation. He began by symbolically attacking the buildings in the grandiose square of Bellecour with a silver hammer. He was an invalid and wielded the hammer from a wooden wheelchair as he proclaimed the actions to be taken against the city. First among them was the order that the 'sumptuous houses' in the square, their gardens and statues would be destroyed. Eight hundred workers were immediately engaged to commence demolition of the facades of the richest buildings here as well as many of the fortifications that protected the city.[6] Couthon also decreed that 'severe' punishment was to be visited on the people of Lyon for 'having caused the national army to take action against them'.[7] Those found with arms in the city, as well as all the *juges de paix* and municipal functionaries who had been active in their positions from June and throughout the two-month siege that had begun in September, were arrested. Notices affixed to the city walls under Couthon's authority warned that: 'terror should be awakened in the souls of the brigands and traitors.'[8]

For some historians, the 'Terror' has been seen as a tactic used by the radical revolutionaries in Paris – those usually associated with Maximilien Robespierre – to 'radicalize the conflict, create new dangers and new fractures' in their ongoing quest for political power.[9] While at first Couthon's use of the word 'terror' seems to validate the idea that France had entered into such a 'Reign of Terror', with Lyon an example of the increasingly harsh measures taken to consolidate the Jacobin Republic, this theory has been recently challenged. Michel Biard has questioned the utility of writing 'terror' with a capital 'T' when at the time it was only ever used with a lower case 't'.[10] Timothy Tackett has highlighted the deep convictions and

Figure 0.1 *Destruction des édifices de Lyon* (Destruction of the Facades of Lyon). Engraving by Georges Touchard-Lafosse, inv. SN 299 © Musée Gadagne (Lyon).

volatile emotions of the period that better explain terroristic episodes, and Marisa Linton has shown how many of the deputies themselves were the most terrorised because of such emotions. Both Tackett and Linton suggest that emotions of the period were exacerbated by fears of 'conspiracy', a very real and enduring fear, which adequately explains the use of contingency laws among the revolutionaries rather than a more intractable policy of 'Terror'.[11] Peter McPhee has most recently surmised that the retrospective use of the concept of 'Terror' to describe the revolutionary period has too easily been accepted because of modern descriptions of Islamist terrorists as latter day 'neo-Jacobins'.[12]

Understanding the 'mental world' of the revolutionary period has been seen as crucial by other historians. Robert Darnton argued that punishments meted out to those guilty of crimes well before the Revolution had been brutal, and the language of this world continued to be used to respond to fears of conspiracy and counterrevolution as they were then perceived.[13] Ian Coller has shown how the emotion of 'enthusiasm' could have a positive connotation when it was pursued with 'disinterest', but it also had the potential to develop into 'fanaticism' in its negative connotation, the powerful feeling that clouded judgement and was decried by Voltaire.[14] Looking at the language used by the Lyonnais judges in this way, we do see 'enthusiasm' in its positive sense evident among those who took on the new judicial and municipal offices in Lyon from 1791 and who remained in office until 1793. It was clearly an emotion of the revolutionary period and was considered to be troublesome only when 'it tipped over' into the 'fanaticism' that we also subsequently see with many of the accused who came before the military tribunals, established soon after Couthon's visit. New fears and passions were engaged among the citizenry of Lyon as political factionalism grew in 1792 and 1793, and the judges of the period appear to have felt the same fears and passions as other citizens of the time. Increasingly, they used words like 'conspiracy', 'fanaticism' and 'terror' to explain their decisions in the revolutionary courts.

Couthon's use of the language of 'terror' when he was sent to Lyon in early October was referencing the discussion before the Convention on 5 September 1793. National deputies were suggesting that 'terror' should be the 'order of the day' and that it should be the required response to internal troubles.[15] In this discussion, terror was seen as a positive force empowering the Republic against those who appeared to be conspiring against the nation. Ronald Schechter has suggested the revolutionaries at this time 'characterised terror as a property of the law, deeming it exemplary, restraining and therefore "salutary"'.[16] And because Lyon was suspected of having broken away from the one and indivisible Republic to become such an enemy in need of restraint, a policy of 'terror' was called for. The strongly felt 'convictions' of the period appear to have provided an 'explosive combination' when mixed with the prevailing 'circumstances'. In the words of Peter McPhee, they justified a policy of 'Revolution until the peace' against internal and external enemies.[17].

Many books have been written about the debates and the personalities of Paris during the Revolution, but few recent books have looked at the important provincial cities like Lyon or personalities who lived there rather than in the capital.[18] The judicial archives in Lyon are voluminous, and we can find in them the history of less well-known provincial magistrates like Chalier and Ampère. The reader can then appreciate the revolutionary experience of some 'enlightened' actors, who, although having similar backgrounds, came to astonishingly different views about the law and exceptional justice, which culminated in a turn to violence. The events in Lyon appear to have triggered many of the profound fears of the time. Yet, the impressions of Laukhard also show vividly the extent of the tragedy that befell Lyon and directly raise the question of why and how Lyon and its inhabitants were so harshly dealt with. To understand the decision to use 'terror' to subdue Lyon, we thus need to revisit what happened in the city from the very earliest stages of the Revolution.

Notes

1. W. Bauer (Trad.) *Un Allemand en France sous la Terreur: Souvenirs de Frédéric-Christian Laukhard* (Paris: Perrin, 1915), 269.
2. Bauer, *Un Allemand en France*, 272.
3. See the Historic note, 14 December 1790 signed by Ryard, where municipal officers searching his home in Poleymieux stated that Ampère had been more than willing to show them his property and had accompanied them 'candle in hand' to the peripheries of his courtyard; quoted by L. Dupré-Latour, *Bulletin de la Société des Amis d'André-Marie* 3, 58.
4. M. Edelstein, *The French Revolution and the Birth of Electoral Democracy* (Farnham, Surrey; Burlington, UT: Ashgate 2014), 282. M. Crook, *Elections in the French Revolution: An Apprenticeship in Democracy, 1789–1799* (Cambridge and NY: Cambridge University Press, 1996).
5. The most comprehensive analysis of the 'federalist' revolts that suggests they were neither 'federalist' nor 'royalist' in their original motivation is contained in P. Hanson, *The Jacobin Republic Under Fire: The Federalist Revolt in the French Revolution* (University Park, PA: Pennsylvania State University Press, 2003), 100.
6. E. Herriot, *Lyon n'est plus: La repression*, vol. 3 (Paris: Hachette, 1939), 49.
7. Herriot, *Lyon n'est plus*, vol. 3, 5.
8. G. Couthon, 14 October 1793, Archives départemental du Rhône [hereinafter ADR] 1 L 981.
9. P. Gueniffey, *La politique de la Terreur: Essai sur la violence révolutionnaire 1789–1794* (Paris, 2000), 338.
10. M. Biard and H. Leuwers (eds), *Visages de la Terreur* (Paris: Armand Colin, 2014), 5–7.
11. T. Tackett, *The Coming of the Terror in the French Revolution* (Cambridge, MA: Belknap Press, HUP, 2015). M. Linton, *Choosing Terror: Virtue, Friendship and Authenticity in the French Revolution* (Oxford: OUP, 2013).
12. M. Biard et al. 'Analyser "la Terreur" dans l'historiographie Anglophone', *Annales Historiques de la Révolution française* 2 (2018), 143–144.
13. R. Darnton, *The Kiss of Lamourette: Reflections in Cultural History* (New York: W.W. Norton, 1990), 11–20.
14. Presentation of Ian Coller, 'Turbans of Liberty: Revolutionary Emotions and Global Emotions', Conference, *Society of French Historical Studies* 10 May 2018.
15. Patrice Gueniffey suggests 1793 was merely the 'official' commencement of 'The Terror', it having actually begun with the exceptional laws of 1791 against émigres: *La politique de la Terreur*, 15.
16. R. Schechter, *A Genealogy of Terror in Eighteenth Century France* (Chicago and London: University of Chicago Press, 2018).
17. McPhee, *Liberty or Death: The French Revolution* (New Haven, CT and London: Yale University Press, 2016), 270–73.

18. The best analyses of Lyon and the Revolution are now somewhat dated: Camille Riffaterre, *Le Mouvement antijacobin et antiparisien à Lyon et dans le Rhône-et-Loire en 1793, 29 mai-15 aôut*, tome 1 (Lyon, 1912), the four volumes of Edouard Herriot, *Lyon n'est plus* and W.D. Edmonds, *Jacobinism and the Revolt of Lyon, 1789–1793* (New York: OUP, 1990).

Part I

INSPIRATIONS

Chapter 1

THE MOST POLISHED TOWN

> Lyon was distinguished before the revolution not only as a place of manufacture, but as a place of literature and science.
>
> — Anne Plumtre, 1810

A writer by the name of Anne Plumtre took advantage of the Peace of Amiens in 1801 to travel from England to see for herself what changes the Revolution had made in France. She was especially interested in the provinces, and in addition to a period of residence in Paris, she made an extended stay in Lyon. Plumtre found the region to be very 'different' and more inspiring than the observations of travellers, who only visited Paris and did not stay anywhere long enough to become 'habituated' to the people.[1] Plumtre got to know the Lyonnais and was most interested in their stories, especially as they related to the period leading to the Revolution. Lyon, she observed, was 'reckoned before the Revolution, the most polished town in France, after Paris' with its buildings, its academies, its theatre, its famous college and library, and these famous landmarks were still to be admired when she lived there. She estimated its population at some 120,000 (historians now suggest it was more like 150,000), many of whom were involved in the lucrative silk trade, which had become the predominant industry.[2] The city, its trade and its population, she noted, had been uniquely affected by the Revolution. To appreciate how Lyon navigated the changes the Revolution brought, we do need to imagine what life there looked like at the time.

Silk had become the predominant trade in Lyon from its origins in 1562 and was known generically and simply as 'La Fabrique'. Lyon had

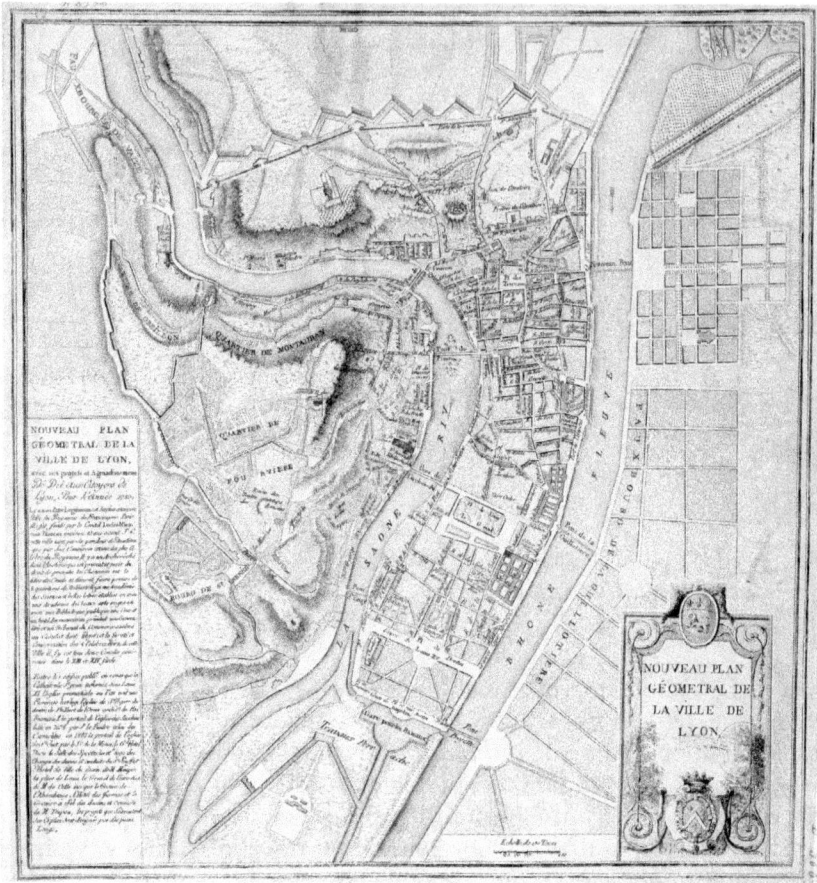

Figure 1.1 *Plan géometral de Lyon*, 1789 (Map of Lyon). Bibliothèque Municipale de Lyon.

grown to become the largest provincial city in France because of this trade in silk, and a number of important consequences flowed. Because silk was a commodity needed for the court of the French kings and for other European courts, it meant the city gained a sort of notoriety and uniqueness. By the time of the Revolution, this notoriety was not one the citizens welcomed. The special status gained by the city for producing the luxurious fabric of silk for the royal court encouraged various careers in the silk industry, but there was less opportunity for other occupations. No university or *parlement* (independent court) was established here. There were also fewer noble families in the city but an influential mercantile elite who flourished because of the silk trade. These unique characteristics of the emphasis on a mono-industry were not considered a problem until a series of crises impacted the production of silk from 1782. Until then, the benefits of a creative and large workforce were widely admired. 'Universal' fairs were held here four times a year, when merchants from overseas and from within France congregated in the city to buy and sell wares.[3] 'Thousands of workshops' operated to supply elaborately worked fabric, which was sold by the 'hundreds of merchants' of the city.[4] Silk was by far the biggest export of the city, and at the time of the Revolution the trade extended to North Russia, Germany, the Levant and to a lesser extent to Spain and Italy.[5]

The richer silk merchants at first hung their *blasons* inscribed with their coat of arms in the most coveted addresses of the Rue Juiverie in the Saint-Paul area of the old city (Vieux Lyon).[6] Financial transactions took place in a palatial building known as the Loge de Change, close to the Saône River, and there were many turreted houses owned by silk merchants that extended up the Fourviere hill in the narrow, winding medieval streets. Monasteries and churches in gothic and medieval style mingled with the remains of the ancient Roman city that had been established here on the right bank of the Saône River in 43 BCE. Gradually, as the silk industry attracted more workers, however, the commercial centre moved from the cobbled streets and the hotels and shops to the peninsula. An imposing Bourse (Stock Exchange), the Hôtel de Ville, the neo-classical buildings of the Place Terreaux and the mansions that surrounded the square of Bellecour with its equestrian statue of Louis XIV were constructed. The hospital called the Hôtel-Dieu situated on the right bank of the Rhône was extended by the architect Jacques-Germain Soufflot in the 1760s and became an important place for medical research. Businessmen could now hail a 'batelière', one of the numerous women who touted for business at the port and manoeuvred their small craft skilfully across the Saône using large metal poles (known as Harpics).[7] There was a stone bridge where pedestrians could also cross from the Loge de Change to the newer centre on the peninsula, and on the other side was the newer wooden structure of the Pont Morand.

The two navigable rivers, the Saône and the Rhône, flowed around the peninsula. The fortresses that had dominated the surrounding hills were still there but had been allowed to fall into disrepair because, despite the proximity of the city to Piedmont-Sardinia, there had been a century and a half of peace along the southern border.[8] Offices of the *négociants* (the grand merchants) in the city centre remained closer to the River Saône, which was less tumultuous than the Rhône, and thus had more useful ports. The silk weavers moved higher up the hill known as the Croix-Rousse to specially constructed houses with long windows that maximised the light but were sufficiently far away from the humid conditions near the rivers not to damage the silk. A series of covered passageways called *traboules* were used by journeymen to carry the cloth from their buildings higher up and through the stone flagged buildings that led down to the port. The specially constructed route, of deep stairs and long corridors, enabled the heavy bolts of silk to be carefully manoeuvred whilst being protected from the sun and rain. The valuable cargo was loaded onto the ships that would take them to the European clients.

Clients were sought by enterprising merchants, like Joseph Chalier, who travelled widely in Europe. He had been born to a bourgeois family of solicitors at Beaulard, in the mountainous region of Piedmont, and was sent to Lyon for his education. Here he took some lessons in design and architecture and was offered employment with Soufflot. However, he was more attracted by another offer of employment from one Muguet, who gave him a job as a silk *négociant*, which involved travelling in Europe and the Orient, visiting foreign clientele of the commercial enterprise. Chalier wrote of his success in his endeavours, recovering a creditable tally of debts for his employer over some fifteen years.[9] As his experience indicates, work as a top-level *négociant* was lucrative. Merchants dealt with all aspects of the trade, including sourcing the thread and negotiating with the clients and the artists who made the patterns. They also sold the raw silk, the patterns and the orders to the weavers. When the work was completed, they then negotiated what was paid to the small manufacturers, ensuring that the market price of the worked silk stayed competitive.[10] In effect, they retained profits when the manufacturers could sometimes barely make ends meet. This inequity was widespread, in spite of the fact that the manufacturing process demanded special skills and equipment that the silk manufacturer himself possessed. Even though Chalier himself was later to become active in revolutionary justice and politics, many others in the silk trade continued to aspire to the wealth and independence that becoming a *négociant* promised.

Jean-Jacques Ampère was another *négociant* who would also become a judicial officer after the Revolution. He had a strong family connection with the silk industry, as the second of four sons of François Ampère, a master silk worker. His brothers were also master silk workers, but Jean-Jacques himself had become a high-level trader by the age of 25.[11] At the time of his marriage in 1771, one of his brothers (Jean-François) and Claude Joseph Desutières-Sarcey, his father-in-law, were also listed in the matrimonial record as *négociants*.[12] His trajectory also suggests that until 1782, when he decided to leave the silk industry, upward mobility was still possible in the industry. There was, however, also an unusual cosmopolitan mix of talented artisans in the urban centre of Lyon, many of whom had become impoverished silk workers and who wanted to see real and lasting change in their work conditions as well as those who had become established as a mercantile elite and who wanted their privileges to remain virtually unchanged.

The manufacturers involved in the silk trade had typically learned the various aspects of the career over their lifetime. They worked in a type of cottage industry team that rarely exceeded five workers. Most of the work was actually done by members of their own family, including women and children from the age of 13 or 14. Women were paid less than men, often nothing at all if they were in a family business, but they were not able to progress in the hierarchy. Some girls were encouraged to work for five or six years to help secure a dowry.[13] The long period of apprenticeship of men silk workers, of five years plus a further five years as a *compagnon* (traveller), and their ownership of the tools of the trade, meant they were ambitious and personally invested in the industry.[14] Known as *canuts*, after the tool they used in the weaving process, the workers felt proud of their status and put in long hours to get ahead. They aspired to become a *maître-ouvrier* and then possibly a *marchand* and finally a *négociant*.

The reliance on the silk trade, so critical to the commercial success of the city, became by the time of the Revolution a liability to the larger workforce because of the limited focus of those involved in it. The 'proto-industrial' structures of the industry meant that by the late eighteenth century the majority of workers were tied to a lowly paid trade. There was a desperate need for increased investment to ensure continued growth.[15] A temporary decline in demand for silk in 1778 coincided with increased costs of financing new methods of production, and this led to a crisis point in 1782, when stagnation and even bankruptcies were reported.[16] Because consumers of the luxury fabric were usually only the aristocrats and the royalty, the financial difficulties experienced at Versailles before the Revolution also had a huge impact on Lyon. Marie-Antoinette's decision to dress in more simple fabrics and the Eden Treaty of 1784 aggravated the poor economic situation.[17] This treaty was the result of an agreement to reduce tariffs on imported cottons and linens, made cheaply in factories in England, which then made these fabrics more competitive against locally produced silk. Such a series of crises only increased the dependence of interests of those heavily invested in the industry.

Some *négociants* at the highest level avoided the crises of the eighteenth century because they were able to diversify and lessen their risk of losing money by investing in property. They actually continued to accrue wealth from the profits they made from rents and the returns on providing capital for business.[18] However, others did not accumulate enough to participate more actively in the property market.[19] Those who were able could choose to invest in the newer residential buildings that were going up in St Clair, or the proposed redevelopment of the marshy area called the Brotteaux, which was planned as an amusement park, and increased their wealth. For instance, Jean-Antoine Morand (who built the new wooden bridge to the Brotteaux in 1774) and Antoine-Michel Perrache (who pushed the confluence of the two rivers further to the south) were funded by richer merchants, who helped to develop these innovative urban plans.[20]

Wealth and economic progress amongst the higher classes led to other opportunities as well as making profits from contracts and investments. Public spaces were becoming an important part of the profile of the city and places where opinions could be researched and expressed. The interactions of like-minded people in reading rooms and libraries, where they had access to print media like journals and novels, encouraged informal supportive connections. Jürgen Habermas described the formation of a Europe-wide 'bourgeois public sphere' in the new mercantile world of private individuals where, in the eighteenth century, 'reason' was used to criticise and transform society.[21] Slowly, but inexorably, the 'enlightened' bourgeois of the new liberal public sphere in France began to criticise the absolutist monarchy, its regulation of justice and its administration of taxes and duties. In Lyon, where educated bourgeois had unparalleled access to such places of discussion, connections grew stronger between those who successfully used the power of 'public opinion' to question the abuses of the *ancien régime* and who would eventually become active in revolutionary change in the city, especially as it related to reform to the institutions of justice.

The voluminous library of the Collège de la Trinité became available at first to 'interested persons' soon after the Jesuit order of teachers had been expelled from the school in 1762. By 1765, this enormous marble-tiled library with its 'prodigious number of volumes' was regarded as one of the finest and most beautiful in Europe.[22] In November 1789, the library was passed to the city in its entirety. So too were the objects in the Cabinet of Curiosities, which included Egyptian, Roman and Greek antiquities, Chinoiserie, botanic specimens, medals and coins. The observatory constructed for the College in 1701 also became more available to members of the public after the Revolution. These magnificent spaces encouraged exchanges of knowledge. There were in addition various reading rooms in Lyon where journals could be perused and discussed, as well as the latest novels, travel memoirs and the expensive *Encyclopédie* of d'Alembert and Diderot. There were smaller public libraries – including one in the Hôtel des Flechères (a building adjacent to the courthouse and prison on the Saône River), where collections were available for public access – and bookshops where the latest literature could be purchased.

For those who wanted to engage with the scientific discoveries and ideas of the time, there were a number of societies or 'circles' who welcomed new members after 1755, including the Société philosophiques des Sciences and the School of Veterinary Science. The latest journals and ideas were discussed in these meeting places. There were also thirty different lodges of Freemasonry in the city, which appealed to many bourgeois largely because of the novel ideas explored there and the interesting visitors who attended. Merchants and *négociants* comprised some sixty per cent of the members in Lyon.[23] Jean-Baptiste Willermoz, a doctor who would work in the prisons, was one of the leading exponents of this movement, which had a number of adherents in Lyon and provided a preliminary forum for exploring cosmopolitan ideas of the Enlightenment. Although this was a movement marked by elitism, it was also a creation that helped to spread radical ideas before the Revolution.[24] Willermoz along with Jean-André Périsse Duluc and Jacques Millanois (both elected deputies to the General Assembly of 1788) were intellectual leaders in the movement. They also belonged to the Third Estate in Lyon, and in the critical revolutionary years they would go on to express views that tended to align them with the 'camp of the Jacobins, as much as their tastes and their relations classed them with those of the moderates [*modérées*]'.[25]

The most exalted forum for intellectuals of the Third Estate, and the one most difficult to become a member of, was the Académie Royale des Sciences, Belles-Lettres et Arts de Lyon. Many future municipal and national leaders, such as Palerne de Savy, Louis Vitet, Jean-Emanuelle Gilibert and Roland de la Platière, were members.[26] The first public 'séance' was held in 1724. Voltaire presented a public talk here in 1750 because of the keen interest shown in his work by the Lyonnais.[27] The Académie offered a programme of activities and competitions intended to have a wide-ranging educative function, including demonstrations of the Mongolfier brothers' aerostatic balloon experiments in 1784.[28] In 1787, Antoine-Francois Delandine, a librarian and academician, catalogued what he thought was one of the most significant initiatives of the local academy: the collection of prizes that the Academy had sponsored for various *concours* (competitions). He was of the opinion that the number of competitions held in Lyon and offered to members of the public on matters of serious import had led to a growth in 'the number of overall ideas'.[29] These ideas included suggestions on ways to improve the factories of Lyon, sometimes focusing on the manufacturing processes of silk-working but also on more general topics like how to increase happiness (a competition in 1793 that was contributed to, though not won by, Napoleon Bonaparte).[30] Men and women, amateurs or specialists were encouraged to enter competitions by the awarding of accolades and cash prizes in the various local Academies throughout France.[31]

The variety of contests available in the Academy of Lyon confirms the fact there were some forward thinkers here and also suggests that the influence of 'Enlightenment' thinking had diffused into the general community. Certainly, the entries from Lyon suggested a large number of Lyonnais were thinking and opining about matters that went beyond their own material improvement and dealt with more universal issues of humanitarian concern, like the enslavement of Africans. Although not at first touching on political or religious matters, the Academy of the eighteenth century decided to ask for public views about slavery and the colonial impact of Europe in the Americas. The Abbé Guillaume Raynal sponsored thirty-three such prize competitions in Lyon over the course of the 1780s, mostly on the question of whether the discovery of America was more 'harmful' than 'useful' to humankind. It is believed Raynal wanted to incorporate the public discussion he had initiated by these competitions into his third edition of the *Histoires des deux Indies*.[32] A large number of entries were received on the question from interested Lyonnais, but the competition was withdrawn in 1790 without the monetary prize being awarded because no work was considered innovative enough. Only some of the debate was published, and most entries remained anonymous. However, according to an overview of the responses made in 1791, most authors did concentrate on the barbarity of the slave trade.[33] Individuals were concerned about growing inequities in the world, as the competitions show, and they did have informed opinions. However, many of the competitions expressed local concerns: about the customs duties that so heavily impacted the manufacturing city; the judicial institutions, which were so barbaric; and inequalities and inequities, which were so widespread. Those who read and discussed history and current affairs widely were thinking of alternative ways in which society could be administered. Many professional men of the Third Estate of Lyon did submit entries.

Other poorer groups of Lyonnais were also discussing their grievances or their ideas for a future that was fairer and more just, but the social gulf that separated them from the more professional members of the Third Estate continued to widen. There were other venues, including taverns and dance halls, where the various discontents of the working population could be aired. The city was a hot house, looking forward to the possibilities of the future but also afraid of the pressures that were threatening to explode its very fabric. Yet, the many competing groups with which workers could identify also meant effective and prolonged action was slow to begin. As well as the identification with different levels of career within the silk or other industries, there could also be an identification with where one lived: the different *quartiers* of the city.[34] Most inhabitants of the city lived in the midst of the institutional and administrative buildings, with some *quartiers* housing the very poor and others, close by, housing the very affluent. These neighbourhood groupings in Lyon were as important for a sense of belonging and support as David Garrioch found they were in Paris.[35] They provided the local meeting places around cafés, wells, markets, or at the *perruquier* (wig-maker) or the wine shop, where sociability was also encouraged.[36] The *quartiers* would become important in the future because they became the basis for the electoral *sections* used for voting purposes during the Revolution.

Lyon in the 1780s was at this stage still ruled by Consuls and by an Intendant appointed by the king. The Consulate had been formed to protect the city and its finances through local consuls (*échevins*). Admission to the political position of consul was only granted to those who had progressed through the merchant class. These consuls were elected from a small hierarchy of *notables* in the three provinces of Lyon, Forez and Beaujolais. They could become ennobled after serving two years in the office. This meant that, although originally gaining influence from their engagement in the commercial enterprises of the city rather than from the hereditary nobility as in other parts of France, the ruling elite gradually became removed from the mercantile interests of the city. The leaders seem to have become increasingly more worried about their own advancement than the general improvement of the industry and soon came to resent any criticism or agitation from the silk workers themselves. They bought larger and better houses with their fortunes, keen to increase their 'social prosperity'.[37] The burgeoning intellectual elite, however, became highly critical of the rich merchants. Manon Roland spoke for them when she lamented to an acquaintance in Lyon just prior to the Revolution: 'The gains of commerce have meant the proliferation, in our walls, of the ennobled, the privileged, the rich or those who hope to become rich.'[38] Jacones Imbert-Colomès, the leading consul in 1789, was a chief target of the more 'enlightened' bourgeois, but he had originally been a notable of modest means. He had married into wealth and this rise was typical of the new social hierarchy.

The tendency of merchants, who had profited from their successes in industry to disguise their commercial origin, only increased alienation within the social hierarchies. The new 'monopoly of the bourgeois' who had made their wealth with the silk trade and could then advance in status or diversify their risk rather than share the losses caused by the downturn in the silk industry made the inequities seem even more pronounced.[39] Rich merchants could be ennobled as a result of taking on the role of consul, and once they served in such a role they became ever more estranged from those who were not so lucky in their careers and were becoming overwhelmed by subsistence problems. The vagaries of employment would later unite workers as *sans-culottes* (those who did not wear aristocratic breeches).[40] At this stage, the workers or *menu peuple* (common people) did not protest their conditions as a strong and united group. They had little power, and although the silk workers had a sense of collective identity and did unite with smaller groups like the hat makers and strike for better conditions in 1786, the benefit of the action was short-lived and their grievances continued to simmer.[41] Most silk workers before the Revolution accepted that they had to wait for more favourable conditions to advance up the social ladder, and until then they had to trust in the benevolence of the Church and charitable individuals.

The Catholic Church was the other significant entity impacting everyday life in Lyon, and attitudes to its predominant position were also beginning to change during the 1780s. Lyon had long been one of the most important dioceses in France, with many monasteries, convents and churches dotting the city and the banks of the river. The imposing Saint-Nizier church with its tall spires and buttresses and the Church of the Cordeliers, which had seven chapels attached to it, were situated in the peninsula. The cathedral of Saint-Jean towered over Vieux Lyon. Every canton – the administrative divisions within the district of the Ville de Lyon – had a number of local churches and monasteries. The priests that lived here were not the simple *curés* found in smaller cities or villages but were strong and powerful leaders with economic and social stakes to protect. The *chanoines-comtes* (members of the cathedrals) who led the institutions often identified more as nobles than simple men of the church and had the comfortable lifestyle in keeping with one of the most important 'chapters' of the kingdom.[42] They continued to represent themselves as 'fathers of the people' in the struggle of the poor and oppressed against La Fabrique leading up to 1789.[43] However, the great number of monasteries and churches in the city itself encouraged discontent because of the amount of land they owned and occupied. In 1790, for example, there were 833 religious personnel housed in 33 convents spread across the city.[44] Because of the geographical situation of Lyon, there was little space to expand, and these holdings meant the city grew more overcrowded.

Initiatives were supported by the church to help the poor and indigent through charitable ventures, but these had varying degrees of effectiveness. Many of the monasteries and other organisations had to support their own members, who did not contribute to society but lived in contemplative orders, and this suggested how unresponsive the church was to the changes of the modern world. The institution itself was becoming increasingly irrelevant to many Lyonnais. Workers had become disengaged from religious observances and were more likely to attend the taverns of the Brotteaux or those along the banks of the Saône on a Sunday rather than church.[45] Church involvement in education was also becoming less accepted. At this time, the school system in Lyon was run by the church and based on the limited programme offered by the colleges of six or eight years of study for boys from the age of eleven or twelve. It was less usual for girls to have the opportunity of secondary schooling. Jesuit priests had been the teachers in such schools until 1762 and were responsible for the strict curriculum, which included Latin and rhetoric. Although the Jesuits had since been replaced by secular teachers of the Oratorian and Dominican orders and the French language was now emphasised, still the curriculum was criticised for being limited, rigid and slow to adopt the natural sciences.[46] The appropriateness of religious instructors in schools became one of the many debates in Lyon as to the place of religion in society more generally.

Jean-Jacques Ampère, former *négociant*, made a radical decision in 1782 to move away from Lyon to relocate his young family to a country environment where there was no school. His decision to give up his secure and high-status job and himself educate his son in the village of Poleymieux was the beginning of a promising future for the young André-Marie, who would become famous for his work on electromagnetic theory. It cannot be doubted that the impact of the difficulties of the silk industry in the critical year of 1782 contributed to his decision. It is also clear that such a decision to live a more simple and moral life and impart this wisdom to the next generation, although unusual, appeared laudable at the time. The Ampère family, however, would be set apart as being among the better-off members of a largely peasant community despite the fact that they were so clearly imbued with the idealism of the age.

Notes

1. A. Plumtre, 'A Narrative of a Three Year's Residence in France', (1810) in S. Bending and S. Bygrave, *Women's Travel Writings in Revolutionary France*, Vols 5–7 (London: Routledge, 2008). Plumtre offered the memoirs of her reflections and researches of this time to the press sometime after her journeys. She observed that while many other writers had written of their experiences during the revolutionary years, hers were of greater significance because of her longer stay and deeper focus on the provinces (see pp. x–xi).

2. Most recent studies accept this figure, which included, as Bill Edmonds observed, a transient or floating population of about 20,000. W.D. Edmonds, *Jacobinism and the Revolt of Lyon, 1789–1793* (New York: Oxford University Press, 1990), 9.
3. Edmonds, *Jacobinism*, 20.
4. Archives Municipales de Lyon [hereafter AML]. Archives en ligne: La Vie économique: la grande fabrique de soie.
5. E. Herriot, *Lyon n'est plus: Jacobins et Modérés*, vol. 1 (Paris: Hachette, 1937), 40–41.
6. N. Noyer-Ohlmann, *Rue Juiverie; rue aux blazons, rue des artisans d'art* (Lyon: Broché, 1995).
7. A. Delaigue and M. Martinet, 'Les Lyonnaises pendant l'Ancien Régime', in B. Angleraud et al., *Femmes de Lyon* (Lyon, 2016), 59–60.
8. M. Garden, 'Effacement politique contradictions culturelles et tensions sociales', in A. Latreille, *Histoire de Lyon et du Lyonnais* (Toulouse, 1975), 255.
9. M. Wahl, 'Joseph Chalier: Étude sur la Révolution Française à Lyon', *Revue Historique* 34 (1887), 3.
10. L. Trénard, *La Révolution Française dans la région Rhône-Alpes* (Paris: Perrin, 1992), 71.
11. He was described as having the profession of 'négociant' when he witnessed the marriage of his older brother Jean-Joseph on 14 November 1758: AML: registres paroissiaux et d'état civil, accessed 1 May 2015, http: www.archives-Lyon.fr.
12. Ibid.
13. Delaigue and Martinat, 'Les Lyonnaises pendant l'Ancien Régime', 94.
14. L. Trénard, 'La Crise sociale Lyonnaise à la veille de la Révolution', *Revue d'histoire modern et contemporaine* 2(1955), 12.
15. Trénard, *La Révolution*, 106–7.
16. Trénard, *La Révolution*, 106–7.
17. Trénard, *La Révolution*, 109.
18. See the discussion of capital growth among bourgeois employers in H. Heller, *The Bourgeois Revolution in France, 1789–1815* (Oxford: Berghahn, 2006), 4.
19. According to Trénard, barely a quarter of Lyonnais merchants who called themselves *négociants* could buy their own homes in the city, whereas those with noble status owned a whole *hôtel* or buildings that they rented to further augment their wealth and power. *La Révolution Française*, 65. Ampère used 10,000 livres that his wife obtained on her marriage from her uncle towards the purchase of the property, which cost 20,000 livres including furniture and animals that came with the farm.
20. Garden, 'Effacement politique', 273.
21. J. Habermas, *The Structural Transformation of the Public Sphere*, trans. T. Burger (Cambridge MA, 1989), 24, 51–54.
22. B. Marion, 'Le Collège de la Trinité: Histoire d'une Bibliotheque de son Cabinet de Curiosités' (Mémoire de Masters, Université de Lyon, 2014), 59.
23. Garden, 'Effacement politique', 277.
24. G. Kates, *The 'Cercle Social', the Girondins and the French Revolution* (Princeton NJ, 1985), 90–91.
25. A. Joly, *Un Mystique Lyonnais et les secrets de la franc-maçonnerie: Jean-Baptiste Willermoz 1730–1824* (Paris, 1938), 283.
26. Joly, *Un Mystique Lyonnais*, 338, 176–77 and 339.
27. J.-B. Dumas, *Histoire de l'Académie des sciences, belles-lettres et arts de Lyon* (Lyon, 1839).
28. Dumas, *Histoire de l'Académie*, 170.
29. J.L. Caradonna, *The Enlightenment in Practice: Academic Prize Contests and Intellectual Culture in France 1670–1794* (Ithaca: Cornell University Press, 2012), 149.
30. Caradonna, *The Enlightenment*, Appendix A.

31. Caradonna, *The Enlightenment*, 100–17.
32. Caradonna, *The Enlightenment*, 157.
33. Bertrand Van Ruymbeke suggested the fact that there were close to fifty responses to this particular set of competitions was unusual because such competitions in the major cities like Lyon usually only drew some five to ten responses. He noted that the names of contributors were separate from the essays and so unless a prize was awarded they remained anonymous. Talk given at the Johnson Collection, East Melbourne, Victoria: 'The French reflect on America and on Slavery', 29 August 2017.
34. M. Garden, *Lyon et les Lyonnais au 18e siècle* (Paris: Les Belles Lettres, 1975), 275–78.
35. D. Garrioch, *Neighbourhood and Community in Paris, 1740–1790* (Cambridge: Cambridge University Press, 1986), 16.
36. Garrioch, *Neighbourhood and Community*, 24–26.
37. Trénard, *La Révolution*, 65.
38. Trénard, *La Révolution*, 64.
39. Garden, *Lyon et les Lyonnais*, 353–54.
40. This tendency was noted by George Rudé in the Parisian context but is also observable in Lyon. *The Crowd in the French Revolution* (Oxford: Clarendon Press, 1959), 22.
41. D.L. Longfellow, 'Silk Weavers and the Social Struggle in Lyon during the French Revolution, 1789–94', *French Historical Studies* 12(1) (Spring, 1981), 11–12.
42. P. Chopelin, *Ville patriote et ville martyre: Lyon, l'église et la Révolution, 1788–1805* (Paris, 2010), 17–18.
43. Chopelin, *Ville patriote*, 22.
44. Chopelin, *Ville patriote*, 47.
45. Chopelin, *Ville patriote*, 68.
46. R.R. Palmer, *The Improvement of Humanity: Education and the French Revolution* (Princeton, NJ, 1985), 12–18.

Chapter 2

LIFE IN THE COUNTRY

> The air of Poleymieux is fresh and healthy, because it is a mountainous country, but as most of its inhabitants are forced to go to bring in the harvest in the swampy country . . . they unfortunately report fevers . . . for their pain.
>
> —Minutes of the first Municipal Assembly of Poleymieux held 25 May 1788

At the time of the Revolution, the vast majority of French people lived in the countryside and were deeply concerned about the management of their unique environments.[1] Their livelihoods were often tied to an agricultural economy over which the local *seigneur* exercised predominant control. He received *rentes* or dues from his subjects at the time of harvest. He made sure hunting and collection of wood was regulated and taxed and had strong control over food, with his own mills and ovens often used to produce it. The judicial officer, known as the *fiscal procureur*, was his legal agent in the regional courts of justice and was thus often wholly concerned with taxes and dues owed rather than with pursuing criminal prosecutions.[2] The poorer classes in the seigneurial domain sometimes owned land, but even when they did not own land, they were well aware of the possibility of the feudal system being abused. They were therefore vocal in expressing their complaints against the nobles or clergymen, who would unfairly profit from their labour. Many historians now contend that the inhabitants of the countryside in France helped ensure a democratic future by their actions at the time of the Revolution just as much as their urban brothers.[3]

Poleymieux provides a useful starting point for understanding the Revolution from the point of view of the country inhabitants of Lyon. It was a small commune, part of the Sénéchaussée of Lyon and the parish of Neuville-sur-Saône.[4] Neuville was at the foot of the Mont d'Or (Golden Mountain) and straddled the banks of the Saône River so was easily reached by carriage or boat from Lyon. From there, access could be had to the small villages dotted up the sides of the mountain, including Saint-Romaine, Chasselay and Limonest. Poleymieux was one of the most unspoiled and beautiful areas of the region, with woods and gentle streams that fed into the gushing Thoux River. It had lush meadows on which ewes (called *brébis*) would graze, their milk processed into the famous cheeses of the region. A vista of picturesque hayfields and fruit trees, including limes, bordered the forest of the Garenne, according to an eighteenth- century chronicle called *Géographie du Rhône*.[5] Feudal constraints were nevertheless impacting more and more on the lives of those who chose to live there.

Some richer residents of Lyon spent time in country homes and appreciated the natural environment as an escape from urban life. They included one Pierre Poivre, who had commenced his career in Lyon as a *négociant* in the silk industry and later became a colonial administrator in India and famous for the botanical specimens he collected on his travels.[6] Jacques-Pierre Brissot, a Parisian journalist, visited Poivre and his 'heavenly' family in 1782 and described their immense and 'delicious' gardens filled with exotic plants, rocks, grottoes and gently murmuring streams, which transported him straight into the world of 'Héloise' – the tragic heroine of Jean-Jacques Rousseau's immensely popular novel.[7] Jean-Jacques Ampère – who had worked in the silk industry, as had Poivre – was so impressed by the transformational ideas for society suggested by his namesake Rousseau that he too decided to become one of a small number of bourgeois families who lived in Poleymieux. The bucolic surroundings provided the place to 'fix your eyes on nature, follow the path traced by her' and thus bring up children who would become worthy citizens as Rousseau advised in *Emile*.[8]

Country life had become much less tranquil in Poleymieux, however, as the locals became increasingly upset about those who were using their wealth and privileges to negatively affect communal interests. Residents were forced to contest their rights over common land in a law suit begun by one Marite de la Barrollière, a Swiss landowner who had taken over a public road, making it even more difficult for the villagers to travel to neighbouring towns like Limonest.[9] Although proud of their region, the poorer inhabitants began to express despair and rage about the unfair dues and obligations required of them – as the minutes of the first municipal assembly of Poleymieux quoted at the beginning of this chapter so clearly expresses. While there were some peasant landowners in the country areas surrounding Lyon, most inhabitants rented land or worked for feudal landlords, including the local *seigneur* and the Church. Their lives represented a sharp contrast to those of the Lyonnais in the city. There was little access to education; roads and transport were poor; and the inhabitants were dependent on the climate and resources of the areas in which they lived to make a living. All over France, the growing dissatisfactions of the peasants impacted by the feudal system in the country areas like this small commune were becoming more pronounced.

The municipal assembly of Poleymieux, which first met on 25 May 1788, drew up a comprehensive document that put in writing some of the dissatisfactions. Prominent members of the village met on this particular Sunday to document the community's economic and fiscal statistics. They advised the authorities that there were eighty modest farmhouses in the village and five 'bourgeois' families, who were the only landowners to make even a very small (*modique*) living from producing wheat and wine. It was pointed out that it was only the two *privilégiés*, the *curé* and the *seigneur*, and three of the bourgeois families who owned the few steers used to sow seed. They also owned most of the 50 cows and the 100 *brébis* in the village, which produced milk to make cheese. Even for these comparatively wealthy landowners, however, things were difficult. The rigours of winter in the mountain, the poor soil and poor terrain meant a very mediocre production. Commerce was impeded by the roads, which became impassable in bad weather. There were no doctors, midwives or schools in the village and no mills to grind wheat.[10] There were twenty poor households receiving alms. The church itself was in dire need of repair, and there was little hope of improving the situation because of the poverty of most of the inhabitants. This report obviously had the purpose of signalling to the king the penury of the area and the thin living that could be extracted from its fields. A major complaint was that the *dîme* exacted from the inhabitants by the Church was set at a higher value than was required in neighbouring villages. It was noted that there had never been any registering (*cadastre*) of the value of the land. Meetings of the municipal assembly were subsequently held every Sunday, after the church service, from this point on. Those who took on the local roles were to remain active in Poleymieux politics for some time, writing letters to Lyon or Paris to alert the government of local problems or issues and more often than not to complain about the negative effects of the seigneurial system on the peasants.

Although aspiring to a more 'natural' education for his children and a simpler life for himself, the advantages the Ampère family had over their neighbours meant there was always a wide chasm between them. This may well be the reason that Jean-Jacques failed to take a leadership role in the Municipal assembly in 1788 even though he was nominated for the post of mayor.[11] Ampère was recorded as one of the leading 'bourgeois' living in Poleymieux, and a brief study of his life shows the sharp social differences that were evident in many such provincial areas. His house and farm had been purchased the month before his marriage in 1771. Ampère's wife was descended from the aristocratic Desutières-Sarcey family of Paris and her significant dowry paid half the value of these purchases.[12] The property included sheep, cows and a bull, chickens, a cellar filled with barrels of wine (some twenty-two barrels aged for more than five years) and wine presses. It also included a small building at nearby Albigny-sur-Saône and rights to work fields, including a vineyard and orchard, and some rights to cut timber. An inventory taken at the time suggests a well-furnished house, with numerous feather beds, tapestried armchairs, armoires, dressers, a fireplace and a well-appointed kitchen, including a number of pie dishes.[13] However, the farm with its potential income from cheesemaking and wine pressing was left to managers.

Figure 2.1 *Maison d'Ampère* (Ampère home – now the Musée d'Ampère). Photograph by the author.

Even when the family made their life-changing decision to move to the country to live in the Poleymieux property they could return to Lyon for the coldest months of the year.

While Ampère did have a typical farmhouse he thus avoided the inherent problems of agriculture in the village precisely because he was not required to work full time as a farmer.[14] He employed workers. At the time he purchased the property, the contract included a lease over meadows, orchards and vines nearby, rented from the Notre Dame convent in Lyon. The original contract of sale of the property stipulated that Ampère had an obligation to pay wages and food for domestic cultivators for a year following the purchase of the property in 1771.[15] The extensive stables, barns and storage rooms housed churns and ovens for making cheeses and perhaps for drying meats. There were presses, vats and casks for wine. The space was also used for housing animals and for storing grain and the straw necessary to fill beds and cover the floors for warmth in winter. Twenty years later, a search of the property by municipal authorities described haylofts overflowing with 'heaps of wheat and other crops', a 'huge heap of hemp', barns full of wood, stables full of manure, a working pigeon house and vegetable garden and a courtyard with a 'prodigious heap of straw'.[16] The family had the resources both financially and culturally to sustain themselves.

Ampère used his financial resources to purchase an administrative role in the local Gruerie as *procureur fiscal* for a period of two years, which helped support a life of relative ease for his family.[17] Payment for such roles (known as the 'venality of office') was a common practice in seigneurial justice and has been shown to have actually ensured some independence among the fiscal officers because they were not so beholden to the *seigneur* if they had paid money for the right to hold office.[18] The purchased position, however, did not promise a high recompense for Ampère, because Poleymieux was a small jurisdiction that only dealt with cases of 'middle justice', such as hunting rights and harvest dues, rather than cases of 'high justice', which dealt with other civil and criminal matters.[19] The Gruerie mostly heard cases of contraventions against the rights of the king and the *seigneur* over land and the wood that could be cut from the forested areas.[20] In 1782, when Ampère took up his position, the *seigneur* was Servan L'Aîné (the Elder) a popular member of a family from the area. He had been administrator of finances, in charge of collecting the dues owed to the king for the region for some years. Ampère worked under the Châtelain (the chief judicial official), Brunet, and the chief local magistrate, the judge Garin from nearby Neuville. There was also a *juge gruyer* (M. Rieussec) from Lyon, attending when there were disputes to be litigated.[21]

Figure 2.2 *La Gruerie Poleymieux* (The Forestry Court). Anon., postcard. Archives départementale du Rhône.

Most of the local peasantry had little cause to litigate commercial contracts, but they did have disputes with the forest wardens and with the payment of taxes. As the records of the commune show, the collection of the *dîme* was considered most unfair by the local population because it was a tax that was sent away from the community to the ecclesiastical institutions in Lyon.[22] The peasants and small landholders could not see the justification in contributing a large proportion of their harvests to the church headquarters in the city as well as having to meet the exactions of the feudal *seigneur*. Their economic viability was threatened by these taxes, but while the *seigneur* and his agent were accommodating and considered the welfare of the families in their domain disputes did not escalate.

Ampère believed himself to be an 'enlightened' bourgeois, motivated by the power of modern ideas of the *philosophes* – especially those of Rousseau – and he was often described as 'wise' and 'pacific' in his judicial interactions.[23] He had also used his savings to buy some of the core Enlightenment texts of the eighteenth century, which became the foundation of a significant library installed in the farmhouse and were handed down through the generations of his family. Ampère had become convinced from his reading that personal change could make a difference in French society. Rousseau believed fathers were in fact the best first tutors and should educate by guiding their children.[24] Providing an education that allowed the growth of reason to occur in a natural context was the 'duty' Rousseau believed a father owed to the state and humanity.[25] Only a 'natural' education based on strengthening an inbuilt 'moral order' would save the young from the dissimulation and lies that modern society seemed to encourage.[26] This happy state could be achieved by 'guidance rather than instruction' if the student was allowed to 'find out for himself'.[27] Moving to the country was a choice at this time, a choice that promised an education for the Ampère children that included 'learning geography by walks, natural history by object lessons, the ideas of violence, of justice, and of prudence, by being subjected to violence, injustice and imprudence and so on'.[28] A natural education minimised the likelihood of the child accepting the prejudices of his teacher and was considered the most appropriate education for children who would become part of the 'enlightened' world that philosophers like Rousseau suggested was possible. That this philosophy was so heartily embraced by the family confirms the strength of Jean-Jacques' beliefs.

Studies have found that the *sensibilité* evoked from the works of Rousseau was a 'significant trait' among its readers after 1760. Rousseau's works 'had a profound effect upon life and it transformed practical habits quite as much as it did ideas'.[29] Ampère had been so affected, and this meant his children, including his son André-Marie, were encouraged to learn in an unconventional way. The family dabbled in poetry and writing.[30] André-Marie recalled in a series of autobiographical notes the benefits of the education that set him on the path for his future groundbreaking contributions to the field of electromagnetic theory. He explained that his father began to teach him and encouraged him to learn only when and what he had a desire to know.[31] His father 'never ceased to be interested in publications of French and Latin literature as well as several branches of science' and inspired in him a 'love of learning'.[32] The children were taught to read at home from French primers, and André-Marie was even given the rudimentaries of Latin so he could further his study of calculus once he developed an interest in botany and maths. The library contained various contemporary novels, works of history, the theatre and authors of antiquity.[33] The greatest space was reserved for seventeen volumes of the famous Encyclopaedia of Diderot and D'Alembert. André-Marie became immersed in whole sections of the Encyclopaedia, which he memorised until temporarily diverted by his inability to understand the articles on calculus.[34] Numerous historical texts and some works on the nervous system and on vegetarianism by the local doctor, Jean-Baptiste Pressavin, were also part of the library. Pressavin, who was later to become involved in revolutionary politics on the local municipality and in the National Convention, had a novel way of seeing the world, which allowed him to embrace and contribute many new ideas to society.[35]

These works in the library show the curiosity of the Ampère family about new scientific ideas. While one cannot definitively say whether members of the family read all the works in the library, the type of education and influences they valued is clear. The range of works, including the variety of Latin texts, prompts the assumption that the father had been taught by the Jesuit order in Lyon. The fact that he did not send his son for an extended time to the school when it was staffed by the Oratorians meant that he favoured the more modern ideas of Rousseau and Voltaire, which were critical of the limitations of this type of learning. André-Marie had a much more eclectic and interest-driven education and recalled the fun he had in his youth memorising and declaiming famous scenes of the classical playwrights.[36] He also claimed to have been well acquainted with works about history, including that of England and the United States.[37] We thus know that the family appreciated and used their library. The education he provided his children shows the practical application of the ideas Ampère had gained from the lessons of both classical and contemporary history. The recollections of André-Marie as to how the family treasured their books suggest the family knew the value of 'enlightenment' texts.

The Ampère family were somewhat unusual both for the decision to disconnect from the commercial world by moving to the country as they did for the books they chose to buy and for the decision they made to educate their children. Until a new *seigneur* purchased the castle and its lands in 1785, Ampère's position of *procureur* at the Gruerie was undemanding, and the work required him to walk only a few hundred metres from his house to the feudal court. While Servan was *seigneur*, there was little trouble in collecting the dues owed because he was respected by the inhabitants and his claims were generally accepted. Things did change abruptly when the new incumbent, Guillin Dumontet, purchased the *seigneurie* in 1785, after Servan died. Then, Ampère's quasi-judicial position gave him an insight into the problems of the feudal system when it was dominated by a particularly grasping *seigneur*. Ampère was forced to again make a change in the family circumstances when confronted by the excesses of the new *seigneur*.

The castle of Poleymieux, originally constructed in the fifteenth century, had an imposing aspect, which appealed to the new incumbent of the *seigneurie*. It was surrounded by a low wall with four small conical towers at its corners, enclosing a garden with orchards, vineyards, a large circular fountain with a jet of water and an enormous pigeon house. The main structure was added to by numerous farm buildings and cellars. It was overhung by a tall tower with a small window crossed with iron bars.[38] All the towers had narrow slits, called *meurtriers*, through which archers could fire arrows at besiegers. The castle literally and metaphorically towered over the villagers, who would wend their way up to the summit of the Mont d'Or every Sunday for church services at the church building, which abutted the castle. The castle also bestowed on its owner the status and privileges that Guillin was also eager to avail himself of. He was often seen walking around his estates with two mastiff dogs and a gun-wielding Senegalese retainer, ready to attack anyone who crossed him.[39]

The new *seigneur* had had a career as a colonial administrator in Senegal before he purchased the castle. His previous naval position had seen him engage in some questionable practices in the rubber trade, including illegal use of the King's navy.[40] According to the nineteenth-century historian Audin, he brought to his new position 'the behaviour of a man used to slave trafficking and to the tyrannical governing of a colony far from all controls'.[41] Rather than expressing a benevolent attitude to the people under his care, Guillin was more concerned with reviving and enforcing dues and privileges that were traditionally due to him. Such actions of *seigneurs*, although criticised, were common. The more grasping of *seigneurs* and their *procureurs* could allow dues to accumulate and then claim arrears for up to twenty-nine years in a lump sum.[42] Historian Anthony Crubaugh has looked at how such positions worked in provincial areas and found that *seigneurs* sometimes only engaged *procureurs* who 'ensured that inhabitants paid their seigneurial dues and generally respected the rights and honors to which the lord laid claim'.[43] To do this, they avoided the sale (or venality) of the position, preferring to hire or fire *procureurs* as they wished.

While at first Ampère visited the castle and interacted with the new *seigneur* in his function as *procureur*, it would appear from the Almanac records that his position was not extended.[44] Indeed, he became one of those impacted by the harshness of the new *seigneur*.[45] His own property was subject to a demand for payment of dues that had fallen into disuse and so were inflated by 1786, and his family shared in the disillusionment of the local community. Guillin was especially notorious locally for his actions of digging up the bones of the dead buried in the church cemetery and his annexing of this land. Some claimed that he actually used the bones as fertiliser for his gardens.[46] Brunet and the inhabitants of Poleymieux wrote to Paris frequently complaining about the practices of the *seigneur* from this time.⁴⁷ Although there is some evidence he helped the poor during a disastrous winter, by allowing them to gather around his fires day and night, he appeared to be more concerned that they acknowledged debts owed to him rather than that he should honour any obligations he may have owed as their lord.⁴⁸

Once Ampère retired from service with the *seigneur*, he and his family considered themselves part of the community, and they had made some sacrifices to become so, but ultimately their life was cushioned by profits made in the commerce of the city and from managing their various investments in the country. After giving up his work at the Gruerie, Ampère was able to devote himself to the increasingly obvious genius of his son, André-Marie, who was at the age many boys went to formal school. Since there was no school in Poleymieux, his father continued to augment the family library to cater for the boy's special interest in calculus. He facilitated his son's correspondence with another, slightly older, friend in Lyon about problem-solving experiments.⁴⁹ Finally, he helped him present a solution to a complex theoretical problem to the Académie des Sciences in Lyon. In 1788, André-Marie presented a thesis for examination to Claude Roux in Lyon.⁵⁰ Their connection to Lyon was thus to remain important, and the family spent the winter months there, accessing the vibrant social life of the city, including its theatre, reading rooms and the Academie. The printing/bookselling family of Périsse-Duluc became friends with the family when Ampère frequented their shop in the rue Mercière in Lyon.⁵¹ For those interested in scientific progress, this was a gathering place where the latest philosophical ideas were read and discussed. André-Marie was given some opportunity to attend lectures at the Collège de la Trinité while they were in residence in Lyon over the winter months. He spent some months under the supervision of M. Daburon and M. Mollet, Oratorian professors who taught mathematics and physics there after the Jesuits were expelled.⁵² Jean-Jacques was also able to obtain chemistry books from the library of the Collège as his talented son grew more interested in mathematics.

The very unusual nature of the library of the Ampère family and the progress of André-Marie's education further established a stark contrast with the lives of the more usual inhabitants of Poleymieux. Other small farms in Poleymieux like that of Ampère, although of similar construction, with barns and drystone walls built from the golden sandstone that gave the mountain its name, did not offer such a fulfilling life to their inhabitants. Most Poleymoriots were entirely reliant on agriculture for their livelihood. In good times they produced copious amounts of wine, hay and wood, but winters were very harsh.⁵³ Arable land was in short supply and was often rocky and hard to till. While some peasants worked their own small plots, most had to work as farmhands or cut wood for a living. They were vulnerable to natural disasters like that recorded on 2 February 1789, following heavy rains in December, when 'melting snow formed torrents of water so large that they ravaged almost all the fields sown with wheat . . . spread stones and gravel in the valley . . . and so degraded the roads that they are impassable by foot and impossible for vehicles'. Wood that had been collected and cut by the inhabitants was washed away and icy conditions ruined the fruit on the trees.[54] Such disasters were challenging for the whole community but especially for those who could not diversify their businesses as the leading bourgeois and the *seigneur* could. They would be especially vulnerable to the crises of 1789.

Notes

1. N. Plack, 'The Peasantry, Feudalism, and the Environment, 1789–93', in P. McPhee (ed.), *Companion to the French Revolution* (Chichester: Wiley Blackwell, 2015), 213–15. She suggests an estimated 22 million people of the 28 million total population at the time of the Revolution lived in the country, and they voiced their concerns about the degradation of their environment.
2. A. Crubaugh, *Balancing the Scales of Justice: Local courts and Rural society in Southwest France, 1750–1800* (University Park, PA: The Pennsylvania State University Press, 2000), 111–14.
3. J. Markoff, 'Violence, Emancipation and Democracy: The Countryside and the French Revolution', in G. Kates (ed.), *The French Revolution: Recent Debates and New Controversies* (London: Routledge, 1998), 246. He argued that the tensions created by an active peasantry were essential to the formation of truly democratic institutions.
4. F.A. Varnet, *Géographie du département du Rhône* (Lyon: Gallica, 1897), 28.
5. Varnet, *Géographie*, 35.
6. C. Perrat, 'Un Lyonnais à la veille de la Révolution: "Pierre Poivre, Ancien Intendant des Iles de France et de Bourbon"', *Annuaire-Bulletin de la Société de l'histoire de France* 74(1) (1938), 99–116.
7. Perrat, 'Un Lyonnais', 104.
8. J.J. Rousseau, *Emile*, trans. B. Foxley (London: Everyman's Library, 1974).
9. ADR (Poleymieux), 153/1, 7.
10. ADR (Poleymieux), 153/1.
11. ADR (Poleymieux), 153/1.
12. His wife's contribution is mentioned in Ampère's letter to her after his trial: ADR 42 L 62.
13. Inventory attached to the contract of sale of 3.6.1771. Documents form part of the collection held in the Fonds Ampère, AAS, Paris.
14. The Ampère house is today preserved as it was when the family lived there and now functions as a museum of electromagnetic theory in honour of André-Marie.

15. Contract of sale between the Veuve Rougnard and J.J. Ampère effected 3.6.71. Fonds Ampère, AAS, Paris.
16. Report of Ryard, 14.12.1790, quoted in L. Dupré-Latour, 'Historical Note on the Poleymieux House', *Bulletin de la Société des Amis d'André-Marie Ampère* 56 (Oct. 2012), 58.
17. Ampère mentions a sum of 3,000 *livres* from his capital that he had paid for a position of two years duration upon his retirement from commerce. Letter to his wife of 23 November 1793. ADR 42 L 62.
18. Crubaugh, *Balancing the Scales*.
19. For the distinction between different feudal systems of justice see Crubaugh, *Balancing the Scales*, 90–91.
20. There was no criminal justice dispensed at this level of court, but disputes concerning taxes were dealt with.
21. Almanach astronomique de la ville de Lyon et des provinces de Lyonnais, Forez et Beaujolais pour 1782. Musée d'Ampère.
22. ADR (Poleymieux), 153/1.
23. A. Audin, *La Conspiration Lyonnaise de 1790 et le drame de Poleymieux* (Lyon: Éd. lyonnaises d'art et d'histoire, 1984) 65. This description of Ampère comes from the nineteenth century.
24. Rousseau, *Émile*, 15.
25. Rousseau, *Émile*, 15.
26. J. Storobinski, *Jean-Jacques Rousseau: La transparence et l'obstacle* (Paris, 1971), 14.
27. Rousseau, *Émile*, 19.
28. D. Mornet, *French Thought in the Eighteenth Century*, trans. L.M. Levin (Hamden, CT: Archon Books, 1969), 170.
29. Mornet, *French Thought*, 240.
30. The father would write a political play based on a story of an enlightened monarch called Artaxerxes in 1792, and the son also attempted to write historical plays and poetry.
31. André-Marie Ampère, *Autobiographie*, AAS, chemise 326.
32. Ampère, *Autobiographie*.
33. Dûrr, 'Liste des livres' Fonds Ampère, AAS, Paris, Chemise 292.
34. Ampère, *Autobiographie*.
35. J.-B. Pressavin, *Nouveau traité des vapeurs ou traité des maladies des nerfs* (Lyon, 1770).
36. Pressavin, *Nouveau traité*.
37. Ampère, *Autobiographie*.
38. Audin, *La Conspiration Lyonnais*, 68.
39. A. Raverat, *Lyon sous la Révolution, suivi de la liste des condamnés à mort* (Lyon: La Découvrance, 2006), 22. Baron Raverat wrote a lively account of the events that transpired on this day in 1883, based on eyewitness accounts but also using the more rightwing viewpoint of Alphonse Balleydier, *Histoire politique et militaire du people de Lyon pendant la Révolution Française, 1789–1795* (Paris, 1816).
40. Audin, *La Conspiration Lyonnaise*, 58–63.
41. Audin, *La Conspiration Lyonnaise*, 141.
42. Crubaugh, *Balancing the Scales*, 68–69.
43. Crubaugh, *Balancing the Scales*, 12.
44. Ampère's name is not mentioned in the 1787 Almanac records, and it would appear he had retired or been dismissed by the *seigneur* before that year. Extracts of 'Almanach astronomique de la ville de Lyon et des provinces de Lyonnais, Forez et Beaujolais pour 1786'. Musée d'Ampère.
45. Audin, *La Conspiration Lyonnaise*, 64–65.

46. Lettre I, ADR (Poleymieux),153/3.
47. Archives Nationale [herefter AN], D/XXIX/65.
48. Raverat, *Lyon sous la Révolution*, 23.
49. AAS, Chemise 323–72. Correspondence with Mr Jean-Stanislas Couppier.
50. Trénard, *La Révolution*, 88.
51. P. Marion, *Le Génial bonhomme Ampère: Le roman de sa vie* (Lyon: Mémoire des Arts, 1999), 25. This book is a quasi-fictional account of the life of the Ampère family but does provide some material of local provenance. André-Marie would later tutor the children of the Carron family, who lived in Saint-Germain, Mont d'Or and were also connected by marriage to the Périsse-Duluc family: H. Chevreux, *Journal et correspondance de André-Marie Ampère* (Paris: Hetzel, 1872), 10.
52. Ampère, *Autobiographie*. These lessons were taken during their winter residence in Lyon, and M. Daburon also came to the country to see André-Marie and inspired in him a desire to progress in mathematics.
53. Ampère, *Autobiographie*.
54. ADR (Poleymieux), 153/1.

Chapter 3

CRISES AND REVOLUTION

A just and beneficent king, beloved of his people, gathers together the representatives of the nation . . . reminding all Frenchmen of the imprescriptible rights of a free and generous people, he wishes, in concert with them, to begin the reform of abuses . . . May he have eternal grace!
—Cahier of the Third Estate of the Sénéchaussée of Lyon
Archives Parlementaire (AP), 1789, 608

We have charged those we deputise to request that nobles or others, born in Lyon can receive the Order of Malta, as Chevaliers of justice, bearers of arms, or monastic clergy, on giving all necessary proofs of nobility . . .
—Cahier of the Second Estate of the Sénéchaussée of Lyon (signed the Marquis of Mont d'Or and others representing the nobility)
AP, 1789, 608

A growing fiscal crisis combined with a particularly severe food crisis in 1788 ignited public discontent and brought *ancien régime* France to the point of Revolution in 1789. The national budget of 1788 had been made public, and it showed a shocking imbalance of debt and interest payments on loans taken out by the state to monies received.[1] This exceptional state of affairs facing the king led to the decision to call the Estates-General to Versailles in May 1789. By assembling all the Estates of the kingdom to the discussion, different strata of society were empowered and began to imagine political change as part of the process.[2] The process became quite radical as it followed on from catastrophic harvest failures and popular rioting. In July 1788, violent storms had destroyed country harvests across France and manifested in food shortages, unemployment and bankruptcies.³ Such shortages regularly led to riots throughout the country, but the particularly harsh winter that followed led to anger that hoarders or merchants were stockpiling grains and depriving the poor.⁴

* * *

Conditions in Lyon were exacerbated by the freezing of the Rhône and the interruption to supplies brought in by boat, which caused shortages of food and associated misery in the city. Silk workers, still suffering from declining demand for their product, were especially affected because of the mono-industry they were involved in, and their livelihoods became ever more vulnerable. Weavers had had a long series of grievances against the merchant élite but were becoming less and less able to challenge them and the consuls who supported them politically.⁵ The corporations controlling the industry were making increasing demands on the workers and took reprisals on those who participated in further disputes after the successful strike action in 1786.⁶ Although the silk workers remained loud in their demand for some solution, they had very few avenues of redress. Many had already been reduced to large-scale begging in the streets and outside the theatres as conditions continued to worsen.⁷

The workers in Lyon turned to the 'provincial assemblies' (which were convoked in the regions of France at the same time as the Assembly of Notables in 1787–89) to express their strong opinions on their situation as did many other groups in France.⁸ The Lyonnais showed great enthusiasm for these assemblies as well as expressing their 'violent oppositions' in numerous pamphlets also written at the time.⁹ Denis Monnet, a leading weaver during the strike of 1786, continued to be involved in social agitation.¹⁰ He led the activists in the assemblies as they registered their protest against unfair practices, which were making it impossible to earn a living from their trade. As the minutes of the assembly convoked in the small commune of Poleymieux from 25 May 1788 attest, the rural population were also expressing their dissatisfactions.¹¹ The assemblies gave people a political voice and an education in how to demonstrate their concerns. In the urban and country areas here, as elsewhere in France, people then also clamoured to have a say on national problems, advising the king about what should be done.

The call for a nationwide meeting to address the successive crises became widely seen as an effective solution. Because a gathering of the different orders had not been held for 175 years, the many preparations required, including the writing of *cahiers de doléances* (Notices of Grievances) awoke a new excitement among those who felt they had grievances and who believed the king would listen to them. The *cahiers* of Lyon show how differently the various orders of society viewed the converging crises and thus how remedies should be conceived. The Marquis of Mont d'Or led the nobles in a predictable reassertion of their ancient rights and suggested privileges should be increased in the *cahier* of the Second Estate. However, the suppression of unfair privileges and abuses, once taken for granted, was strongly supported by peasants in the rural areas. The excerpts from the Lyonnais *cahiers* at the beginning of this chapter are illustrative of the different views at the heart of the debate about to take place in the meeting of the Estates-General. They show the universality that many of the Third Estate would bring to the question of future change and the selfishness that other Estates continued to believe was acceptable. Comparisons of the *cahiers* show how enthusiastically and how differently even those among the Third Estate viewed the request by the king to think of practical solutions to the crisis.[12]

While the Second and First Estate *cahiers* made some suggestions for constitutional reform and regular meetings of the Estates-General, the greatest engagement in the preparation of such documents was amongst the Third. This was the largest order and comprised the majority of people in the French state. Conversations about a fair and just society – which continued to gain traction in the 'public sphere' of reading rooms, bookshops and cafes of cities like Paris and Lyon – were now written up. Discussions amongst the less literate but equally revolutionary peasants also took written form in the documents of the Third. Some *cahiers* raised the question of whether society should even be organised in terms of 'estates' but rather should have an equality of taxation and rights. In Paris and the provinces, people began to question the privileges and injustices that they knew were no longer supportable – whether or not they had read Rousseau or Voltaire – and they widely believed the king would accept the necessary changes.

As well as there being a self-conscious intellectual movement called the 'Enlightenment', which contributed to the new discourse about rights and equalities among the educated Third, historian Peter McPhee also identified a 'shift in behaviour and belief', which had come about subconsciously among the vast majority of ordinary people who were lumped together as part of this estate.[13] The ideas and suggestions of the Third and lowest order clearly show this shift in their novel and wide-ranging suggestions. However, it was the very multiplicity of the responses of the Third in Lyon and their suggestions for change that are particularly informative. The Lyonnais *cahiers* of the Third all reveal the strong social activism and interest in reform present in the city and the country areas. There were separate *cahiers* from the 'Third Estate' Lyon (Ville) and of *Des bourgeois de la ville de Lyon* in March 1789, which were somewhat more tempered than the primary document. Rural parish and urban collective groupings also produced their own documents, including those of the Beaujolais and Forez areas.[14] While the *cahiers* of the First and Second addressed a common concern that all abusive practices, including taxes, should be remedied and that financial privileges and exemptions should be limited, the various documents of the Third went further and suggested they be suppressed.

The primary document of the *Sénéchaussée* (Third Estate) was written up immediately (*sur-le-champ*) after it was discussed (because of the insistence of the enthused country inhabitants) and thus contained 'errors' according to a note added to the record.[15] It began by praising the king for his initiative in requesting their views, then setting out concrete suggestions that would make their hardships easier (as the Second Estate document had done), but it also expressed a more comprehensive vision of a constitutional government with oversight by the Estates-General, bolstered by judicial and taxation reforms and the abolition of the *octrois* or internal tax barriers. The national constitution was to be the 'expression of the general will of the nation, sanctioned by the king, as approved and consented to by the general will of the nation'. While there was recognition of the domination of the Catholic religion, the *cahier* called for the suppression of the *dîme*. The third and fourth chapters concerned the justice system and proposed prescient changes: a code for civil and criminal laws to make them uniform throughout the kingdom; the abolition of venal office; the establishment of one or more *juge de paix* (Justice of the Peace) to provide mediation services; and a declaration that seigneurial justice and feudal rights were 'abusive and against the common good'. As to general police matters, it was proposed that 'useful citizens' should be encouraged by the provision of public education. Respect for *curés* (priests) in country areas, freedom of the press and fixed and fair prices on subsistence foods were also recommended. Other sections related to measures to make agriculture and commerce fairer and included the proposal that the manufacturers of Lyon should be 'protected from total ruin' by imposts that should be reformed. The bold grievances in the principal document of the *Sénéchaussée* were thus paired with equally bold suggestions for change.

The wide engagement of the *Sénéchaussée* (Third) document with particular local issues intimated how active the *menu peuple* were to become in challenging injustice perpetrated by the merchants of the city – also members of the Third – but who saw themselves as of higher status because of their property and wealth. The separate document from the 'Bourgeois' of the city was drawn up by some of those merchants whose primary concerns were 'ruination' of business by 'voracious men of justice' and the excessive imposts on necessities and subsistence goods, which lessened their profits. Changes to the chaotic taxes and charges that affected the livelihood of those in the city were the major suggestion, especially the 'ruinous taxes' believed to be impeding the commerce of the city. These two documents of the Third thus clearly set out the major concerns of the silk industry: the difficulties faced by the poorer workers as well as those articulated by the richer merchants. They identify the fault lines that would later divide the Lyonnais in their attempts to achieve a fairer social and economic balance in the urban areas. The input of the 'peasants' in the rural areas was also clearly present in the sections that inveighed against the abuses of seigneurial justice. The primary document contained well-considered suggestions of the changes needed to both civil and criminal justice. In this respect, the primary *Sénéchaussée* document is in line with findings by Shapiro and Markoff that those *cahiers* with larger and more general grievances were often from areas in which there were later found to be popular uprisings.[16] Lyon and its surrounding communes had significant local and general issues to present to the king, and the potential for increasing agitation was causing some fear in the city.

The meeting of the Estates-General also necessitated elections within the three estates to appoint deputies, who were required to take the grievances to the king. The deputies elected then took part in the countrywide effort to contribute their opinions to the historic meeting of the Estates-General before the king at Versailles. The process was fraught with complexity, and Louis XVI was indecisive even when the deputies arrived in Versailles from May 1789. There were tensions over the purpose of the meeting and how votes would be taken to resolve the financial and other matters to be discussed, and the Third Estate gradually took on radical positions.[17] From 17–19 June, the Third declared themselves a sovereign National Assembly and were joined by most of the First (the more egalitarian of the Clergy). Together, these deputies took an oath on 20 June to remain united until they had drafted a new constitution. Shut out of their hall by the king and faced with the uncompromising attitude of the Second, the Assembly began to meet in a small building used to play the new game of *Jeux de Paume* (hand-tennis). The king ordered the remaining outsiders to join with the Assembly on 27 June.

Barely a month later, on 14 July, Parisians, enthusiastic about the new developments and anxious about a possible military coup being prepared to reverse the situation, managed to gather 8,000 rioters in front of the fortress prison of Paris and lay siege to it.[18] Although there were few political prisoners held in the fortress Bastille at the time, there was an arsenal that was ransacked for arms and gunpowder, and the sheer brazenness of the attack on this formidable building in the city of Paris had left the kingdom reeling. The fall of the Bastille had suddenly made clear to the king and the privileged classes the unequivocal political power of the people. The action helped convince some of the clergy and nobles who were still refusing to meet on equal terms with the more numerous Third Estate to reconsider the very basis upon which the monarchy had until then been organised. The appearance of the king himself at the National Assembly on 15 July ushered in a new era of popular politics, which resonated across the country.[19] Popular revolts in the capital had already drawn attention to wage cuts in the urban factories in April of 1789, and they continued in early July over the crises in prices of subsistence foods. The suddenly successful attempt to attack the Bastille became a turning point that convinced the *menu peuple* of their power.

Insurrections in Lyon were not at first as successful as they were in Paris, but emotions were still high. Rumours of the Third's attempt to be recognised as equally powerful as the other traditional orders in society slowly filtered down to Lyon and from there to the country regions. The Ampère family were ecstatic at the news of the fall of the Bastille in Paris. We know the moment was significant for Jean-Jacques because he used the Bastille as a backdrop in a play he was soon to write about the new wise king France could expect.[20] His son Andre-Marie later claimed the day was as important to him as his first communion.[21] Popular riots continued through the months of July and August in Lyon. The local issues were different to Paris but no less political.[22] Violent attacks were made on the internal tax barriers, which were overturned in a week of protest from 3 July 1789 by urban workers. The city was unusual because of the number of weavers who still operated in the urban area.[23] The limited focus of the militant weavers and hatters was also unusual, being largely confined to the customs barriers collecting the *octroi*, the tax on goods coming into the city.[24] The silk workers otherwise remained somewhat politically conservative because they were tied to the systems of production of La Fabrique and still aspired to become part of the hierarchy of merchants. The particular local idiosyncrasies of 'pride, solidarity in finding an economic solution', persisted.[25] There was a willingness to find a solution within the industrial structures in place, despite the difficulties and the complaints by the weavers.[26] Because of this conservatism, and despite the quite radical nature of the Third Estate *cahiers*, consular officials initially remained firmly in control of Lyon, and the attacks on the tax barriers did not lead to their abolition.

The commitment of the Consulate to making changes without impacting the rights of personal property was initially accepted by early Lyonnais 'patriots', but the repression used against the rioters eventually caused consternation. At first, the destructive attacks on the offices of the tax collectors, when records were burnt and thrown into the river, served to reinforce a fear amongst the propertied classes of popular violence and worked as a powerful disincentive to being known as a 'patriot'.[27] Gradually, the recognition of the difficulties for smaller businesses within the industry did grow along with a realisation that the only solutions proposed by the Consulate involved increasing violence. Militias drawn from local aristocratic families or from abroad were engaged and helped ensure that social divisions were becoming increasingly divisive.[28] Their use of repression meant a 'great gulf' had been opened up in Lyonnais society.[29] The mercantile elite approved of the measures of the Consulate, but a growing group of 'enlightened' bourgeois were becoming much more sympathetic to the problems of the poorer classes and contemptuous of the mercantile class.

In Paris, the historic vote of the National Constituent Assembly (NCA) occurred on 4 August, when deputies vowed to abolish the feudal system itself by a series of decrees. Aristocratic titles and privileges were renounced on this day, and commitments were made to accelerate new rights and liberties. On 29 August, the Declaration of the Rights of Man and Citizen was tabled and became the blueprint for the new constitutional monarchy, spelling out the equalities, rights and the ultimate sovereignty residing in the nation. These decrees had a powerful emotional effect on the deputies themselves and the rest of the nation.

The fundamental dissatisfactions of the urban poor in Lyon, however, continued to be ignored while the traditional elites – the rich merchants, the ennobled Consuls and the Church hierarchies – remained in power. Although the Church continued in its efforts to help the less fortunate, anger and political unrest continued to grow among the silk workers as the 'search for economic remedies' and the 'pride of belonging to La Fabrique' began to fail.[30] The conservative leadership of the Catholic Church was called into question because of its active role in criticising any acts of popular agitation. Monsignor Marbeuf had been appointed head of the diocese in 1788 and remained resolutely counter-revolutionary.[31] He posted an order in the city, condemning social activism after the first riots in 1789.[32] What was seen as an insensitive dismissal of real problems helped harden opinion against him and other Church leaders and ultimately against the role of the Church in society.

While the Marquis de Mont d'Or made an appearance in the body now called the NCA for the Second Estate of Lyon, he was often absent during the course of the ongoing deliberations, claiming illness.[33] The deputies of the Third Estate of Lyon sent to Versailles, on the other hand, were very active. They were mostly urban 'notables' who had the status of *négociant* or were prominent merchants. However, among them was also a doctor, a tanner and the two most vocal representatives of their team: Jean-André Périsse-Duluc (a printer) and Jean-Jacques Millanois (a member of the Académie), both also Freemasons.[34] Périsse-Duluc observed that the clergy and nobles who now joined the NCA 'along with a lesser number of commoners' began to immediately form a team and were so strong because they would 'never differ on their votes'. They became known as the Monarchiens, and although the Third at first went 'out of their way to encourage the participation of their new colleagues', according to Timothy Tackett those deputies of the Left (among whom he included Périsse-Duluc), many of whom would later become known as 'Jacobins', were in October feeling in the minority.[35] By October, the market women of Paris took the further unprecedented action of escorting the king and his family to the capital.[36] The National Assembly also moved to the Salle du Manège (stables) of the dilapidated palace of the Tuileries in Paris by early November.

By December 1789, the Third had managed to gain stronger control over the NCA with the formation of the political club 'Amis de la Constitution', known as the Jacobins. Tackett shows that the Jacobins, who were overwhelmingly from the Third, were then able to counter the right-wing factions that had become a bloc in the voting of the NCA and themselves become a strong political force.[37] The clubs began to spread outside of the capital and became particularly strong in Lyon. Their proliferation ensured that discussions grew about the feudal and religious privileges that impacted the lives of both urban and country Lyonnais and the economic and social problems that had still not been addressed.

Notes

1. J.-P. Jessenne, 'The Social and Economic Crisis in France at the End of the *Ancien Régime*', in P. McPhee, *A Companion to the French Revolution* (Chichester: Wiley Blackwell, 2015), 36–40. Expenses of 620,000 *livres* were noted compared to receipts of 500,000.
2. T. Tackett, *The Coming of the Terror in the French Revolution* (Cambridge, MA: The Belknap Press of Harvard University Press, 2015), 42. Initially discussing fiscal reform, the Assembly was reconvened in 1788 to discuss the organisation of a meeting of the Estates-General in 1789.
3. Jessenne, 'The Social and Economic Crisis', 39.
4. According to Tackett, this 'harrowing' winter was 'the coldest that century': Tackett, *The Coming of the Terror*, 52.

5. L. Trénard, 'La Crise sociale Lyonnaise à la veille de la Révolution', *Revue d'histoire moderne et contemporaine* 2 (1955), 14.
6. Trénard, 'La Crise sociale', 18–19, 35.
7. Trénard, 'La Crise sociale', 37–38.
8. Tackett, *The Coming of the Terror*, 43.
9. M. Garden, 'La Révolution et l'Empire', in A. Latreille, *Histoire de Lyon et du Lyonnais* (Toulouse: Privat, 1975), 288.
10. B. Edmonds, 'A Study in Popular Anti-Jacobinism: The Career of Denis Monnet', *French Historical Studies* 13 (1983), 215–51.
11. ADR (Poleymieux), 153/1.
12. G. Shapiro and J. Markoff, *Revolutionary Demands: A Content Analysis of the Cahiers de Doléances of 1789* (Stanford, CA: Stanford University Press, 1998), 103,114.
13. P. McPhee, *The French Revolution 1789–1799* (New York: Oxford University Press, 2002), 62.
14. *Cahier des doléances du Beaujolais par les États-Généraux de 1789* (Lyon: Imprimerie Nouvelle Lyonnaise, 1939), 2.
15. AP, *Cahier des doléances pour les États-Généraux de 1789* [Sénéchaussée de Lyon]. Accessed 1 December 2015, http://gallica.bnf.fr. 'Nota' (1).
16. These authors compared and analysed the various *cahiers* to determine the pronouncements they contained and what that revealed about later revolutionary action in the various provinces of the country, Shapiro and Markoff, *Revolutionary Demands*, 419.
17. Tackett, *The Coming of the Terror*, 48–51.
18. P. McPhee, *Liberty or Death: The French Revolution* (New Haven and London: Yale University Press, 2016), 75–78.
19. Tackett, *The Coming of the Terror*, 57.
20. Jean-Jacques Ampère, '"Artaxerxce": Tragédie du père d'Ampère, papiers de André-Marie Ampère', Fonds Ampère, Archives d'Académie des Sciences [AAS], Paris. Série J. Chemise 292.
21. J.R. Hoffman, *André-Marie* (Oxford: Blackwell, 1995).
22. Donald Sutherland suggests all rioting in 1789 differed in the way it addressed fiscal and subsistence questions from Paris: D. Sutherland, 'Urban Crowds, Riot, Utopia, and Massacres, 1789-92', in P. McPhee, *A Companion to the French Revolution* (Chichester: Wiley Blackwell, 2015), 237.
23. D. Longfellow, 'Silk Weavers and the Social Struggle in Lyon during the French Revolution, 1789–94'. *French Historical Studies* 12 (1981), 11.
24. W. Edmonds, *Jacobinism and the Revolt of Lyon, 1789–1793* (New York: Oxford University Press, 1990), 13–16.
25. Trénard, 'La Crise sociale', 45.
26. Longfellow, 'Silk Weavers', 4–9.
27. Edmonds, *Jacobinism*, 47–49.
28. B. Edmonds, 'The Rise and Fall of Popular Democracy in Lyon 1789–1795', *Bulletin of the John Rylands Library* (1984), 411.
29. Edmonds, 'The Rise and Fall', 411.
30. Trénard, 'La Crise sociale', 45.
31. P. Chopelin, *Ville patriote et ville martyr: Lyon, l'église et la Révolution, 1788–1805* (Paris: Letouzey et Ané, 2010), 15, 74.
32. A. Champdor, *Lyon pendant la Révolution 1789–1793* (Lyon: Albert Guillot, 1983), 12.
33. E.H. Lemay, *Dictionnaire des Constituants: 1789–1791* (Paris: Universitas, 1991).
34. See the biographical details of Lemay, *Dictionnaire des Constituants*.

35. T. Tackett, 'Nobles and Third Estate in the Revolutionary Dynamic of the National Assembly, 1789–90', in G. Kates (ed.), *The French Revolution: Recent Debates and New Controversies* (London: Routledge, 1998), 202–208.
36. D. Garrioch, 'The Everyday Lives of Parisian Women and the October Days of 1789', *Social History* 24(3) (Oct. 1999), 245, 249.
37. Tackett, 'Nobles and Third Estate', 214–17.

Chapter 4

THE CANDLE FLARES

> Finally we left Monsieur Ampère [after a thorough search of his house, cellars and lofts], overwhelmed with his evident honesty, and his wish to accompany us, candle in hand, far from the boundaries of his property.
>
> —Ryard and the National Guard, December 1790

The geopolitical changes that were put in place in Lyon and its surrounds during 1790–91 were huge. From September 1789, the kingdom had been divided into eighty *départements* and within each of them another nine districts and then a series of nine cantons. The aim of the NCA was to achieve a mixture of country and urban areas in each administrative unit and a measure of uniformity throughout the nation.[1] Voting for citizens to hold administrative office, one of the most important steps towards modern democratic practice, took place in primary assemblies based in the *départements* or in additional units called *sections* in the bigger cities like Lyon.[2] Even some of the smallest parishes in the country, like Poleymieux, were given renewed status as communes and the power to elect a municipality.[3] The *départements* each had a *chef-lieu*, a centre of administration. Civil judicial functions were completely reimagined and began with the establishment of a law court in each of the new districts, with its officers also elected. Lyon retained its premier status in the region as the *chef-lieu* of the Département du Rhône.[4] The physical transformations required a correspondingly huge personal transformation among the Lyonnais, what was often called at the time a 'regeneration'.

* * *

The Lyonnais found the first year of Revolution an emotional time. Great enthusiasms about changes were ignited among those who identified as 'patriots' in the city, but at the beginning of 1790 the Consulate retained political control and took greater account of the fears of the property owners and the mercantile elites than the needs of the *menu peuple*. Imbert-Colomès, chief Consul, refused to disband the militia responsible for stopping protests and riots.[5] As a result, social activists and concerned reformers began to unite in opposition to his policies. The Consulate wanted to keep using Swiss regiments to patrol vulnerable spots in the city rather than support the election of the new National Guard. When they blatantly arranged for a large contingent of foreigners to reinforce the security of the arsenal on the hills above the Saône, a confrontation was planned. On 7 February 1790, a revolutionary crowd invaded the arsenal, took weapons and gunpowder from its stores and managed to rout those sent to disperse them.[6] Reinforcements were unable to prevent the attack from spreading to the Hôtel de Ville.[7] The Consulate recognised its defeat and sat in its last session on 12 April 1790, and Lyon finally achieved the 'municipal revolution' that the patriots were demanding in March and that had taken place in Paris the previous year. Those who had attacked the arsenal were never called to account, and their weapons remained dispersed amongst the *menu peuple*, who had instigated the action.[8] Patriots were enthused by the positive changes and were encouraged by the fact that changes would soon be made that would pacify the poorer groups in society.

Others could only see the negatives. Despite the electoral changes, the *menu peuple*, who did not earn enough to be eligible to vote, were dismayed that the rich and powerful were still in control as 'active citizens'. They felt powerless unless they rioted. Many property owners then feared the increasing violence in the city, and this fear was reflected in the choices of those elected to the municipality in March 1790. Fleury-Zacharie-Simon Palerne de Savy became the Mayor. He was a high-ranking magistrate from the *ancien régime* commercial court. Most of the other municipal officers were also fairly conservative choices; *négociants*, bankers and ex-consuls. There was just one baker and one draper elected with the lowest property requirement.[9] The group as a whole were still more likely to support the property owners than support radical change. By July 1790, the workers were again expressing their disillusionment. They were not impressed by the celebrations planned to celebrate the anniversary of the storming of the Bastille. They wanted flood relief and other immediate concerns of shortages of bread and coal addressed. An attempt to foreground the ceremony of giving the Pierre-Scize prison (known as the 'Bastille Lyonnaise') to the people as part of the celebrations did not appease them, because 'the people recognised that they were only spectators'.[10] They saw the marked disjuncture between an appearance of support for the Revolution by the traditional elite and any comprehension of the needs of the poor and disaffected in Lyon. The *octrois* barriers, which had been re-erected after their destruction a year earlier, were again smashed.

The *octrois* barriers had become an enduring symbol of oppression for the *menu peuple*, but the municipal administrators ensured they remained in place. Foreign troops continued to be used, as in the past, to repress the riots, which started during the celebration of Bastille Day in July 1790. The Swiss regiment brought in to guard the customs barriers from attacks had no sympathy with popular concerns, and many could not even speak French. The violence soon escalated against them until, in August, a Swiss soldier by the name of Antoine Lager was knifed and killed. His body was strung up on a lamp post and mutilated by a group of rioters. The attackers were later convicted and subjected to a correspondingly horrible reprisal following their conviction:

> Denis Saulnier had his arms, thighs and waist broken, his body exposed on the wheel to there finish his days and the said Dalou had been hung and strangled, both with a sign before and behind them proclaiming: *séditieux* and *assassins*.[11]

This judgment has been seen as the final episode of aristocratic reaction against the *menu peuple*.[12] Rather than the disturbances themselves, it was the high-handed attitude of the ruling élite that continued to ignite the political consciousness of the *menu peuple* and also encouraged support for the struggle against such repression among the rest of the Third Estate.

The campaign for a new system of criminal justice to end such horrendous punishments as the 'breaking on the wheel' continued in the growing club movement. Bourgeois professionals and artisans became vocal about the need for justice and expressed these and other concerns in the forum of the new Société des Amis de la Constitution (Friends of the Constitution). This group had officially formed in September 1790 when it allied with the Jacobin club in Paris, but some of its members had earlier been part of the Club du Concert. By August 1790, the latter club became known as the 'Feuillants', and those who remained were mostly conservative merchants.[13] The newer Jacobin Club was a predominantly bourgeois movement with a strong connection to the Masonic lodges and circles of the former regime.[14] It had some forty bourgeois members, a high subscription fee to join, and met on Sunday after boules.[15] One of the most prominent members was Jean-Marie Roland. Roland had been active in the Academy des Belles-Lettres of the *ancien regime*, a Masonic lodge and the Société d'agriculture and had worked as an inspector in La Fabrique but had become in the eyes of some a 'dangerous and outspoken radical' during the late 1780s.[16] Another prominent founding member of the club movement was François Billiemas, a court official, who had also been a Freemason.[17] His stated aim was to move the *menu peuple* away from violent riots and into more egalitarian-structured popular clubs in the *sections*.[18]

The popular societies, based on the political organisation of the *sections*, grew more quickly than the original Jacobin club.[19] They were characterised by a much less onerous property qualification and a wider representation across the working professions. Sectional club members soon numbered 3,000, and each *section* was able to send three delegates to meet as a powerful Central Club.[20] The clubs gave the Third Estate a political voice, which helped achieve relative peace. Roland felt that hope for the future lay in the formation of the sectional clubs of the *quartier* with their 'educating mission', and it was this benefit rather than greater social or political participation that he wanted to encourage among the poorer groups of society.[21]

The bourgeois clubbists as well as poorer workers who joined the popular clubs were 'early choosers' of Revolution, those who historian Peter Jones has suggested had a 'Rousseauvian' enthusiasm for change at this point. They were 'men with a sense of commitment ... a self-selected group who had served an apprenticeship to the cause'.[22] They volunteered for committees, which took on much of the work required to reorganise the administrative units and also the new judicial institutions of the country.[23] François Billiemas was such a 'chooser' and became involved with the implementation of the new judicial changes as well as organising the more accessible popular clubs. He was a staunch defender of the constitutional monarchy who saw the 'advantages of the victory of the bourgeoisie' and who used Rousseau to fight against the 'ignorance and superstition'.[24] Roland was also a leading 'chooser' at this stage and was supportive of both 'patriot' clubs.

Roland was, however, strenuously opposed to social disorder and was unable to understand the propensity to violence of the *menu peuple*.[25] Yet, he did express himself in radical ways to would-be reformers in a pamphlet in January of 1790, which clearly stated what steps were most necessary for revolutionary advancement. These were 'a total regeneration of ... [*les moeurs*]' of the city to address the inequalities between the social classes and the abolition of some of the most hated taxes, including the *octroi*.[26] Roland began to demand greater help for the poor than many other 'respectable' reformers.[27] He supported the production of cheap bread and policies designed to appeal to the popular classes precisely

Figure 4.1 *Jean-Marie Roland de la Platière*. J. Chinard, inv. H2054. Bibliothèque et documentation, Musée des Beaux-Arts Lyon.

because they would obviate the need for violence.[28] Social inequities would be adjusted, he argued, if unfair taxes and import duties were abolished. During his time as a supplementary officer (*notable*) in the municipality, his *ardeur démocratique* continued to grow.[29]

Roland continued to devote himself to the question of customs duties because of the wider benefits he saw for the city. He and his wife, who adopted the name Manon, were open to a more egalitarian way of living, even considering a radical communal life with like-minded friends for a short period.[30] They became instantly popular when on 8 July 1790 they presented a petition, in the presence of a huge crowd of spectators, demanding the suppression of taxes on foodstuffs.[31] The liberal bourgeois in Lyon did follow much of his advice even when he moved to Paris to pursue the issue of tax relief for the local municipality. When the *octrois* taxes were abolished as a result of his intervention in early 1791, the alliance of bourgeois reformers and those more popular clubbists elected from the sectional clubs did then become strong and stable and they continued to look to Roland as a leader. There were fewer riots because the artisans, especially the silk weavers, had influence through those they supported and elected through the sectional clubs and the Central Club. Roland was looked upon as a mentor 'by a slightly younger generation of local revolutionaries' although he was recognised as being 'irritatingly virtuous'.[32] His suggestions, however, often inspired fear in more conservative voters.

The clubs and their members gradually became more involved in politics to counteract the reactionary element in the city.[33] The evolving forms of the political clubs in the regions of France and in Paris during the Revolution eventually provided a choice between two political views, the Girondin (moderate) or Montagnard (radical) in the national sphere.[34] This basic duality was reflected in Lyon. The less radical Jacobins were more usually called 'Rolandins', in a derogatory sense because of their belief in economic liberalism, which was contrasted to the popular economics espoused by the Chalier-Jacobins.[35] Neither nomenclature represented a truly unified or cohesive group. Luc-Antoine Champagneux became an influential republican and associated first with Chalier and later with the more moderate group. He began to print his own radical newspaper in September 1789, called the *Courrier de Lyon*.[36] He had been a lawyer but had become disillusioned with the local reactions to the Revolution. He explained in September 1790 why he had done so:

> I was full of admiration for the decrees of the legislative body ... I regarded as the most deplorable of men those who, putting on a mask of their attachment to the new constitution, and thus attracting the confidence of electors, then brought into the posts they thus obtained, all the ideas of the *ancien régime*.[37]

Champagneux aimed to bring the local community closer to the 'incredible happenings' in the National Assembly in Paris and, in addition, to provide a forum for the debates that challenged the traditional hierarchies of Lyon.

Clubbists in Lyon were able to discuss the latest news from Paris because of the availability of a number of journals like Champagneux's *Courrier*. This paper was only one of a number of newspapers that noted the day-to-day problems that were being faced by the Lyonnais, including the economic and social crises, but that also published news of revolutionary ideas and political changes as they happened in the capital. The Lyonnais could also subscribe to *Le Moniteur*, which recorded the debates in the National Assembly from 1789, and Brissot's *Le Patriote française*, which often included some critical articles written by the Rolands. Manon contributed to this paper under the name of the 'Roman woman' because she felt so close to the democratic impulse that had begun in antiquity.[38] The *Affiches de Lyon* printed announcements of events and was published weekly. In 1784, the *Journal de Lyon* took over much of this operation. Such journals could be read in the bookshops and in various libraries in Lyon, both public and private, if readers were unable to purchase a subscription.[39] The enormous library of the Collège de la Trinité had been open to the public for two days a week since the Revolution and was a popular place to read the wide array of journals in the city.[40]

Champagneux's paper throughout the year of 1790 performed an educative function, reassuring readers of the benefits of revolutionary change.[41] There were articles about the *octrois* taxes and the reason for the riots against them, commentaries about the new system of revolutionary justice that had been promulgated, and opinion pieces about the state of the prisons, which Champagneux felt also needed to be reformed. A number of issues were devoted to explaining the proposed judicial changes and particularly the crucial role of the *juge de paix*. There was a discussion about the laws concerning the new magistrates, about their proposed payment, about their election, about the sharing of judicial power with the government and society and, finally, about what made a good judge.[42] Other issues debated generally in this year were the financial concerns of the city and rising incidences of forgery as a consequence of the new paper money (*assignats*) put in circulation to enable the purchase of *bien nationaux* (property that had previously belonged to the Church).

The *Courrier* usually began with an editorial piece, but Champagneux often included anonymous letters about revolutionary issues. Some of these letters were written by Jean-Marie Roland and others by his wife.[43] One anonymous letter, typical of the newspaper's stance, was published in the third issue of September 1790 and concerned the abolition of noble titles in August of the previous year. The author was a man of 60 years of age, who had renounced 'with pleasure' his position as *secrétaire du roi*, a venal title he had bought under the previous regime. The letter expressed a whole-hearted recognition of the wisdom and the justice of the decree and the author's welcoming of his new title of 'citoyen françois'.[44] During 1790, the *Courrier* chronicled similarly happy reactions of its readers, people like its principal author, Champagneux, who were passionate about revolutionary change, but also included debates from those worried about some of its less positive implications. Until he retired from writing in September 1790, Champagneux dealt serially with such important issues and their reception in the local society. Matters of concern, such as the number of poor driven to suicide and the devastation caused by the flooding of the local rivers, were included with very little comment. Notices were given about what was happening in the local theatre. All these topics show the preoccupations of the Rolandins: the need for change, the promise of new ideas of justice, and optimism about how it could be achieved, and, of course, the important question to many Lyonnais of what was showing at the theatre.

The changes of 1789–90 that Champagneux described were considered transformational by the urban professional classes but were not immediately understood in the same way by the peasants in rural and country areas, who continued to owe harvest dues to their *seigneur* and the *dîme* to the Catholic Church. It was soon realised that these 'peaceful' inhabitants needed their own instruction in the laws and the events that were affecting them, partly to ensure that they remained peaceful. From September 1790, another important subscription newspaper called the *Feuille Villageoise* became available. It was a nationwide paper sent into the provinces with a more obvious pedagogical emphasis. The weekly was directed at local *curés* or landholders, who were expected to relay the articles to their own non-literate peasant communities.[45] Like the *Courrier*, this paper provided explanations of the many revolutionary changes, including those to the judicial system, and advised people how the new *juges de paix* and juries would work.[46] The *Feuille Villageoise* was founded by the Abbé Joachim Cérruti, who wrote articles in it until his death in 1792 and who had a strong focus on the religious changes supported by the constitutional clergy.[47] This abbé had in fact been a professor at the Jesuit Collège de la Trinité in Lyon before his religious order was expelled in 1762. As a result of his influence, the paper also offered a radical interpretation of the more general changes as they concerned the traditional institutions of the Church. It was supportive of a reformed Church committed to reducing the proprietorial abuses and returning to more fundamental principles of simple *curés*. When 'seditious' bishops attempted, in early

1791, to turn the local *curés* against making the required oath to the constitution, which enabled them to be paid by the state, the paper explained the 'duty' of *curés* to provide civil as well as religious instruction.[48] While it did provide a forum for rural problems, the paper emphasised in each issue the primary educative function it served to those who needed to be 'regenerated' rather than giving villagers a political voice.[49] For example, soon after the paper appeared, it used a dialogue between an angry peasant and his *seigneur* to educate the people about the wider implications of the feudal issues that the countryside was particularly affected by. Rather than encourage divisive opinions, the rural newspaper concentrated on the need for restraint and trust in the moderate patriots.[50]

The small country town of Poleymieux was having its own debates about feudal changes, and there was increasingly a feeling that something must be done about the *seigneur*, who had purchased the local castle and who was seeking more dues from members of the small commune. Grumbles and stories circulated of his latest excesses.[51] At this stage, Jean-Jacques Ampère purchased a subscription for the *Feuille Villageoise*, evidence of his strong belief in the possibility of personal change, religious change and ultimately changes to the absolutist monarchy that had ruled France for centuries.[52] The future of France, he thought, depended on citizens embracing new ways of thinking, but that depended on an orderly process of education, which this rural paper provided. According to Melvin Edelstein, the *Feuille Villageoise* was one of the most popular papers in the period, not least because of its claim to be apolitical.[53] Its biggest concern became to disseminate an interpretation of Christianity that emphasised the 'close alliance of a reformed Catholic Church and the larger project of national regeneration', as another historian, Anthony Crubaugh, also noted.[54] The paper suited the intellectual outlook of Ampère, and he presumably did discuss with his neighbours the ideas the paper was attempting to disseminate – quite possibly on a Sunday after the church service held by the local constitutional *curé*.

A reformed church was a popular idea among clergy and their rural parishes; however, many urban Lyonnais preferred other avenues of sociability and discussion. Those involved in the popular forum of the Freemasons continued to meet regularly. Their lodges had divided into those supportive of the Revolution and others, such as those part of the group known as the 'Cercle des Maçons de la Bienfaisance', who were more critical of the new order. One of the leading Freemasons, Jean-Baptiste Willermoz, along with Jean-André Périsse-Duluc and Jacques Millanois (deputies of Lyon to the NCA), were of the former group and had views that tended to align them with the 'camp of the Jacobins,

Figure 4.2 The route to the local church. Photograph by the author.

as much as their tastes and their relations classed them with those of the moderates [*modérées*]'.[55] Other 'circles', including the Maçons de la Bienfaisance, regularly discussed the news from Paris.[56] They were places where the 'rather messy interaction between the concerns of literary men ... and merchants' took place but that were predicated on 'one's having a certain position in the property order'.[57] The taverns in Lyon were also places of 'daily sociability' and discussion. Official opening hours had extended to 11 PM after the Revolution, and their numbers increased despite the concerns of the local priests.[58]

By the end of 1790, the most significant political discussions in Lyon centred on the growing alarm among 'patriots' that many political leaders were becoming overtly counter-revolutionary. High-ranking nobles and aristocrats, including Imbert-Colomès, were believed to be planning a royalist plot, which would see the king brought to Lyon and then 'liberated' to the court of Turin across the border in Italy. According to Amable Audin, this plot was a barely disguised secret.[59] Denunciations and allegations of those involved further split the Freemasonry movement.[60] The 'aristocratic' conspiracy had in fact become increasingly unlikely to eventuate when the king himself refused to come to Lyon, yet the plotting continued. These machinations were uncovered in December 1790 and the leaders were indicted.

Unrepentant royalist leaders were imprisoned, and many others who were implicated, including Imbert-Colomès and Monseigneur Marbeuf, were finally expelled from the city.

Another aristocrat heavily involved in the conspiracy was Guillin de Pougelon. He was imprisoned in Paris and charged with counter-revolution. He was in fact the brother of the *seigneur* of Poleymieux, Guillin Dumontet. This connection only encouraged suspicion of the *seigneur* and his activities in the area where he lived. The *seigneur* had by now effectively turned most of the inhabitants of Poleymieux against him. He had long been seen to be acting against the interests of the local Poleymoriots and was only concerned about his own aggrandisement as a letter he sent to the municipality of Lyon at the beginning of 1790 showed. In the letter, the *seigneur* complained about 'the beasts that roamed unchecked over his land', up to his very windows where their noise prevented his wife getting any sleep.[61] The deliberations of the Poleymieux commune frequently discussed the problems the *seigneur* caused the locals, including the unprovoked firing of a gun at a peasant on 1 February 1790. On 23 April 1790, Brunet, the former *châtelain* and now *procureur syndic* in Poleymieux, was 'forced' to denounce the *seigneur* to the National Assembly because of the latter's 'unheard of treatment' of his subjects and demands of excessive feudal dues, which 'could not be checked by the poor inhabitants'.[62] Brunet complained in his letter that those affected by the demands of Guillin Dumontet were, however, too poor to pay to verify his claims, with the result that he alone profited. Brunet asked for 'prompt justice' to the 'prayers of the poor'.[63]

It was becoming apparent to the Poleymoriots that their heavy burden of feudal dues was not going to be simply abolished but transmuted into even more flagrantly unfair obligations that had to be paid out by those who wanted to be free of them. Rather than a lessening of feudal dues owed to him, Guillin Dumontet insisted upon increased compensation for the loss of his rights, which effectively meant his constituents had no relief at all.[64] Dumontet claimed the National Assembly had authorised him to 'insist that the Commune verify his demands as *seigneur* according to the compensation provisions of the August decree'.[65] The peasantry thus had a parallel experience of the Revolution to the nobles and the bourgeois, as Anatoli Ado showed was common in the country. They got little benefit from the sale of *biens nationaux* of the Church because they could not afford to purchase confiscated land, but they were more than ever affected by the redeemable dues that *seigneurs* claimed and that the 'bourgeois' lawyers assessed and ratified.[66] Active citizens of Poleymieux began to raise their voices in the commune meetings, held every Sunday after church in the mayoral offices.

Ampère, the former *procureur* of Poleymieux, was one of the five bourgeois families of means in Poleymieux. Although nominated for a position on the local assembly, he was, however, not elected to any significant role.[67] This result was more than likely because of his former work for the *seigneur* in the local Gruerie, which may have compromised him in the eyes of his neighbours. Seigneurial justice was believed to have helped 'transform the country in the bourgeois sense' by validating the triumph of 'agrarian individualism' that Guillin Dumontet represented.[68] Given the worsening relations between the villagers and the grasping *seigneur*, any alliance with him, no matter how short-lived, would likely be considered negatively. Ampère had a slightly higher property assessment than Brunet, who was elected on 1 January as *procureur*, and Antoine Royet, who was also then elected mayor.[69] After the disappointment of not being chosen for a local role, Ampère appears to have attended fewer of the local meetings, and this withdrawal could be expected to further heighten suspicion of his status.

In nearby Chasselay, the members of the revolutionary clubs were particularly keen to make sure that the homes of the so-called aristocrats, including the châteaux of the *seigneur*, were kept under observation for any counter-revolutionary activity. On 14 December 1790, Ampère's home and the castle of Poleymieux were both subjected to searches following rumours that arms and counter-revolutionaries were suspected of being hidden in the village. In an account of the events by the commissars, it appears Ampère consented to the search of his home. He even encouraged a more assiduous checking of his 'heaps of hemp' and the straw the household used to stuff their bed mattresses. Ampère opened his cellars, granaries and stables with such goodwill that the search was cut short; the searchers were 'overwhelmed with his evident honesty and his wish to accompany [them], candle in hand, far from the boundaries of his property'.[70] While the *seigneur* also consented to a search at this time he only did so grudgingly, all the while asserting his rights.[71] In another six months' time, another search would lead to a spectacular eruption of violence. The rural areas were unconvinced by the transformations of the Revolution.

Despite the rural disaffection, there was a more hopeful mood in the city in late 1790. Many of the old élite were banished or imprisoned, and the municipality of Lyon became the focus of real change. With the removal of Imbèrt-Colomes, more committed revolutionaries gradually came to the fore. At the municipal elections in November and December 1790, Roland and like-minded others who had been elected earlier as *notables* moved into the role of municipal officers. Roland became the chair of the finance committee.[72] The burgeoning club movement introduced new members to the electors of Lyon. It thus encouraged a politicisation of the artisanal class and 'placed new weapons in the hands of the *menu peuple* ... the *section*, the concept of citizenship, and the even more subversive concept of equality of rights'.[73]

Changes to criminal justice were as high on the agenda for these newly elected Lyonnais politicians as they were for Parisians, and Ampère would soon also be attracted to the city to help this group implement them. These changes were to be based on 'clear and coherent principles, the first of which was an assertion that justice was a public power with the sovereign Nation as its source'.[74] The aims to be achieved in the new institutions were signalled by Adrien Duport, a deputy in the NCA. He was a member of the Second Estate when elected to the Estates-General, originally a career magistrate in an *ancien régime Parlement*, but he soon became a member of the left side of politics and a Jacobin and argued for extensive judicial changes.[75] Talking of the jury system, Duport connected this initiative to the ideals of 1789:

> This blessed institution of juries, alone, can banish from the heart of the citizen the fear and the numerous vices that this bred and gives to him that confidence ... [that] he is not alone on the earth; that there exists for him a protection against injustice and that this protection he will find amidst those who surround him, amongst the neighbours who only ask, in return, the same dispensations on his part. There is the true way to give to moral men, a deep humanity, the love of equality and fraternity. [76]

Given his experience of the social problems caused by seigneurial justice, the ideals expressed by Duport would have resonated strongly with Ampère. Judicial reform was a rallying point for him as it was for other 'enlightened' bourgeois in Paris and in Lyon, in the cities and the country. The laws of the NCA of 1791 were beginning to make the extraordinary changes to the judicial and administrative systems that reflected the ideals of 1789 and the bourgeois who committed to revolutionary change as well as the *menu peuple*, who having become more politically radical were more confident that real and lasting change was being effected.

Notes

1. I. Woloch, *The New Regime Transformation of the French Civic Order, 1789–1820* (New York: W.W. Norton and Co., 1994), 37.
2. M. Crook, *Elections in the French Revolution: An Apprenticeship in Democracy, 1789–1799* (Cambridge: Cambridge University Press, 1996).

3. Woloch, *The New Regime*, 31.
4. F.A. Varnet, *Geographie du département du Rhône* (Lyon: Gallica, 1897), 35. By 1793, it changed to the Départment du Rhône-et-Loire.
5. L. Trénard, *La Révolution Française dans la région Rhône-Alpes* (Paris: Perrin, 1992), 199.
6. Trénard, *La Révolution Française*, 199.
7. W. Edmonds, *Jacobinism and the Revolt of Lyon, 1789–1793* (New York: Oxford University Press, 1990), 50.
8. Edmonds, *Jacobinism*, 50.
9. Edmonds, *Jacobinism*, 312.
10. This prompted the inked inscription on an aquatint held in the Musée Gadagne of the château Pierre-Scize, describing the event ironically as the 'ridiculous image of the château de Pierre-Scize'. S. Wahnich, *Des Objets qui racontent l'histoire: Collections du Musée Gadagne* (Lyon: ÉMCC, 2003), 24.
11. B. Benôit, 'Analyse des violences urbaines à l'époque révolutionnaire: l'exemple Lyonnais', in B. Benôit (ed.), *Ville et Révolution Française: Actes du Colloque International, Lyon, Mars 1993* (Lyon: Presses universitaires de Lyon, 1994), 149.
12. Benôit, 'Analyse des violences urbaines', 149.
13. Trénard, *La Révolution française*, 265.
14. G. Kates, *The 'Cercle Social', the Girondins, and the French Revolution* (Princeton, NJ: Princeton University Press, 1985), 90–91.
15. M. Wahl, *Les Premières années de la Révolution à Lyon 1788–1792* (Paris: Armand Colin, 1894), 226.
16. S. Reynolds, *Marriage and Revolution: Monsieur and Madame Roland* (Oxford: Oxford University Press, 2012), 108–11.
17. Trénard, *La Révolution Française*, 252.
18. W. Edmonds, 'The Rise and Fall of Popular Democracy in Lyon 1789–1795', *Bulletin of the John Rylands Library* (1984), 408.
19. Wahl, *Les Premières années*, 226.
20. Trénard, *La Révolution Française*, 265.
21. Trénard, *La Révolution Française*, 123–24.
22. P. Jones, 'Choosing Revolution and Counter-Revolution', in P. McPhee (ed.), *A Companion to the French Revolution* (Chichester: Wiley Blackwell Publishing, 2015), 279–81; 285–86.
23. E.H. Lemay and A. Patrick. *Revolutionaries at Work: The Constituent Assembly 1789–1791* (Oxford, 1996), 6–9.
24. Trénard, *La Révolution Française*, 265.
25. Reynolds, *Marriage and Revolution*, 122.
26. Reynolds, *Marriage and Revolution*, 117.
27. Reynolds, *Marriage and Revolution*, 111.
28. Reynolds, *Marriage and Revolution*, 124.
29. É. Bernardin, *Jean-Marie Roland et le Ministère de l'Intérieur 1792–1793* (Paris: Société des études Robespierristes, 1964), 12–13.
30. Reynolds, *Marriage and Revolution*, 126–33.
31. AML 1 CM 1. 8 July 1790.
32. Reynolds, *Marriage and Revolution*, 294–96.
33. Reynolds, *Marriage and Revolution*, 124.
34. M.L. Kennedy, *The Jacobin Clubs in the French Revolution, 1793–1795* (New York and Oxford: Berghahn Books, 2000), 8–9.
35. Wahnich, *Des objets*, 66.

36. G. Feyel, *Dictionnaire de la presse française pendant la Révolution 1789–1799*, Tome 1 (Paris: Centre International d'étude du XVIIIe siècle, 2005), 293–370.
37. *Courrier de Lyon*, 27 September 1790.
38. Reynolds, *Marriage and Revolution*, 114.
39. Trénard considers these papers the first examples of a local press and notes subscriptions were held by the public libraries, *La Révolution Française*, 98–99.
40. S. Van Damme, 'Sociabilité et culture urbaines', *Histoire de l'éducation* 90 (2001), 89.
41. Champagneux noted the attempted suicide of a woman of 50 years old, 'poussée par la misére', who threw herself into the Rhône on the morning of 8 September 1790 and a man who on the same day suicided in his rooms. *Courrier de Lyon*, 15 September 1790.
42. *Courrier de Lyon*, 4 September 1790; 1 September 1790; 15 September 1790.
43. Reynolds, *Marriage and Revolution*, 113–14.
44. *Courrier de Lyon*, 3 September 1790.
45. *La Feuille Villageoise*, Gallica BNF.
46. *La Feuille Villageoise*, 156.
47. See the entry on 'Cérruti' by Serge Bianchi, in A. Soboul (ed.), *Dictionnaire historique de la Révolution Française* (Paris: PUF, 1989), 199.
48. *La Feuille Villageoise*, 384–85.
49. M. Edelstein, '*La Feuille Villageoise*, the Revolutionary Press, and the Question of Rural Political Participation', *French Historical Studies* 7 (1971), 176, 178.
50. *La Feuille Villageoise*, issue 3.
51. The *seigneur* was alleged to have limited citizen access to common lands and shot at alleged trespassers. Letter sent to the National Assembly in April 1971 by the mayor Chomel and Secretary Botton, Poleymieux, AN D/XXIX/65.
52. See M. Dûrr, 'Liste de livres de bibliothéque Ampère', Fonds Ampère, AAS. Chemise 364.
53. Edelstein, '*La Feuille Villageoise*', 177.
54. A. Crubaugh, 'The Peasant at the Gates of Heaven: *La Feuille Villageoise*, Religion, and the French Revolution, 1790–1791', *Journal of the Illinois State Historical Society* 38 (2010), 3.
55. A. Joly, *Un Mystique Lyonnais et les secrets de la franc-maçonnerie: Jean-Baptiste Willermoz 1730–1824* (Paris: Ed. Télètos, 1938), 283.
56. Trénard, *La Révolution Française*, 265.
57. J. Landes, *Women and the Public Sphere in the Age of the French Revolution* (Ithaca, NY: Cornell University Press, 1988), 43.
58. Trénard, *La Révolution Française*, 258.
59. A. Audin, *La Conspiration Lyonnaise de 1790 et le drame de Poleymieux* (Lyon: Éd. lyonnaises d'art et d'histoire, 1984), 29.
60. Joly, *Un Mystique Lyonnais*, 285.
61. ADR Archives Communale (Poleymieux) EDEPOT 153/3, Lettre IV.
62. AN, D/XXIX/65.
63. Ibid.
64. Article 1 of the August decree on feudalism. While it abolished those dues based on 'real or personal servitude', it allowed others to be redeemable and stated that 'the price and the manner of the redemption will be set by the National Assembly'. See 'The August 1789 Decrees on Feudalism', in P. Dwyer and P. McPhee (eds), *The French Revolution and Napoleon: A Sourcebook* (Hoboken: Taylor and Francis, 2002) e-book, 24–28.
65. Dumontet's claim was mentioned in the Brunet letter, AN D/XXIX/65.
66. A. Ado, *Paysans en Révolution: Terre, pouvoir et jacquerie 1789–1794* (Paris: Société des Etudes Robespierristes, 1996), 254.

67. ADR (Poleymieux), EDEPOT 153, 31 January 1790.
68. Ado, *Paysans en Révolution*, 254.
69. ADR (Poleymieux), EDEPOT 153.
70. Report of Commissaire Ryard, quoted by L. Dupré-Latour, *Bulletin de la Société des Amis d'André-Marie* (Oct. 2012), 58.
71. Audin, *La Conspiration Lyonnaise*, 74–75.
72. Audin, *La Conspiration Lyonnaise*, 124–25.
73. Edmonds, *Jacobinism*, 66.
74. A. Crubaugh, *Balancing the Scales of Justice: Local Courts and Rural Society in Southwest France, 1750–1800* (University Park, PA: The Pennsylvania State University Press, 2000), 131.
75. T. Tackett, 'Nobles and Third Estate in the Revolutionary Dynamic of the National Assembly, 1789–90', in G. Kates (ed.), *The French Revolution: Recent Debates and New Controversies* (London: Routledge, 1998), 217.
76. Quoted in R. Allen, *Les Tribunaux criminels sous la Révolution et l'Empire 1792–1811*, trans. J.S. Bryant (Rennes: Presses Universitaires de Rennes, 2005), 14.

Part II

ASPIRATIONS

Chapter 5

Patriots and Traitors

> Persons who were eyewitnesses will leave no doubt about the atrocious conduct of Seigneur Guillin and the wisdom of the Municipal Officers of Poleymieux and the National Guard of the neighbourhood who were with them ... the judges who will be seized of this affair will take the cautious steps necessitated by fairness and by the extremely delicate circumstances in which the empire found itself ... suddenly everyone had learnt the news of the flight of Louis XVI.
> — Report of Eustache of Trévoux, to the Assemblée Nationale

The municipality of 1791 in Lyon began the slow work of regenerating local politics and implementing the changes that the August decrees and the Declaration of the Rights of Man had promised. The municipal officers were especially excited about the establishment of a new judicial order. Amongst those elected at the end of 1790 were the former *notables* Louis Vitet and Jean-Baptiste Pressavin. Vitet was a doctor of anatomy, who had undertaken ecclesiastical and then medical studies and wrote about veterinary science. In 1789, he had been president of the Société des Amis de la Constitution and he was chosen as mayor at the beginning of 1791 and again in 1792.[1] Pressavin, a surgeon, now elected to a municipal position, also spent some time as the city attorney (*procureur*).[2] Pressavin was a radical thinker, who had written about nervous and venereal diseases and developed a theory about the deleterious effects of meat-eating on health.[3] He was enthusiastic in his new political role and took on various projects as required by the municipality and the department. Both Vitet and Pressavin identified as 'patriots' but also as part of the political group led by Champagneux and Roland. This group were at the forefront of the first administrative and judicial changes of the Revolution.

The so-called Rolandins were genuinely concerned about improving social and economic conditions in the city. However, their commercial and property interests meant they were also supportive of the liberal policy of free trade. Although they promised to abolish the most onerous of the taxes still in force, they reminded the people that they had to be paid until another fiscal solution could be found.[4] Those Lyonnais who were more resolutely oriented towards commerce alone did not have an active role in local politics, because they did not have the support of the bourgeois or the popular classes as the Rolandins did at this time. The mercantile elite appeared to be happy to let the new political institutions operate as long as tranquillity and public order was maintained.[5] Other patriots elected included Antoine Vingtrinier, Joseph Chalier and Antoine Nivière-Chol.[6] The latter group had similar aims to the Rolandins at this stage.

The least controversial of the issues the municipal officers addressed early on was the administration of justice. The first changes had already been made on 4 August 1789, when all the former judges had to give up their purchased or hereditary jobs (known as the venality of office). Previously, magistrates would purchase their office and then pass the role on within their families. The local and national grievances in the *cahiers de doléances* had repeatedly expressed concerns about the failures of the seigneurial system of justice, based as it was on this principle of venality. The former practices meant an 'infrequency of session in small jurisdictions' and an unwillingness to deal with local criminal matters because the judges preferred the more lucrative work in the cities.[7] It also meant the civil power of the *seigneur* was reinforced in the provinces rather than his duty to oversee the criminal power also delegated to him. This was because he had the power to appoint the justices, who then were required to pursue his private interests.[8] Criminal justice in the country areas had become unworkable, and many people thought it should be suppressed because of the unwillingness of the feudal *seigneurs* to enforce it.[9] Criminal justice administered in the cities during the *ancien régime* was also subject to extensive criticism before the Revolution for the repressive punishments and arbitrary decisions that characterised it. The punishments against those who attacked the customs barriers, for instance, were widely criticised as barbaric. The king's power to imprison people by a secret *lettre de cachet* was also considered harsh and unpredictable. All these problems were addressed by the legislative changes, but the decrees establishing a new criminal justice system were the last to be enacted.

The laws of the NCA of 16–24 August 1790 first set out the procedural laws intended to ensure both uniformity and predictability in the new systems of justice.[10] The foundational role of *juge de paix* (Justice of the Peace) was developed to ensure all citizens were able to access judicial equity in the civil jurisdiction. There was to be one such officer elected in each canton who was authorised to determine civil matters promptly and, where possible, to encourage mediation between litigants. Those who voted for the new *juges de paix* were participating in what Melvin Edelstein and Malcolm Crook have considered one of the most important and innovative steps towards representative democracy in the modern world.[11] The *juge de paix* was paid by the state to assist the people of his canton in the exercise of their civic rights. The Third Estate of the *sénéchaussée* of Lyon had actually suggested in March 1789 that there should be established 'one or more *juges de paix*, elected by the parish, to conciliate the disputes of inhabitants' as well as a charitable council in each arrondissement to help the poor 'in the exercise of their rights'.[12] The truly modern part of the actual legislation however was the role of the citizen in electing these functionaries. One national deputy in February 1791 described the role of the *juge de paix* as the 'masterpiece of the National Assembly' and 'a gift from heaven'.[13] This single change made 'each citizen a direct adversary of all infractions of the social laws'.[14]

The role of *juge de paix* had all the elements of the 'practical and the idealistic' that were typical of the National Assembly, according to Crubaugh.[15] The new magistrate was to be 'a mediating amateur whose paramount qualifications ... [included] a sense of fairness instead of familiarity with a body of legal knowledge'.[16] Eligible citizens were now central to the new judicial system no matter where they lived, both in terms of electing the *juge de paix* in their canton and then bringing matters before him. They could approach the *juge* in their local canton for all their legal needs as a first step, and these officials were empowered to deal with many cases immediately and without appeal. If the gravity of the charges required the matter to go to a hearing before a higher court, the matter was still initiated at the local level. Elected magistrates also staffed a series of new civil courts set up in each district capital.[17] The uniform territorial divisions already established for the local administrative units thus ensured better access to justice than had ever been the case in the past.[18] Although those first elected were predominantly men of law, gradually voters made sure their *juges* came from more diverse backgrounds and were the amateur conciliators that had been envisaged by legislators.[19]

Voting for the 'citizen magistrates' was by written and secret ballot, and the choosing process could take many days. 'Substitutes' had to also be chosen, in case the first candidate elected did not accept office or later resigned, as well as two assessors to help carry out the judicial tasks of the canton. Because of the complex procedure, and the fact that pre-printed lists were not allowed, the elections necessitated commitment from voters. In Lyon, there was a strong commitment to the election of these judicial officers. Although the cantonal elections of 1790 showed a slightly below average participation in relation to municipal elections, turnout was high for the election of the *juges de paix*.[20] This was largely because of the diversity of those willing to take on the role; they were not, as a rule, the previous 'men of law', who were the only choices in many other parts of France.[21] While those experienced in judicial practice from the *ancien régime* were often dismayed by the loss of the prestige and status that they had previously enjoyed, the new functionaries came with no such expectations.[22] The official himself was only identified by a small badge of office.[23] Nevertheless, there was a lot of enthusiasm for the role amongst the Rolandins. Chalier, Champagneux and Billiemas, all originally municipal 'notables', became judicial officers at the end of the year, as did one François-Joseph L'Ange. L'Ange was an 'artiste' of the silk industry and was driven by a concern for social justice. The new magistrates voted in at the canton and district level worked for two years in the judicial roles, and from 1792 they could also hold simultaneous municipal or district office.[24]

Pressavin was a municipal officer involved in the judicial project from the beginning, but he was also involved with other matters of administration including the establishment of a local National Guard in February 1791. This militia slowly superseded the foreign military groups previously thought necessary to control outbreaks of popular violence.[25] Pressavin came to believe that the duplication of functions between the municipality and the departmental authorities should be suppressed in favour of the smooth running of 'public life' (*chose publique*), but he continued to interact with both bodies.[26] From February, Roland was appointed a special deputy to the NCA to advocate the need for fiscal reform in Lyon to help resolve its reliance on the *octrois* tax. This tax was abolished in May 1791.[27] The indebtedness of Lyon was also significantly reduced when the NCA decided to forgive some loans on 5–10 August as a result of Roland's petitioning in Paris.[28] The achievement of these popular initiatives meant the lessening of social agitation, especially in the urban areas, and continued support for the Rolandins.[29]

Other national decrees had a more mixed reception. From October 1789, the 'tentative' decision to sell Church lands had been taken, and it was followed within months by the ending of religious vows of nuns and the ejection of monks from monasteries of the 'contemplative and mendicant orders'.³⁰ The sale of ecclesiastical properties began in November 1790 and continued into April 1792 in Lyon. Churches, monasteries and gardens, which had taken up an enormous amount of space between the two rivers, were valued and then sold at auction as *biens nationaux* after their religious occupants were turned out of them.³¹ Pressavin reported to the Conseil Municipal on the work required. He outlined the estimation and inventory of all the property that had been dealt with, the steps taken in working out the true state of indebtedness of the relevant churches and monasteries, including recovering the titles and relevant papers and finally calculating the actual sales. He reported that the bidding for land was intense in Lyon, and the income that went to the coffers of the district authority exceeded expectations. He suggested that citizens should be heartened by the success of the national plan of putting paper money (*assignats*) into circulation for these purchases.³² A significant gain for citizens was the appropriation of the former Cordeliers monastery in the heart of Lyon city, which in 1792 was assigned to the canton Halle au Blé. However, while some properties were retained for municipal services, many monasteries were demolished and replaced with luxury homes that only the rich could afford.³³ The number of bishops was also reduced. The changes, thus led to some profound anxieties, especially in the less affluent urban areas, where there was a worry about the charitable work of the Church being discontinued and about amalgamations of parishes.³⁴ Despite Pressavin's assurance, the growing use of the *assignat* failed to allay the fears of the populace because it contributed to growing inflation, and few of the poorer Lyonnais were able to benefit from the sale of Church property anyway.

The most challenging religious decree had been that of 27 November 1790, which required all priests to swear an oath to the Civil Constitution.³⁵ This strong measure had a predictably divisive effect on many Lyonnais. While many members of the Church wanted to be seen as supporting the reforming initiatives that attacked outmoded privileges, there were also many leaders resistant to real change. The new regulations allowed the clergy a fairer salary, but the most controversial requirement was that they must now be elected. Those clergy who had actively sought reform were quite happy with these conditions and prepared to swear the oath. Some found the decrees impossible to accept, especially after the Papal edict of 13 April 1791 observed that the reforms would lead to a 'schism' in the Church by the attempt to impose this 'baser form' of governance.³⁶ In country areas, like Poleymieux, where there had been significant dissatisfaction with the amount of taxes going to the bishops in Lyon, there was little problem with the local *curé* taking an oath to the Revolution. The *curé* Buisson in Poleymieux did take the oath, on 2 January 1791, and an armed contingent of the National Guard were there at the ceremony to help ensure he did so.[37]

Initially in Lyon, the *curés* of all fourteen parishes also took the oath in 1790. Although many withdrew their oaths when the implications of the Pope's warnings were understood, the number of constitutional clergy in Lyon was relatively high according to Paul Chopelin, who closely studied the local church reforms.[38] Yet the 'refractory' clergy, those who refused to take the oath, created tensions by their opposition (and the opposition of their parishioners) to those 'constitutional' clergy who swore the oath to the revolutionary state. Refractories were quite prepared to take political action, as did Archbishop Marbeuf, who joined in the royalist conspiracy of December 1790. After this date, Marbeuf was dismissed, and Lamourette, who represented the constitutional priesthood, was elected archbishop. Still, the refractory clergy continued to encourage defiance, especially among the women in the congregations of the non-conforming churches.[39] Chopelin found strong evidence of some provocative refractories, notably the ecclesiastic Linsolas of the Saint-Nizier church, who continued to encourage defiance.[40] He was rumoured to have ripped his own surplice to create an incident. On 17 March 1791, Linsolas and two other refractory priests were imprisoned by an order of the municipal council signed by three municipal officers.[41] Soon after, on 25 March, the minister for the Interior in Paris countermanded this order. He could see no pretext for the municipality to have had the refractories arrested and ordered their immediate release.[42] Divisions between the different priests and their congregations, however, remained acrimonious. There were continuing attempts to prosecute some troublesome refractories. On 22 July 1791, the Abbé Berthier was denounced to Billiemas in his function as judicial officer, and the priest would be convicted a year later for continuing to practise without taking the constitutional oath.[43]

The king himself became anxious about the extent of the religious changes. He was concerned that he had approved the decrees establishing the 'Constitutional' Church despite the opposition of the Pope in April 1791.[44] Largely because of this issue, he felt impelled to betray his own oath to support the NCA and become involved in an escape plan. Although he had refused to take part in the Turin conspiracy uncovered in December in Lyon, the king was hugely upset about not being free to attend Easter festivities outside Paris. A Parisian crowd, convinced he was avoiding a service conducted by constitutional priests, refused to let him leave the palace, which the family now considered a 'prison'.[45] Soon after, the king agreed to attempt an escape to Austria. Although the escape was ultimately unsuccessful, the recognition of the duplicity of the king would change politics irrevocably. The king and his family were captured at Varennes on 21 June 1791 and escorted back to Paris. While he continued to lead the constitutional monarchy for another year, there were many renewed debates about what power the king should have. The events had clearly demonstrated that his position as a 'good father' to the new state was disputed by the very subjects who had long deferred to him. The possibility of having no king at all was even being suggested. The king was now widely seen as a 'parjure': someone who could not be trusted, because he could so easily abandon his solemn oath.[46]

At the same time as the king had become disaffected by the religious changes and attempted to flee the country, the Poleymoriots had become more defiant against their *seigneur*. He had become the symbol of the feudal constraints that continued to impact the peasants in the area, despite the promised reforms of the French Revolution. His brother, Guillin de Pougelon, had already been implicated and arrested for his participation in a counter-revolutionary plot, which had involved a plan to kidnap the king in December of the previous year. Now, days after the news reached Poleymieux that the king had been caught actually fleeing from the country, suspicion and betrayal erupted in the village and Guillin Dumontet became the logical target.

Local officials were impelled to act by the radicalised peasantry, who were expressing their renewed distrust of local aristocrats. From 24 June 1791, the 'young and hot-headed clubbists' from the town of Chasselay – which was the administrative centre of the region – had begun calling again for searches of the homes of 'the propertied' in the environs of Poleymieux, convinced of 'political danger'. The anger against the king conflated with the anger felt towards the local *seigneur* and became a 'violent desire to finish with feudal constraints'.[47] Hundreds of National Guard members and supportive locals came together to surround the castle of the local *seigneur* on 26 June, and when National Guard officers from Chasselay prepared for a search, their mood was clearly an aggressive one.[48] A similar phenomenon has been noted in many other departments in France, where peasants acted out their traditional method of rebellion: 'they attacked the castle ... the punitive reaction, inseparable from the popular Revolution'.[49] An official report later sent to the National Assembly claimed there were credible fears of the *seigneur* hiding a cache of weapons in subterranean caverns leading to the church yard. It was believed there were pieces of artillery, barrels of gunpowder and guns.[50] The Chasselay contingent had called on neighbouring villages to have their National Guard augment theirs, which was feared to be too small, and to help block the roads if a transport of arms were to appear. The search team collected onlookers as they wended their way to Poleymieux early on the Sunday morning for the scheduled meeting

Figure 5.1 Castle tower remains, Poleymieux. Photograph by the author.

outside the castle, which was to take place at 11AM as the regular service at the church was finishing. Those delegated to conduct the search waited until the appointed time when the National Guard unfurled their flags and banged their drums. They knocked on the door.

The *seigneur*, forewarned by the unusual activity in the area during the night, was waiting for events to unfold. He denied the *commissaires* entry and wounded one of the delegates when a gun he had in his hand discharged. As the *commissaires* ran for cover, Guillin took aim at the crowd from his tower with an ancient firearm known as a 'tromblon' (blunderbuss). He encouraged his Senegalese servant to do likewise. The sight of them both wielding their weapons and dressed in colonial military uniform escalated the situation.[51] Anger was brewing among the onlookers because the *seigneur*'s actions seemed to validate all the worst excesses that feudalism continued to represent.[52] The 'tocsin' was rung to bring more reinforcements, and the National Guard took shelter behind the low surrounding walls and hedges. After some time had elapsed, the delegation began negotiating with Guillin's wife and they were allowed to go inside. They found a number of weapons including a canon, historically used at ceremonial occasions in the village, but also – and more alarmingly – some arrow heads were found soaking in poison. The delegation continued looking and disarming the weapons they found.[53]

Despite admitting the delegation to the castle, the *seigneur* left them to lock himself in his tower and again threaten the overexcited crowd. His aggressive posturing increased the tensions outside, especially when he began to hurl stones out the window.[54]

Guillin next fired a pistol, this time hitting and wounding some bystanders. The crowd then became determined to break in, convinced that the delegation inside was in danger. The official report claimed that many 'unknown' agitators had by now joined the onlookers. They rushed to the window with ladders, heaped straw up in front of the heavy wooden door and started a fire, while crying out for vengeance. When the door fell open, the crowd flooded in, with more sustaining injuries. The cries of the fifteen persons injured urged the others on in their quest to punish the perpetrator.[55] As the crowd entered, it would appear that Guillin's wife either misguidedly opened the door of the cellars to divert the crowd or they were pried open.[56] The cellars were pillaged, casks of wine breached and 'disorder was at its height' as some men began to drink and act like 'wild beasts'. Unwilling to listen to their leaders, they forced their way into the tower.[57] All restraint was gone as angry men ran up the stairs and confronted the *seigneur* with farm tools, axes and swords. According to later accounts, he was attacked from every side, and a killing blow was struck with an axe. Several of the municipal officers and the mayor of a nearby village tried to protect the wounded *seigneur* during the fracas, but they were unable to prevent his being killed or dismembered. Guillin's body was hacked apart, his ears were cut off as trophies, his limbs and various body parts flung out the windows into the fires still burning in front of the castle.[58] Some hours later, a spectacular act of ritual cannibalism was enacted when some young men attempted to eat the charred remains of his right hand and heart. The gruesome account of these events was supported in the court records by three witnesses.[59]

Once the immediate crisis calmed, judicial officers began to progress the complicated legal questions that arose by means of the processes of justice in place at the time. Because only the civil changes to judicial procedure had so far been put in place, the criminal courts were not yet established to hear the matter. A number of different delegations of judges, however, were sent to investigate the facts. One delegation commenced a criminal inquiry focusing on the assassination of the *seigneur* and reported finding parts of his charred body when they visited the site two days after the events, amongst the debris scattered around the ruined castle. Another part of the investigation focused on the recovery of property stolen from the castle. A judge and his team were sent to the surrounding villages but had little success in finding anything significant. Inquires continued in July in Neuville, where the seigneurial judge responsible for Poleymieux

Figure 5.2 *Seigneur Guillin Dumontet*. Unidentified newspaper clipping. Courtesy of Musée d'Ampère.

usually sat. Further inquiries were conducted later in Lyon. In all, the investigations resulted in the generation of masses of written documentation, which by September comprised some sixty-one depositions and 235 pages of text, according to the nineteenth-century historian Amable Audin.[60] This prolixity of written briefs had been one of the most criticised aspects of *ancien régime* justice. The preparation of such evidence encouraged expensive and prolonged proceedings, with the accused held for long periods without trial. After the gathering of the relevant evidence in the Poleymieux case, some twenty-five arrests were made of those who had used excessive violence or were guilty of pillaging. The accused were incarcerated pending the operation of the principles of the new judicial order mapped out by the NCA.

Madame Guillin also began civil action through her attorney on 28 June to require the return of objects stolen from the castle and for the return of the remains of her husband's body.[61] She moved to Paris and continued to press for compensation and gave evidence before the National Assembly in August, also begging that the deputies release her brother-in-law – Guillin de Pougelon. She had little success in these actions although her harrowing tale reportedly affected many of the deputies.[62] Another local delegation from the municipality, led by Eustache the new *juge de paix* of Trévoux, also came to Paris in September to present their contrary version of events. Eustache had been the President of the popular club of Chasselay at the time of the murder and the primary signatory to the fifteen-page document originally sent to the National Assembly explaining the actions of the National Guard.[63] The violence against the *seigneur* of Poleymieux was in fact a relatively rare phenomena, and it was widely deemed to be a horrible but isolated occurrence. Tackett emphasised that it was one of only four such murders after the flight of the king and linked to the retribution of the locals who Guillin had treated so abusively.[64]

While reactions to the king's flight were strong locally, as the Poleymieux events indicate, there was still optimism in the NCA about a new iteration of monarchy regulated by the long-awaited constitution. In July 1791, a majority of the deputies had voted against the Republic that had been suggested as a first response to events. Many deputies broke away from the Jacobins to form the more moderate Feuillants club, and they continued to support a constitutional monarchy. Amongst the group were most of the deputies of the Third chosen from Lyon, including Millanois and Périsse-Duluc.[65] Pierre Goudard, a *négociant* from the silk industry remained a Jacobin, as did Etienne Durand, a tanner.[66] Roland, who was still living in Paris, joined forces with Brissot, who edited the newspaper the *Patriote français* rather than support the 'Feuillants'.[67] Roland himself had now joined the Jacobin club in Paris, and he sent a warning in July 1791 to Lyon that patriots should be careful of those who supported the Feuillants.[68] In Lyon, the Club de Concert did ally with the Feuillants, but their members at this stage were mostly the 'idle rich'. Patriots withdrew their support from this club, and those who had political aspirations severed their ties with them.[69] This was not the case, however, with the national deputies Périsse-Duluc,

Couderc and Goudard, who collaborated in founding a new newspaper called *Le Surveillant* in August 1791 in Lyon, which put across the more conservative viewpoint to their audience.

In July 1791, the dramatic changes to criminal justice were finally being worked out, and they promised to be quite radical. The decrees of 19–22 July extended the powers of the elected *juge de paix* to the criminal jurisdiction.[70] This role again relied on the right of the citizen to begin actions and thereby to invert the social values that the *ancien régime* magistrate had represented. The written statements required previously in criminal cases to commence proceedings were discontinued, and actions were now commenced by the complaint (called a denunciation) made by the citizen to the *juge de paix* of his canton. Citizens were now also to be a part of the system of juries who determined whether the accused were to be tried for crimes and ultimately whether they should be judged guilty of them. The jury system was one of the most significant changes of this 'regenerated' system of justice, but the general oversight of the judicial order remained with the *juge de paix*.

The role of the *juge de paix* in their general police function gave them sweeping powers of arrest and interrogation of suspects and witnesses. They were able to issue warrants for the accused to appear and begin the preliminary interviewing of complainants and witnesses in criminal prosecutions. All appropriate matters had to be investigated and warrants issued within 24 hours of an arrest. The accused was then remanded to either the Tribunal Correctionnel or to the departmental courts, which were established by the decrees of 16–19 September 1791 and known as the Tribunaux Criminels.[71] The Tribunal Correctionnel was composed of at least three *juges de paix* and could quickly decide on less serious matters, which attracted fines of up to 3,000 *livres* or two years imprisonment.[72] Pressavin's report to the Conseil Municipal set out the importance of the new judicial arm of government and highlighted the establishment of the Police Correctionnelle, which would make known to all the 'laws decreed for the maintenance of public order, security and tranquillity of all citizens'.[73] In matters that involved greater penalty or punishment, including 'major challenges to the social and political order' like homicide, rape and rebellion, evidence was required to be sent first to the director of the *juré d'accusation* in the Tribunal de District to determine if there was a criminal case to pursue. If a case was established, the accused was then sent on to a hearing before the Tribunal Criminel, which sat with three judges and the *juré de jugement*.[74]

The facts that had originally been ascertained by the *juge de paix* in criminal prosecutions were required to be presented orally before the respective juries, and the public were able to observe justice being done.

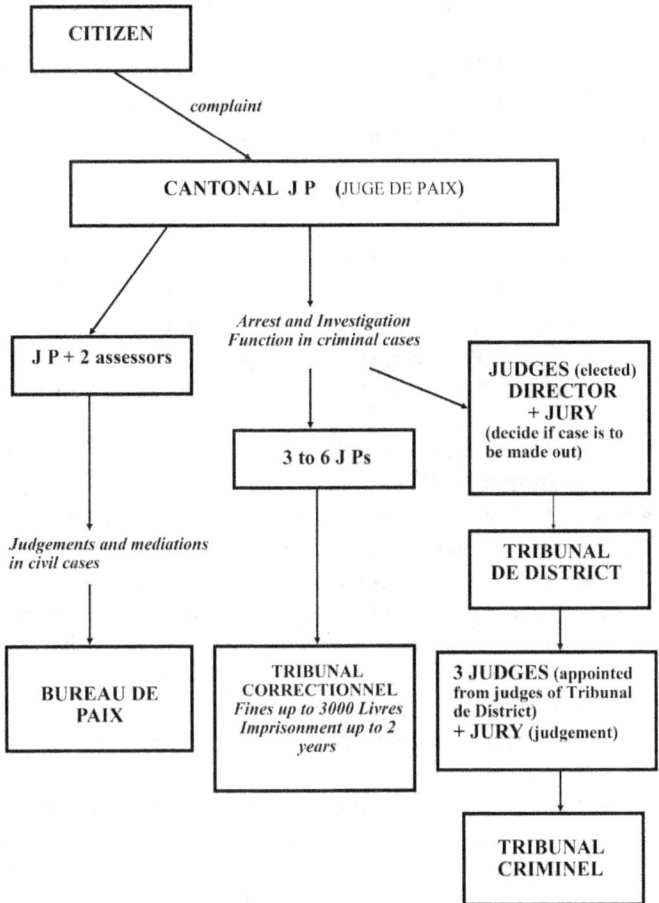

Figure 5.3 Judicial systems in the departments of France; flow chart, 1791–93. Figure created by the author.

Appeals from verdicts of the higher criminal court could be made back to the Tribunal de District that had originally heard the matter. Although there could be an appeal to the Tribunal de Cassation in Paris, this right was only available on the grounds of procedural irregularities.[75] The decrees of 16 and 29 September 1791 promulgated the Code Pénal. Instructions, which accompanied the new code, in effect completed the organisation of criminal justice.[76] There was finally a clear hierarchy of offences to be dealt with by the relevant institutions based on their actual nature and not, as previously, according to the status of the accused.[77] The magistrates merely had to apply the new rule of law, and the unpredictable and barbaric punishments of the *ancien régime* were finally abolished.

The time had finally come for the new criminal institutions to progress the Poleymieux case, but the manner of doing so was not as simple as merely applying the law. According to Audin, the Tribunal de District decided not to prosecute the accused, because of the evidence of patriotism of those involved.[78] The justices stressed the innocence of the National Guard and the municipal officers involved and raised the culpability of the victim himself by bringing up all 'the old grievances, true or false, that the Poleymoriots had against him'.[79] In September, it was decided by the NCA that the accused would be part of a general amnesty granted after the king swore to uphold the new constitution of 1791. They were, however, not immediately amnestied but had to wait until November.[80]

Such incidents of popular vengeance were still being strongly debated in Paris. By December 1791 in Lyon, the more radical sectional clubs strengthened their ties with the Jacobin club of Paris and were not only supporting popular action but urging yet more action against 'aristocrats'. They called for vigorous searches of aristocratic homes. The tensions between what would become moderate and more extreme patriots were beginning to manifest in Paris as well as Lyon, and the collision between popular violence and the 'rule of law' was one of the points of diversion. But the problems that such fundamental differences would create were not immediately apparent as the procedural changes continued to be put in place.

By 19 December 1791, the Conseil Municipal in Lyon had voted for the refurbishment of various rooms in the Hôtel des Flêchères procured for the Tribunal Correctionnel, and funds were allocated to outfit it with a fire, lights, furniture and a concierge to the sum of 500 *livres*. Pay was allocated for its incumbents.[81] These premises adjoined the old prison complex, which remained in its original state with its 'high small windows fronting the narrow cells and sombre vaults, through which the winds blew in winter and the air was trapped in summer'.[82] Although the prisons were not made any more comfortable, there were attempts to change the new courtrooms so they would better reflect the new egalitarian focus of criminal justice. A directive and plans had been sent to departmental authorities throughout France on 22 January 1791 showing how this work should be accomplished. A stepped platform was proposed that would lead to a circular arrangement of seats for the citizen judges, and the audience was given a large auditorium to watch proceedings.[83] From secret interrogations of the accused based on equally secret and complicated briefs of evidence, there was a new oral emphasis and public visibility in the conduct of cases.⁸⁴ Although a judge was still in control of the process, still the inquisitor, he now acted in a much more open and public way because he was elected by the people. Optimism for the judicial structures remained high.

Notes

1. A. Kuscinski, *Dictionnaire des Conventionnels* (Paris: Librarie Rieder, 1916), 609.
2. Edmonds shows the *procureur* was Luc Antoine Champagneux in the December 1791 election and François-Auguste Laussel in the 1792 election. See W. Edmonds, *Jacobinism and the Revolt of Lyon, 1789–1793* (New York: Oxford University Press, 1990), 313. However, Champagneux was temporarily suspended from this position in early 1792 and also spent some time in Paris. During this time, Pressavin and then Nivière-Chol took on the position before the elections of 1792. Their signatures are appended to some cases in 1792; ADR 41 L 7.
3. Edmonds, *Jacobinism*, 506–7.
4. W. Edmonds, 'The Rise and Fall of Popular Democracy in Lyon 1789–1795', *Bulletin of the John Rylands Library* (1984), 418.
5. See Edmonds, *Jacobinism*, 95.
6. Edmonds, *Jacobinism*, 313.
7. A. Crubaugh, *Balancing the Scales of Justice: Local Courts and Rural society in Southwest France, 1750–1800* (University Park, PA: The Pennsylvania State University Press, 2000), 18.
8. Crubaugh, *Balancing the Scales*, 69.
9. Crubaugh, *Balancing the Scales*, 7–18.
10. J.L. Oates, 'The Influence of the French Revolution on Legal and Judicial Reform', MA dissertation (Simon Fraser University, February 1980), 42–43. This dissertation by a legally qualified author provides an interesting technical analysis of the various decrees and laws that established the French judicial administration.
11. M. Edelstein, *The French Revolution and the Birth of Electoral Democracy* (Farnham, Surrey; Burlington, UT, 2014); M. Crook, *Elections in the French Revolution: An Apprenticeship in Democracy, 1789–1799* (Cambridge and NY: Cambridge University Press, 1996), 45, 67. Crook suggests that the initial novelty of attendance at the elections of judicial personnel did fall off but not before many 'modest peasants and wealthier artisans' were elected.
12. AP, *Cahier du tiers-état de la sénéchaussée de Lyon*, Chap. 3, Section 1(4).
13. This comment, attributed to Paul-Marie-Arnaud de Lavie, was quoted by Edelstein, *The French Revolution*, 191.
14. R. Allen, *Le Tribunaux criminels sous la Révolution et l'Empire 1792–1811*, trans. J.S. Bryant (Rennes: Presses Universitaires de Rennes, 2005), 29.
15. Crubaugh, *Balancing the Scales*, 133.
16. Crubaugh, *Balancing the Scales*, 135. Crubaugh looked at a number of provincial *départements* to come to these conclusions about the crucial work of the *juge de paix*.
17. I. Woloch, *The New Regime Transformation of the French Civic Order, 1789–1820* (New York: W.W. Norton and Co., 1994), 30.

18. A. Forrest, 'Reimagining Space and Power', in P. McPhee, *A Companion to the French Revolution* (Chichester: Wiley Blackwell, 2015), 97–98.
19. Edelstein observed that the position of *juge de paix* was so successful it lasted until 1958, although the electoral frequency and number of incumbents was changed in 1795. Edelstein, *The French Revolution*, 191–99.
20. A figure of 49 per cent has been suggested for attendance across the 75 cantons of the city: Edelstein, *The French Revolution*, 118.
21. This increase was noted in the elections of 1790 and 1792, when more socially diverse candidates were elected in Lyon. There were no former *parlementaires*, because Lyon did not have a parliament. Edelstein, *The French Revolution*, 281–84.
22. There was bitter resentment felt amongst former justices at the loss of prestige, but this was felt less in Lyon, where there was no parliament. For the general reaction, see McPhee, *Liberty or Death: The French Revolution* (New Haven, CT and London: Yale University Press, 2016), 139.
23. Their only insignia of office at this level of justice was a red and blue badge stating: *La Loi et la Paix*. Crubaugh, *Balancing the Scales*, fn 141.
24. Crubaugh, *Balancing the Scales*, 193.
25. AML 1 CM 1, 26 February 1791. Pressavin introduced his project on this day to the council.
26. J.B. Pressavin, 'Rapport fait au Conseil de District de Lyon; par M. Pressavin, un de ses membres', in *Divers écrits de Lyon sur la Révolution* (Canberra: National Library of Australia, n.d), 16. Although this report is undated, it appears to have been completed in the latter months of 1791.
27. D.L. Longfellow, 'Silk Weavers and the Social Struggle in Lyon during the French Revolution, 1789–94', *French Historical Studies* 12 (1981), 18. Longfellow noted that suffering continued amongst the silk workers despite the lifting of the *octrois* as the paper money called the *assignat* continued to depreciate.
28. S. Reynolds, *Marriage and Revolution: Monsieur and Madame Roland* (Oxford: Oxford University Press, 2012), 150.
29. A. des Francesco, 'Les Rapports entre administrateurs et administrés à Lyon dans les premières années révolutionnaires (1789–1793)', in B. Benoît (ed.), *Ville et Révolution française: Actes du colloque international, Lyon, Mars 1993* (Lyon: Presses universitaires de Lyon, 1994), 223.
30. J. McManners, *The French Revolution and the Church* (London: SPCK, 1969), 31.
31. L. Trénard, *La Révolution Française dans la région Rhône-Alpes* (Paris: Perrin, 1992), 300–1.
32. Pressavin, 'Rapport fait au Conseil de District de Lyon', 6.
33. Trénard, *La Révolution Française*, 300–1.
34. E.J. Woell, 'Religion and Revolution', in D. Andress (ed.), *The Oxford Handbook of the French Revolution* (Oxford: Oxford University Press, 2015), 256–57.
35. According to McManners, this decree marked 'the end of national unity and the beginning of civil war'. *The French Revolution*, 38.
36. 'The Papal Bull Charitas', in J.H. Stewart (ed.), *A Documentary Survey of the French Revolution* (New York: MacMillan Company, 1951), 184.
37. A. Audin, *La conspiration Lyonnaise de 1790 et le drame de Poleymieux* (Lyon: Éd. lyonnaises d'art et d'histoire, 1984), 76.
38. P. Chopelin, *Ville patriote et ville martyr: Lyon, l'église et la Révolution, 1788–1805* (Paris: Letouzey et Ané, 2010), 139.
39. M. Wahl, *Les Premières années de la Révolution à Lyon 1788–1792* (Paris: Armand Colin, 1894), 467.

40. Chopelin, *Ville patriote*, 189.
41. ADR 1 L 1095.
42. ADR 1 L 1095.
43. ADR 41 L 7.
44. T. Tackett, *When the King Took Flight* (Cambridge, MA: Harvard University Press, 2003).
45. Tackett, *When the King Took Flight*, 44.
46. Tackett, *When the King Took Flight*, 222.
47. Audin, *La Conspiration Lyonnaise*, 82.
48. According to the Rapport to the NA, there were thousands – but this is clearly an exaggeration: AN D/XXIX/65.
49. A. Ado, *Paysans en Révolution: Terre, pouvoir et jacquerie, 1789–1794* (Paris: Société des études Robespierristes, 1996), 248–49.
50. From the printed account or 'Rapport' of the Commissaires of Trévoux to the National Assembly, signed by those charged with undertaking the search, AN D/XXIX/65.
51. 'Rapport', AN D/XXIX/65.
52. Audin, *La Conspiration Lyonnaise*, 82.
53. Audin, *La Conspiration Lyonnaise*, 93.
54. 'Rapport', AN D/XXIX/65, 11.
55. 'Rapport', AN D/XXIX/65, 11–14.
56. Audin, *La Conspiration Lyonnaise*, 98.
57. A. Raverat, *Lyon sous la Révolution, suivi de la liste des condamnés à mort* (Lyon: La Découvrance, 2006), 36.
58. Raverat, *Lyon sous la Révolution*, 37.
59. P. Viola, 'The Rites of Cannibalism and the French Revolution'. Retrieved December 2015 from www.library.vanderbilt.edu/Quaderno/Quaderno3/Q3.C10.Viola, 167–73.
60. Viola, 'The Rites of Cannibalism', 124.
61. Audin, *La Conspiration Lyonnaise*, 116.
62. Audin, *La Conspiration Lyonnaise*, 126–27.
63. 'Rapport', AN D/XXIX/65.
64. Tackett, *When the King Took Flight*, 174.
65. E.H. Lemay, *Dictionnaire des constituants, 1789–1791* (Paris: Universitas, 1991), 668 and 743.
66. Lemay, *Dictionnaire*, 415, 323.
67. É. Bernardin, *Jean-Marie Roland et le Ministère de l'Intérieur 1792–1793* (Paris: SÉR, 1964), 13–14.
68. According to Edmond's research, the deputies were mostly men of 'wealth and conservative views' who supported the Departmental Directory. Edmonds, *Jacobinsim*, 105.
69. Edmonds, 'The Rise and Fall of Popular Democracy', 421.
70. Crubaugh, *Balancing the Scales*, fn.
71. Crubaugh, *Balancing the Scales*, 135–40.
72. Crubaugh, *Balancing the Scales*, 138–40.
73. Pressavin, 'Rapport', 11.
74. Pressavin, 'Rapport', 18
75. Woloch, *The New Regime*, 303–4.
76. Allen, *Le Tribunaux criminels*, 21
77. Allen, *Le Tribunaux criminels*, 32.
78. Audin, *La Conspiration Lyonnaise*, 126.
79. Audin, *La Conspiration Lyonnaise*, 129–30.
80. Audin, *La Conspiration Lyonnaise*, 132.
81. ADR 39 L 12.

82. A.-F. Delandine, *Tableau des prisons de Lyon, pour server à l'histoire de la tyrannie de 1792 et 1793* (Lyon, 1797), 19.
83. K.F. Taylor, 'Geometries of Power: Royal, Revolutionary and Post-revolutionary French Courtrooms', *Journal of the Society of Architectural Historians* 72 (2013), 434–45.
84. K.F. Taylor, *In the Theater of Criminal Justice: The Palais de Justice in Second Empire Paris* (Princeton, NJ.: Princeton University Press, 1993), 6.

Chapter 6

'A LIVELY POLITICAL MILIEU' IN LYON

> Our inquiry into the great questions of the Revolution hardly advance here. It is not from a lack of official notices and papers of all types . . . in a corner by a good fire, in a comfortable salon . . . while lunching in a café, you are brought more than you could want . . . printed at the expense of the clubs and freely distributed . . . [but] people here are detached from the troublemakers [of the Jacobin clubs].
>
> —J.F. Reichardt, 24 February 1792, letter from Lyon

Reichardt, a Prussian visitor to Lyon, wrote home of the wonderful 'meat, fish, bird, vegetables, fruit, wine, all exquisite' available in the gastronomic capital of Lyon in 1792 and the beautiful walks and boat rides by the banks of the river.[1] He also wrote of the 'lively political milieu', where opinions were expressed loudly in the theatre and in the innumerable newspapers. He preferred the Feuillants Club to which he was introduced by Millanois to the dastardly Jacobin clubs frequented by 'old shrews'.[2] But he was deeply unimpressed by the bourgeois of the town, who were 'too rich and absorbed by business to want anything other than internal tranquillity and external peace'.[3] The picture he painted of Lyon in 1792 was one of intractable difference. However, social and political awareness was growing, and the problems of the poorer classes, including their need for basic staples like bread, were beginning to be addressed. Would the new initiatives that the indefatigable team of Vitet and the Rolandins were hoping to put in place make an impact on the deeply divided city?

* * *

In October 1791, the NCA was superseded by the newly elected Legislative Assembly and was supported by a constitution of 14 September 1791, which the king swore to uphold. The former 'estates' no longer existed and so the new deputies were much more diverse in terms of social background. Only 10 per cent were former nobles or priests as compared to the more than 50 per cent who had belonged to the privileged orders in the previous NCA.[4] The municipality elected at the end of 1791 in Lyon was also now characterised by a mixture of professional men of talent and clubbists and was more representative of the breadth of Lyonnais society than at any earlier period.

Elections in Lyon during November and December saw Vitet returned as mayor and a number of Rolandins retain the top positions in politics in Lyon. They were, however, also joined by many artisan and activist clubbists of the *quartiers*, resulting in an unusually high number of Jacobin and popular society members for the provinces.[5] These included two silk weavers, Claude Carron and Jean-François Chalon; a furrier; one mercantile broker; a commission agent; and the *négociant* Joseph Chalier. There were also shoemakers, mercers and master-stocking weavers elected.[6] Billiemas and Roland were returned as *notables*. As the Rolandins had hoped, the *quartier* clubs had become enormously influential in educating people in their civic duties. They had grown to over thirty in number in Lyon and helped members achieve their political ambitions.[7] Kennedy observed that 'by 1791 and 1792 club members, held ecclesiastical, judicial, or public office ... the clubs monitored goings-on in Paris'.[8] They 'deplored religious intolerance'.[9] In them a 'cosmopolitan spirit pervaded'.[10] Vitet still hoped that these more active citizens would be 'guided' by the 'enlightened' bourgeois team he led.

Vitet spoke of his grand vision for the community as a result of the new diversity and support for the Revolution among those elected: 'Love of the *patrie* which has always led us ... with which all citizens are filled, has only one desire, that you will be guided by men who are as enlightened as they are virtuous.' He called on those elected to:

> Abandon the biases of the *ancien régime* ... the formulaic praises (*formules louangeuses*) which are meant to flatter the passions, to blind men ... Slaves need to flatter their masters ... [but] liberty is another language, the only thinking it finds worthy is truth ... it only judges on actions.[11]

But some speakers in the popular clubs wanted to go much further. They had been early proponents of a republic after the flight of the king to Varennes.[12] They remained suspicious of the king and his new powers of veto. By late 1791, the Feuillants, who had made an enormous effort to finish the constitution according to Tackett, and who remained supportive of the king despite his attempted flight in 1791, were strongly opposed nationally by the Jacobins.[13] This development was due to the problematic actions of the king himself. The sweeping law of 9 November 1791, declaring *émigrés* to be outlaws if they had not returned by 1 January 1792, defined those who were enemies of the Revolution. However, the king vetoed this decree, prompting the Assembly then to outlaw non-juring clergy, which decree was also vetoed.[14] These actions meant his commitment to the constitutional oath was again put into question. Patriots were worried that *émigrés* were allying with a coalition of European powers and envisaging war against the Revolution specifically to 'save' the king.[15] Revolutionary laws, however, were not all reactive to cascading events. Those elected locally remained optimistic about achieving change whether in their political role or in the new judicial roles they were elected to.

The long-debated reforms to the administration of justice were still being progressed in Lyon. Many of the hopes and expectations of the Lyonnais revolved around the provision of criminal justice. On 12 January 1792, the newly elected criminal judges were installed in the Tribunal Criminel; Jerôme Cozon was made their President. Champagneux (*procureur*) addressed the judges in these terms:

> Of all the public institutions the jury is the most important ... [and is] one of the most perfect of the constructions of the Constituent Assembly. [16]

The jury was widely welcomed as one of the most significant changes of the 'regenerated' system of justice in the city. Pressavin drew up the first list of thirty jurors who would be available to sit in judgment with three judges of the Tribunal Criminel on 31 January 1792. He also noted that a 'great number of accused' were waiting to be dealt with.[17] The Code Pénal could now be used to determine if a crime was committed, juries could make decisions and the judges of the new criminal courts could sentence criminals according to a uniform set of punishments. The code provided transparency, and criminal justice had become a right that could be sought from the *juge de paix*, whether or not the citizen had sufficient assets. As in the civil matters of disputed debt, a criminal case begun in the *bureaux de paix* required no formal written procedures, no fee, no lengthy reasons for judgment and could often result in immediate and effective justice. The *juge de paix* thus continued to be 'the symbol of the Revolution's commitment to a new type of justice', which was the 'antithesis of the seigneurial judge'.[18] They were servants of the citizens of the state and now squarely in control of criminal justice as well as civil justice.

Figure 6.1 Théâtre des Célestins (constructed in 1792). Photograph by the author.

A case against the constitutional priest of Saint-Nizier, M. Jolyclerc, heard before a jury on 10 April 1792, showed the centrality of the citizens.[19] The sheer audacity of the challenge to a member of the formerly sacrosanct priesthood by an ordinary citizen, though not in the end successful, shows how much things had changed in a short time. This case was begun by the denunciation of a citizen and was directed against the priest, who was one of the *curés* who had taken the Civil oath. The denunciation was presented to the *juge de paix* of the relevant canton, Billiemas. The citizen alleged that Jolyclerc had written a letter that caused a disturbance in his parish and in the canton generally. A printed though unsigned copy of the publication that was claimed to have suggested this fact was presented as evidence. Billiemas had to first find whether there was a law in the Code Pénal prohibiting the publication of such matters. Then he had to find any evidence of witnesses who could say the priest in question was the author of the publication. These two questions were investigated and put to the first jury of citizens, who had to decide if there was enough evidence to put the accused to trial. When the jury ratified the finding that there was no article in the code under which the priest could be charged and further found that there was no evidence he was the author of the printed document, the denunciation was quickly brought to an end. What was in the document was never disclosed because the law did not allow the matter to go any further. This case illustrates the power of the citizen at both initiating and determining the case presented. It also shows how pivotal the role of the *juge de paix* was in the process. He had the task of pursuing the witnesses required, often visiting them in situ, taking statements from them and the complainant, and determining if there was enough evidence to put the accused before the jury of accusation or, in lesser cases, to issue a warrant of arrest. If there was insufficient evidence – for instance, if the accusation was merely vexatious – he could dismiss the proceedings at this preliminary stage. However, whatever the citizen-accuser brought before him the *juge de paix* was constrained to hear.[20]

Although most municipal positions had been filled by the end of the previous year, new elections had to be called in January for the post of *juge de paix* in the canton of Halle aux Blés. It is interesting to look at how this election transpired because it was typical of the processes that took place throughout the city, where there were almost as many *juges de paix* and assessors elected as there were municipal officers.[21] The call had been triggered when the former deputy to the NCA, Périsse-Duluc (now a Feuillant), decided not to accept the position after the first round of elections at the end of 1791. Ampère was then added to a new list of candidates.[22] It is possible that Ampère was recommended for the position by the Périsse family, whose bookshop he is known to have visited, or by the previous incumbent Servan l'Ainé, whose family also lived in Poleymieux.[23] These friends of the family were aware of Ampère's suitability, but it was nonetheless important for him to be seen and introduced to the voters from different parts of the canton. He had to be available – not to canvass votes (which was actively discouraged) but to make himself known to those who had come to participate in voting. Even though voters had to make a special effort to vote a second time in the canton in early 1792, they did so because voting itself was still a novelty and those they elected for the post of *juge de paix* were expected to make a real difference.[24]

Active citizens over the age of 25 were required to attend the headquarters of the canton to cast their vote for the local *juge de paix*. Few of them would have known many of the candidates. Those nominated had to be present as much as possible to listen to the concerns of voters, who had come from far away, and to make their acquaintance. Voters would consult the lists of candidates and exchange views about them.[25] At the second ballot, decided on 12 January, Ampère was elected with a majority.[26] Within weeks of being elected, on 3 February 1792, Ampère was sitting at his *bureaux de paix* (desk) in the former Saint-Antoine chapel, which had been allocated for cantonal business. He had two assessors to help determine the civil matters in his canton, selected from the pool of local *notables*. The furnishings he bought for the official rooms included, as he later described to his wife, the purchase of '15 chairs, two bench seats, a used carpet and some coal'.[27]

Ampère's residence was close by, on the Quai Saint Antoine, along the pedestrian, noisy bank of the Saône. The family lived for part of the year on the third floor (the second level after the ground floor) of an apartment building, and Ampère now had to commit to staying here in the canton in which he had been elected. The region was called Halle aux Blés (wheat) because of the large granary building that hugged the port along the Quai Pêcherie. Ampère could easily walk from the apartment on the Saône, past market stalls and along crooked streets of small businesses and shops, towards the Rhône River and to where the electoral assembly of his canton met. This was a large canton located in the first arrondissement, which stretched from the Saône River to the Rhône. From the stone bridge of the La Change area, it curved around the side of the Church of Saint-Nizier and the middle of the place du Grand-Collège (de la Trinité), up to the highest point in the city known as the Croix Rousse, where the silk weavers lived and worked, and back across the next bridge, the Port-Charlet. It included part of the former Cordelier Monastery and the chapel Saint-Antoine, where the active citizens of the canton met to vote. It also included the Place Terreaux and the Hôtel de Ville itself within its boundaries.[28] The elections held in this canton were especially drawn out because of its large size.

The most important requirement of the role of *juge de paix* was that the officer be physically available to the citizens of his canton to pursue their legal needs, which thus obliged Ampère to move permanently. One can only imagine the difficulty Ampère had in deciding to accept such a post with this condition attached. It would mean he had to leave his family, including André-Marie, for long periods of time. His daughter Antoinette remained ill and in fact died soon after.[29] However, it would seem that his motivation to contribute to the new system of revolutionary justice was great, and he did accept his election. After his failure to be given any role in the elections at Poleymieux, Ampère was prepared to move back to the city to participate actively. The disappointment he must surely have felt when his experience and knowledge was not acknowledged by a seat on the local Poleymieux council would have been more than ameliorated by his election to the prestigious position in Lyon. His success as tutor to his children and also as mentor to the villagers in his local Poleymieux meant he must have felt himself uniquely placed to deliver the wise and considered advice that was now needed to implement a return to

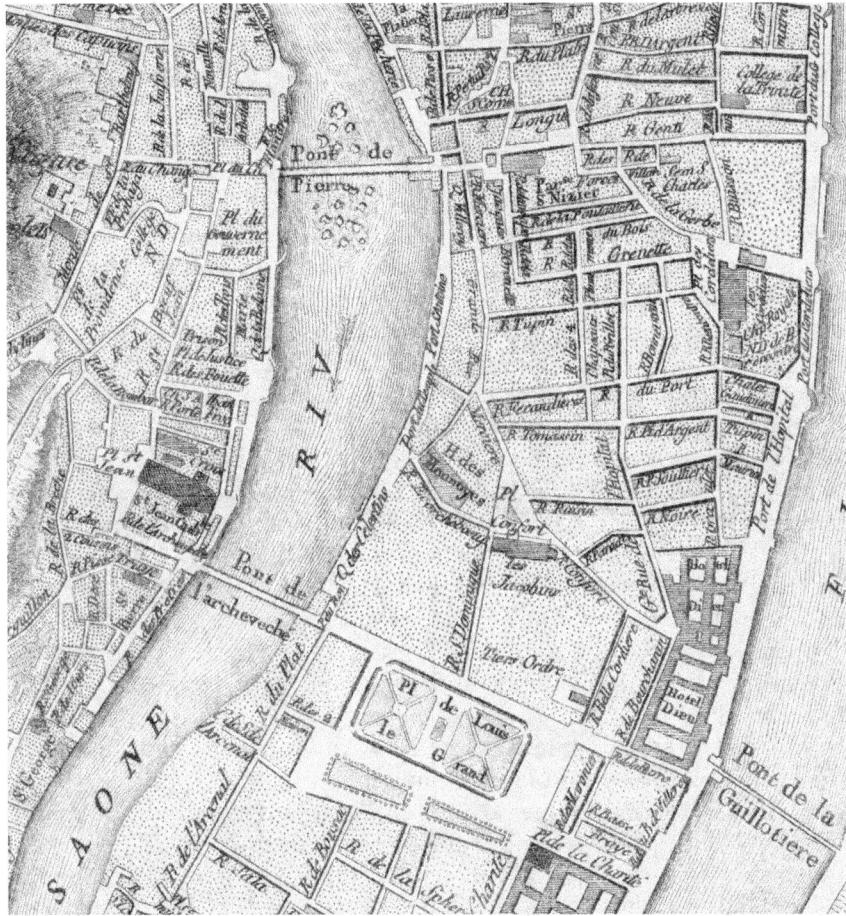

Figure 6.2 Detail of map of Lyon. Bibliothèque Municipale de Lyon.

stability. It would also bring him into contact with other officials in the municipality who had similar goals. It is probable that Ampère took on the role with a sense of excitement and perhaps trepidation about what he would be expected to do. But as *juge de paix* in a large canton, he was now personally empowered to help redefine justice.

On 20 January 1792, Ampère was officially introduced to the mayor, Vitet, in the Conseil Municipal and took his oath to be faithful to the nation, to the law and the king and to maintain the laws of the revolutionary government.[30] Vitet continued to lead the Rolandins and at the same time ensure their policies remained acceptable to the social activists of the popular clubs. He practised a modest lifestyle.[31] He had been active in the Academy of Sciences and had written a *mémoire* on the 'malady' that he called 'aristocracy'.[32] His credentials were impeccable as were those of Champagneux, the Rolandin journalist, who was appointed *procureur*. Billiemas, who became *greffier*, and L'Ange, who continued as a *juge de paix* were also widely recognised for supporting other popular issues as well.

While holding office, L'Ange published a sixteen-page treatise detailing a simple and effective way to stabilise the abundance of crops and the 'just' price of bread, which he thought could be easily achieved by 'a people of citizens'. He thought all that was required was the acknowledgment of the general good that would be achieved by stabilising the cost of such an essential commodity and avoiding famine and then merchants, cultivators and consumers would all help. They would realise the need to prevent speculators from hoarding and abusing their power. The necessary change would not happen by merely banning exports and allowing free trade within the country. He wrote: 'the most alarming and pernicious effect of the present free circulation of foodstuffs, is that it furnishes the aristocracy with the infallible and cruel means of tormenting the people and keeping them shackled.'[33] Stating the problem and presenting the solution was to him a simple task in the climate of cooperation within the municipality, despite the fact that most of the Rolandins followed Roland in advocating internal free trade and the law of the market.

Ampère certainly conformed to the type of 'enlightened' bourgeois representative that the Rolandins thought suitable. He was, like them, one of the 'self-selected' men of 1791 who showed a capacity to commit and accept an 'apprenticeship to the cause'.[34] His first judicial cases were in the civil jurisdiction, determining the validity of commercial contracts or demands for payment made by merchants. There he helped consumers negotiate bill payments and transactions. Debtors mostly appeared voluntarily and often did not dispute the money owed but needed time to pay. Even if matters were disputed, citizens had the right to have matters mediated by the *juge de paix* before they went to a higher court.[35] In these smaller matters, resolutions were quickly made. Ampère's experience in the previous seigneurial jurisdiction of Poleymieux was enough to ensure that he had the required capacity to effect 'equity' in this work.[36] There was no requirement that he should have the legal training or skill in deciphering complicated written arguments that had been required for the position of magistrate in the *ancien régime*. Neither was he required to write up reasons for his decisions. The *juges de paix* were able to give immediate decisions in matters concerning disputed property where the value did not exceed one hundred *livres*.

Ampère heard a case of this type almost every day throughout the months from February to August 1792, and sometimes there would be two or more on a single day.³⁷ An unusual case was that of a woman who claimed civil damages for a 'blow to her right breast', occasioning an injury of 'contusion and swelling' after a popular riot (*rixe*). This case required evidence from a surgeon and within two days Ampère delivered judgment in the matter, granting the woman her costs of medical treatment.³⁸ Although he was the only *juge de paix* in his large canton, Ampère was immediately and effectively working to address the inadequacies of the former civil jurisdiction by ensuring that justice was available to different groups in society, not just those able to afford it. By February, Ampère was also working in the area of criminal justice. He was called on regularly by citizens of his constituency to issue arrest warrants, interrogate witnesses, and collect evidence for matters destined for the higher district and departmental tribunals. He was invariably scrupulous in ensuring the requirements of the law were adhered to. One of the first criminal cases he dealt with that shows the various steps Ampère was responsible for was that of Jean-Baptiste Poquillon, a gardener accused of stealing copper chandeliers from a house on the night of 17–18 February 1792. The very day of 18 February Ampère drew up the arrest mandate and interrogated the accused preparatory to the question of his guilt going before the *juré d'accusation*. He was most concerned that the aggravating circumstances of the robbery were proven. Once the jury in the district criminal court pronounced a 'yes' decision as to the accusation, the matter was sent for final judgment to the departmental Tribunal Criminel and its *juré de jugement*, who were presented with the evidence. On 16 March, the Tribunal Criminel sentenced the unfortunate housebreaker to be placed in a stock on a scaffold for six hours.³⁹

The magistrates in Lyon, including Ampère, had also by this time been performing their designated police function. Typical types of investigations in which they were involved were cases of theft following denunciations from citizens. The steps taken in one such case before Ampère are once again illuminating. In the matter of Maynard, Berthet, Muguet and others he had to make a number of inquiries and a search of the premises of one of the suspects, Berthet, where he found some of the thirty wine bottles stolen on the night of 31 March. His investigations were collated with that of other *juges de paix* charged with investigating the other members of the gang. Ampère then also participated in the final hearing against all the accused, with Billiemas sitting as President of the Tribunal Correctionnel and another *juge de paix*. In another matter of Roussillon against Pascal, the *charcutier* Roussillon brought a complaint to Ampère that his shop was robbed of about forty sausages and two pieces of lard as well as a leather wallet during the night of 4–5 May. Ampère caused an arrest warrant to be effected against the alleged perpetrator and again participated in the judgment when the case was heard by the Tribunal Correctionnel on 28 June 1792.

One of the most important cases, and representative of the questions that now engaged many of the judges and municipal officers, was heard at this time by the Tribunal Correctionnel against a refractory priest. Abbé Berthier was found on 4 July 1792 to have persisted in his refusal to take the constitutional oath of the clergy and had in addition 'distributed seditious works'. Billiemas condemned the abbé to a period of detention and a fine of 500 *livres* on 22 July 1792.[40] From the perspective of the *notable* and *greffier* Billiemas, much had been achieved by the Lyonnais in office by August 1792, and he noted: 'by our union we have prevailed over the aristocracy, and we have had a patriot municipality . . . [which is] why Lyon has enjoyed a constant peace and tranquillity.'[41] This period marked the high point of revolutionary government in Lyon, which was for a time relatively peaceful. The court proceedings at the level of the *juge de paix* ran efficiently and smoothly.

At the municipal session of 21 August 1792, Ampère, with eight other *juges de paix*, officially took the oath to serve on the Tribunal Correctionnel. This judicial function was in addition to the duties already outlined of receiving the complaints made by citizens and the various tasks required of the *juges de paix* in order to initiate the processes of justice. In this jurisdiction, the judges sat together to hear and decide misdemeanours without a jury. Matters heard included complaints brought by citizens who had been the subject of minor assault or crime. As the procedure against Jean-Claude de Pierre later in this year shows, even an assault could have up to eight *juges de paix* (including Ampère) sitting. The case of de Pierre involved an injury to the person of one Coguard. The accused was found guilty and ordered to pay a fine and the costs of the surgeon.[42]

Decisions of the *juges de paix* reflected the tensions that came with revolutionary changes, particularly the religious changes, as we saw in the cases of the Abbé Berthier and the constitutional *curé* Jolyclerc. Economic challenges were also reflected in the many crimes involving the declining value of the paper money called the *assignat*, in circulation since the fiscal reforms of 1790. Life for many people still revolved around the need to procure the most basic commodities. There were thus numerous cases of theft, fraudulent importations and forgery (*faussières*) of *assignats* brought before the Police Correctionnelle, which had the jurisdiction of hearing minor cases.[43] Such cases spoke of the economic crises in the silk industry and also the dislocations of the Revolution, which contributed to the lack of employment and declining incomes for those lower down the social scale in Lyon. A more complex type of problem dealt with by Ampère was the case of Bonnet, a silk worker, heard on 8 June 1792. Ampère ordered Bonnet's arrest on suspicion of complicity in a theft of silk fabric. However, in his later questioning of the witnesses, Ampère came to the conclusion that the accused was actually a man of 'irreproachable' character and may well have been a victim of a false complaint by competitors in the silk industry. The case was nevertheless sent to the higher court, but the accused was in fact found to be innocent as the judge had intimated.[44]

The role of the *juge de paix* was thus a central one in the revolutionary state. Those in the position applied the rule of law as legislated by the state, but they also represented the most insignificant of the citizens in the state. They became intimately concerned with both the positive and the negative effects of revolutionary changes. As Crubaugh suggested, the role was considerably more significant than that of a mere functionary used 'to plug the gaps in jurisdiction left by higher and more important courts'.[45] By August 1792, L'Ange, in his 'address to a thousand Frenchmen of Lyon', reiterated that the new judicial institutions put in place as a result of the changes of 1791 were still relevant because they were created by the 'general will' of the electorate. Because of the genesis of their role, the *juges de paix* as well as the municipal officers had now 'become especially responsible to the entire nation' and did not need to be reconstituted.[46]

The workers and unemployed of Lyon, repressed as they had been by the consular and religious leaders at the beginning of the Revolution, were generally supportive of the Rolandins and the implementation of the national decrees – especially the judicial ones. This had meant an early and immediate abatement of food riots when Rolandins were elected. Yet anxieties continued to rise about employment and the basic requirements of food provision, and these were added to by disagreement about how far religious changes should go. By April 1792, disturbances around non-conforming churches frequently led to riots and fears of counter-revolutionary activity were imputed to the refractory clergy by those who championed the constitutional church. The cessation of employment of domestics in aristocratic households as well as in the monasteries and church institutions that were required to close had impacted the already low employment rates caused by the crisis in the silk industry, and the charitable initiatives of the religious institutions were now curtailed. For many, this unintended result added to the anxieties about change. The religious changes thus remained a source of conflict precisely because they had so many ramifications.

Problems had been encountered from the implementation of the Civil Constitution of the Clergy in 1791, but there were now concerns expressed by the municipality that the directory was failing to implement the laws against those priests who refused to swear the oath.[47] Increasingly, strict anti-religious laws were promulgated in 1792, and the growing intolerance of revolutionaries towards refractory priests meant tensions between them and the constitutional congregations. Protests about religious changes, or about the lack of prosecution of the refractories, were frequent, and the new National Guard had to defuse situations especially in front of the churches used by the refractory priests. On 29 March, a letter informed the Conseil Municipal of incidents taking place outside the church of Saint-Joseph during Sunday mass. The church hierarchy requested that the National Guard should be brought in to quell disturbances here and at other churches. The municipal officers resolved to have guards stationed at the door of the churches.[48] This only increased tensions at the refractory churches. Events came to a head on Easter Sunday, 8 April, when a gathering was formed in the Rue Sala in front of the convent of the Claristes. Women were seized and whipped as they emerged from mass. The intervention of the municipality was again necessary to end the violence. One of the women later died.[49] The next day similar disturbances took place at L'Antiquaille. This violence necessitated the closing of the targeted churches and chapels by the municipality.[50] Throughout the summer, there were more episodes of anti-clerical violence, and the municipality was subjected to accusations that they had not reacted quickly enough to forestall them.

While these religious reactions simmered, there were also other positive signs that the programme of reforms was making headway. There was a high degree of unanimity about making subsistence foods cheaper and more available. The affordability of bread and basic food was still the biggest issue facing the unemployed and the poorer classes. The municipal council session of 1 February 1792 decided to support the initiative of the construction of a wheat storage facility in what had been church property, the Cordeliers Saint-Bonaventure church, which had been assigned to Ampère's canton. The same session, however, also showed the tendency of the more conservative departmental directory to stall initiatives that showed too much reforming zeal. A letter was read out to the municipal officers that was to be sent to Paris, complaining of the attempts of the department to overwhelm the municipality with decrees 'as odious as they are unjust'. These included an order preventing the arrest of a number of departmental members shown to be involved in the conspiracy of 1791 and others that censured the municipality's attempts to put seals on the residences of 'religious fanatics'.[51] Nevertheless, the municipality was not diverted from its primary task of applying the national decrees, despite the pressures from the departmental authorities. The poorer clubs argued that liberty would only be achieved in society when there was also equality, and they supported the election of the *sans-culotte* Julliard as National Guard commandant in March.[52] More radical opinions had begun to flourish.

One of the public spaces most conducive to expressing opinions in Lyon had been and continued to be the theatre. This included the Théâtre des Varietés (later known as the Théâtre des Célestins because it first operated in the old complex of buildings that had formed the monastery of the Célestins). A new theatre building was officially opened in April 1792 and became part of the daily life of many Lyonnais. The plays were not just a diversion from everyday life but reflected the different ideas and views of citizens. While the theatre was a less obvious political forum than the newspapers, it also functioned as a place where egalitarian ideas were gaining a foothold, especially through popular songs. The Assembly at the end of 1791 had legislated for freedom of the theatres, and this law meant a much less regulated venue than during the *ancien régime*.[53] In Lyon, the theatre had always been an important amusement for wealthy Lyonnais, the 'daily rendezvous of all businessmen'.[54] It was now also becoming more accessible to less elitist audiences with the new forms of *opéra-comique* pioneered by the composer André Grétry. Grétry composed sentimental songs that appealed to a wider audience. The plays he wrote were not usually of a radical or patriotic format, but they did inspire passion among the popular classes.

Marie-Joseph Chénier, a radical playwright of the time, anticipated a new *tragédie patriotique* tradition that would speak to the more egalitarian audience of virtuous citizens, but this did not happen quite as he envisaged.[55] A recent study by Cecelia Feilla of the plays put on in the revolutionary decade in France found that although Chénier's ambitions for a pure revolutionary tradition were not fully achieved, there was a larger audience for the mixture of high and low culture that was available. Feilla found 'sentimental and civic notions of virtue blended on stage' and that these productions had 'sometimes competing and contradictory prescriptions'.[56] It was becoming common for playwrights to allude to current political thinking and for audiences to react with boos and cheers. The dictates of taste that had previously defined French theatre and that had led to a rejection of the opera form were thus changing. Audiences were becoming more democratic and were embracing the 'culture of sympathy' that *opéra-comique* represented.[57] This finding is confirmed by the diversity of plays that were presented in Lyon. A number of plays with differing political messages were presented in the two theatres: the more aristocratic Célestins and the Grand Théâtre, which put on the newer forms of *opéra-comique* and operas.[58] There were didactic plays about being a good revolutionary family, such as *La famille patriote* by Collot d'Herbois, but there was also the *opéra-comique* production of *Richard Coeur de Lion* by Sedaine and Grétry, which had popular songs and was intended to heighten the *sensibilité* of the audience.[59]

The variety of themes dealt with in the theatres meant that audiences could be part of the political debate. At first, this freedom was linked with the acceptance of new ideas that the Revolution signified. However, some patriots were uneasy with the freedom to express unpatriotic views in the theatre and called for a ban on such themes. The municipal sessions of 23 February, 6 March and 19 April 1792 dealt with this when they discussed the *spectacle* called the 'Club de Bonnes', which came to Lyon in February 1792 after being shown in Paris in September of the previous year.[60] The play was meant to be a comedy; however, it was increasingly seen by many Lyonnais as a thinly veiled satire against the Jacobins, who were portrayed as bumblers and zealots. The issue came to be seen as more and more serious as the discussions continued, and the departmental authorities ordered it be declared illegal because of the possibility it could lead 'to a tumult with the most serious consequences'.[61] The municipal officers thought there should be more discussion about the issue. The concerns about the play and whether it should be halted also reflected the divided feelings of the city about the influence of the clubs at this time. For the patriots, the play was believed to be responsible for corrupting the morals of young audiences by its denigration of the partisans of the clubs, but for the conservatives on the other hand it was seen as a foil for the 'pernicious influence of the clubs on the masses'. On 13 March, the play was banned.[62] Such issues within Lyonnais society meant there were more pressures on the municipal government and the courts to deal with the changing expectations of their electors.

The connection of the municipal officers and the new judicial officers with Roland, however, continued into 1792, despite the growing sophistication of electors. He was still popular among his followers and even amongst the poorer social groups because of his earlier efforts in abolishing the *octrois*.[63] His sway over local opinion remained strong even though he was mostly absent from Lyon. On 11 January 1792, Roland had been sent to the Assembly with a proposal for the establishment of a commercial tribunal in Lyon, which would deal with the specific economic problems of the city.[64] From this time, he was informed of events in Lyon by letter and he in turn made recommendations to municipal officers by letter.[65] His letters were regularly read out in the council sessions and in the clubs. By March, he had entered the Brissotin ministry and took on the key role of Minister of the Interior.

As Minister, Roland was working nationally to help implement the new changes to the state. He received many communications from the provinces requesting information about the judicial changes as well as queries about how the juries and other court staff should be selected. One of the important issues raised with them was whether *juges de paix* who resigned could be replaced by supplementary officials without a new election. Roland acted as an intermediary in a number of such queries between local administrators and justices of the new courts.[66] Édith Bernardin, his biographer, suggests he at times interfered in the role of the Minister for Justice in providing his clarifications to both minor and significant questions. Some of the concerns he addressed were about tribunals who did not take prompt action against refractories and local volunteer militia and also the 'illegal' requisitions and abusive arrests that were being undertaken by others.[67] This would cause a 'gulf' that would separate him from the Jacobin Montagnards, and it helped establish his reputation as a 'man of order'.[68] However, at this early stage the Municipality was enthusiastic and convinced that the leadership and advice of Roland helped protect the city against popular violence.

Order had been achieved in the vast edifice of justice, and citizens were intimately involved in making sure their rights were recognised. The Code Pénal, the implementation of a system of juries and the election of citizen judges had a profound effect on the way justice was now perceived, from whichever side of politics the new judges viewed events. The ability of each and every citizen to bring infractions of the law to the notice of his cantonal *juge de paix* meant that they were instrumental in bringing a myriad of prosecutions before the courts. They did not need to resort to violence because the courts of law were operating in a transparent and efficient way. Although the popular clubs were ensuring that socially diverse judges and municipal officers were being elected, and the more egalitarian forum of the theatre was ensuring that political debates were across the social divide, the success of the new rule of law was at this stage unambiguous.

Notes

1. J.F. Reichardt and A. Laquiante (trans.), *Un Prussien en France en 1792: Lettres intimes de J.F. Reichardt* (Paris: Perrin, 1892), 186.
2. Reichardt, *Lettres intimes*, 156, 170.
3. Reichardt, *Lettres intimes*, 187.
4. T. Tackett, *The Coming of the Terror in the French Revolution* (Cambridge, MA: The Belknap Press of Harvard University Press, 2015), 149.

5. M. Edelstein, *The French Revolution and the Birth of Electoral Democracy* (Farnham, Surrey; Burlington, UT: Ashgate, 2014), 84.
6. W. Edmonds, *Jacobinism and the Revolt of Lyon, 1789–1793* (New York: Oxford University Press, 1990), 313.
7. W. Edmonds, 'The Rise and Fall of Popular Democracy in Lyon 1789–1795', *Bulletin of the John Rylands Library* (1984), 419–20.
8. M. Kennedy, *The Jacobin Clubs in the French Revolution: The First Years* (Princeton, NJ: Princeton University Press, 1982), 6.
9. Kennedy, *The Jacobin Clubs*, 150.
10. Kennedy, *The Jacobin Clubs*, 230.
11. AML 1 CM 1, 23 December 1790.
12. Edmonds, 'The Rise and Fall of Popular Democracy', 426.
13 13. Tackett, *When the King Took Flight*, 208.
14. P. McPhee, *Liberty or Death: The French Revolution* (New Haven, CT and London: Yale University Press, 2016), 150.
15. T.C.W. Blanning, *The French Revolutionary Wars 1787–1802* (London: Hodder Headline, 1996), 59–61. See also AML 1 CM 1, 23 December 1790.
16. AML 1 CM 3.
17. ADR 39 L 12.
18. A. Crubaugh, *Balancing the Scales of Justice: Local Courts and Rural Society in Southwest France, 1750–1800* (University Park, PA: The Pennsylvania State University Press, 2000), 135–36.
19. ADR, 41 L 8.
20. Allen, *Les tribunaux criminels sous la Révolution et l'Empire 1792–1811*, trans. J.S. Bryant (Rennes: Presses Universitaires de Rennes, 2005), 27.
21. Edelstein, *The French Revolution*, 194.
22. Périsse-Duluc sat on the right in national politics. Edmonds, *Jacobinism*, 105.
23. Servan L'Aîné was the first incumbent of the position. A member of the Servan family he had also been the former *seigneur* of Poleymieux. When he died in 1785 he was replaced by the notorious Guillin Dumontet. P. Marion, *Le genial bonhomme Ampère* (Lyon: Mémoire des Arts, 1999), 36, 41.
24. Edelstein notes that the first elections for JPs were particularly well attended throughout the country: Edelstein, *The French Revolution*, 196–97.
25. M. Crook, *Elections in the French Revolution: An Apprenticeship in Democracy, 1789–1799* (Cambridge and NY: Cambridge University Press, 1996).
26. ADR 35 L 19.
27. 'Instructions pour ma femme'. Letter of 17.10.1793, Archives Departmentale, 42 L 62.
28. ADR 35 L 18. This decree describes the extent of each of the cantons in Lyon.
29. She died on 3 March 1792: 'Généalogies' in L.de Launay, *Correspondance du Grand Ampère* (Paris: Librairie Gauthier-Villars, 1936), x.
30. AML 1 CM 3.
31. Edmonds, 'The Rise and Fall of Popular Democracy', 421.
32. J.-B. Dumas, *Histoire de l'Académie des sciences, belles-lettres et arts de Lyon* (Lyon: s.n., 1839), 342.
33. F. L'Ange, *Adresse à mille Français de Lyon* (Lyon: Louis Cutty, 1792).
34. P. Jones, 'Choosing Revolution and Counter-Revolution', in P. McPhee (ed.), *A Companion to the French Revolution* (Chichester: Wiley Blackwell Publishing, 2015), 286.
35. Crubaugh, *Balancing the Scales*, 139–40.
36. Crubaugh, *Balancing the Scales*, 13.
37. ADR 44 L 110.

38. ADR 44 L 110, Case of Rigoter: 7–9 May 1792.
39. ADR 39 L 33.
40. ADR 41 L 7.
41. This comment was made in August 1792 and quoted in Edmonds, *Jacobinism*, 118.
42. ADR 41 L 7.
43. ADR 44 L 110.
44. ADR 29 L 23.
45. Crubaugh, *Balancing the Scales*, 135.
46. L'Ange, *Adresse à mille François de Lyon*, 4.
47. Edmonds, *Jacobinism*, 92.
48. AML 1 CM 3, 29 March 1792.
49. P. Chopelin, *Ville patriote et ville martyre: Lyon, l'église et la Révolution, 1788–1805* (Paris: Letouzey et Ané, 2010), 190.
50. M. Wahl, *Les Premières années de la Révolution à Lyon 1788–1792* (Paris: Armand Colin, 1894), 468.
51. See the deliberations: AML 1 CM 3, 1 February 1792.
52. Edmonds, 'The Rise and Fall of Popular Democracy', 427.
53. F.W.J. Hemmings, *Theatre and State in France, 1760–1905* (Cambridge: Cambridge University Press, 1994), 53.
54. This observation was made by a prominent Lyonnais and quoted by Hemmings, *Theatre*, 142.
55. Cecilia Feilla quotes his patriotic objectives in the preface to his play, Charles IX, in her book *The Sentimental Theater of the French Revolution* (Farnham, Surrey: Ashgate, 2013), 1.
56. Feilla, *Sentimental Theater*, 16.
57. D.A. Thomas, *Aesthetics of Opera in the Ancien Régime, 1647–1785* (New York: Cambridge University Press, 2002), 202–3.
58. Hemmings, *Theatre*, 145.
59. C. Kradraoui, *Au Théâtre à Lyon de 1789 à 1799* (Lyon: Editions lyonnaises d'art et d'histoire, 1988), 17–21.
60. Kradraoui, *Au Théâtre*, 22.
61. ADR 1 L 1080.
62. See Kradraoui, *Au Théâtre*, 23. On 13 March, the production was stopped, and a demand made that the ban be lifted on 12 June 1793 was also refused.
63. Edmonds, *Jacobinism*, 149.
64. AML 1 CM 3.
65. See the letter of Roland thanking the municipality for the expression of sentiments on his appointment as Minister of the Interior. Here he expressed the hope that the 'administrative corps and all the municipal officers, would deploy the patriotism and the character that distinguished them', and this knowledge would help him in his work: AML 1 CM 3, 14 April 1792.
66. É. Bernardin, *Jean-Marie Roland et le Ministère de l'Intérieur 1792–1793* (Paris: SÉR, 1964), 428–31.
67. Bernardin, *Jean-Marie Roland et le Ministère de l'Intérieur 1792–1793*, 456–57.
68. Ibid.

Chapter 7

NEW JUDGES

> The projects of the émigrés have made us feel our might, and the coalition of foreign powers has increased our courage. Now nothing external will halt France's great destiny ... [but] Lyon has always been split between a great number of privileged rich and oppressors and a greater number of poor.
>
> —Address to the Legislative Assembly by Joseph Chalier, 1792[1]

Most of the elected judges of Lyon in 1792 shared a fervent belief in the regenerated judicial system. However, as well as the age-old crimes of larceny and delinquency brought before them, there were soon new, more serious, crimes to be dealt with. These crimes often involved the plots of *émigrés*, refractory priests and of those who forged the new paper money known as *assignats*. They were crimes with the potential to threaten the state itself. The standard penalties now provided by the Code Pénal meant neither the *juges de paix* nor the citizen in the jury had a great deal of power in ensuring that enemies of the new state were ultimately convicted. If a crime did not exactly correlate to one defined in the code, the accused had to be released without penalty. The biggest question that faced many of the judges in such situations was whether the laws should be applied strictly or whether political issues should influence them. To add to the challenges, the already rampant fears of conspiracies against the new state were 'enormously inflated' by the impact of war.[2] Joseph Chalier was one judge who began to voice popular fears and to think of more radical solutions to the dangers anticipated. For him and the more radical Jacobins of the Central Club, the success of the judicial reforms depended on how those elected to the new judicial positions applied the laws to the new dangers.

* * *

The core changes to the judicial system were largely in place in Lyon by 1792. The courthouse itself was also being physically reconstructed according to the new revolutionary design based on the principle of the more democratic and accessible justice that had been envisaged for provincial courts in January 1791. A newer façade to the courthouse in Lyon was planned to be added to the side of the older prison complex of the Palais de Roanne on the banks of the Saône River but would not be finished until 1793. While the building work was in progress, witnesses were summoned to appear before the magistrates at the Hôtel de Flécheres, at level 2 of the Palais. The layout of the court itself had changed to reinforce the new centre of power of court administration. No longer was the king seen to be the last resort, as the position of his royal seat (known as the *lit de justice*) at the apex of a diamond-shaped configuration once represented.[3] Judges were now accommodated behind a semicircular desk, and facing them, down a flight of stairs behind another curved bench, were the barrister and his client. There was space for an audience because the judges were now accountable to the public who elected them.[4]

Figure 7.1 *La prison de Roanne* (The Prison of Roanne). P.G. Bugniet, inv. 1962–551. Bibliothèque et documentation, Musée des Beaux-Arts Lyon.

Those who accepted judicial office at the time of the Revolution were expected to be 'men of virtue', devoted to the public good rather than subscribing to any form of factional politics. This was a typical conception of the role of the public man in the revolutionary era as described by historian Marisa Linton:

> The new men who came to the fore of political life were obliged to negotiate this changed political landscape in which their own ambition was considered as inherently suspicious, their true identity subject to public scrutiny. They sought to establish their power bases through appropriating the identity of 'men of virtue', selflessly dedicated to the public good.[5]

At the level of the canton and the district court, the judges were especially open to scrutiny by the public. Their provision of a service to the citizen was paramount, and it was considered immaterial whether the judges were entirely new to the law or had previously practised it. Taking on such a position meant those elected were demonstrating a commitment to the state itself and not simply working for their own advancement. The corollary of the moral validation they received from taking on such office, however, was that there could be expected to be other not so virtuous men, who dissimulated, who wore a mask, who pretended support for the Revolution they secretly detested. Despite the rhetoric about 'virtue', the elected judges were drawn from a wide cross-section of society, and they inevitably had their own political opinions.

Ampère was a judge who supported the idea of a constitutional monarchy as can be seen in a play he wrote while he lived in Poleymieux. The play was entitled *Artaxerxes ou Le Roi Constitutionnel* and told the story of the eponymous monarch who had come to see the benefits of a less absolute style of government.[6] The play was a scholarly exercise, written in Alexandrine verse and based on a political translation of a classic opera libretto by Pietro Metastasio. The piece was dated 1789 yet intriguingly was signed *'Montagnard devenu juge de paix'* ('a man from the mountains, now a Justice of the Peace'), which would suggest it was finished after he moved from the mountain of Poleymieux into this judicial position at the end of 1791. It is very unlikely (although not impossible) that he would have meant this title to reflect his support for the left or radical side of Parisian politics, as the higher benches or the 'Montagnards' became known from September 1792. Although never formally published, the play does establish the author's belief in a monarchy based on the cooperation of a king and his people. It also presents his views on the justice that such a monarch should exercise. A debate between the characters Mandane and Sémira begins this discussion:

What judge ever pronounces only on appearances? . . . Mandane: Laws without rigour do not have any authority. Sémira: The authority of the law is nothing without fairness.[7]

This short exchange helps explain Ampère's motivation in taking on an active role at the time he did. He thought equity and fairness were the predominant concerns of the project of the regeneration of justice.

Becoming a judicial officer promised to be transformative for Ampère because he had long championed such revolutionary ideals. Ampère would now potentially work with reformers who truly understood the language of Montesquieu, Rousseau and Cesare Beccaria as his library suggests he did.[8] Beccaria wrote persuasively about the need to confront the horrible nature of punishment as it was meted out in the eighteenth century. This work and that of other philosophers and thinkers whose works Ampère had collected in his library foregrounded the need for judicial change, and the Revolution had provided the context. Choosing to take decisive action as one of the new *juges* must have seemed one of the only ways to take charge of the headlong advance of revolutionary events in the city, as well as being a sensible and creditable thing to do. Jean-Jacques personified the liberal bourgeois who appreciated the need for judicial reform, but he was also aware of the potential for social violence if the rule of law broke down because he had seen such events unfold in the Poleymieux incident. His election signalled a public recognition of his commitment to advance the Revolution as a 'man of virtue'.

The trajectory of Chalier was somewhat different. He had taken on a number of the 'multiple allocations' required of municipal officers in Lyon from September 1791 after some months of European travel. He worked with Roland as a member of the Commission of Commerce and Industry and was part of a 'military bureau'; he was also one of the founding members of a 'committee of surveillance' formed to help uncover conspiracies.[9] Chalier then became a judge of the Tribunal de conservation (Tribunal de commerce) and the Tribunal de District as a result of the elections held in November.[10] He was as industrious and virtuous as any officer could be. Chalier was President of the Tribunal Correctionnel when Ampère was elected as a *juge de paix* in January 1792.[11] Like Ampère, he had no significant judicial experience or training. Although born to a family of notaries, Chalier had decided upon a mercantile career as a *négociant* before the Revolution, as had Ampère. The status that both had gained in the silk industry of Lyon and their abrupt career change on the advent of the Revolution meant they had many similar experiences. However, there was a sharp divergence in the careers of these two men as their political concerns came to the fore.

Figure 7.2 Joseph Chalier, leading magistrate in the Tribunal de District and member of the Jacobin Club. Wikipedia Commons.

Politics was beginning to impinge on the law, and this led to conflict between the new departmental court, the Tribunal Criminel, and the Tribunal de District. According to the nineteenth-century historian Maurice Wahl, 'an ardent struggle' was at play here.[12] The first manifestation of this struggle was the suspension of two municipal officers, Chalier and Champagneux, early in 1792. Chalier had, with the knowledge of Champagneux and another officer by the name of Bonnard, written up the *procès-verbaux* of citizen Meynis in December 1791, charging him with the crime of procuring a knife. Despite the fact that the accused claimed it was only a domestic knife, Chalier went on to pursue the man based on a belief that he had ordered other such weapons be procured for his friends.[13] Chalier and Champagneux were ordered to appear before the Tribunal Criminel early in 1792, when the accused complained of this further action. It would appear he was hyper alert to the possibilities of conspiracy against the new revolutionary state. In another matter, of Reine and François Lacroix, he had undertaken a search of commercial premises on 17 February after being alerted to the possibility of them being used for the forging of *assignats*. His actions were decided by the Tribunal Criminel to have been premature because the denunciation was motivated by personal jealousy of a neighbour and had no basis in fact.[14] Despite his devotion to the pursuit of justice, Chalier was ultimately not seen as a 'man of virtue' by the judges of the higher court. He was seen to be impetuous and untrustworthy.

The Tribunal Criminel was composed during most of this period by the president, Cozon, and two other judges. These judges were elected for six years and tended to be more 'professional' because of a requirement that the judges at this higher level should have legal training or experience.[15] The departmental court consequently tended to be more conservative. It had little connection with the elected *juges de paix* and the magistrates at the canton and district level – that is, those who initiated actions brought to them by citizens. Chalier was found by this more conservatively staffed Tribunal Criminel to have been overzealous in the execution of his duties and was suspended. Although Champagneux, on the recommendation of Roland, was soon after appointed a *procureur* by the municipal council, Chalier was not immediately reinstated. The illuminating municipal session of 1 February showed the conflict between the department and the municipality on the suspension of these two municipal officers. A petition signed by 150 citizens was read out that called for the vindication of Chalier and Champagneux. Also read out were the letters sent to the Assembly and the king, accusing the department of spreading 'the poison of discord' by their actions in this case and more generally.[16] Again the municipal officers were supportive of the role of the *juges de paix*, but they avoided the question of whether Chalier's actions should be censored or left for the Legislative Assembly to decide. Chalier did not wait for a decision but hurriedly departed for Paris to lobby for his reinstatement.

In Paris, Chalier found that many of the deputies in the Legislative Assembly were dividing into political factions. The Jacobins were especially wary of the machinations of the Feuillants in the Assembly, but they had also divided among themselves over crucial issues. Those deputies who agreed with Brissot had begun to urge revolutionary war against Austria. They convinced other moderate deputies that the Pillnitz Declaration of 27 August 1791 by Prussia and Austria, pledging support for the monarch of France, needed to be challenged.[17] The more radical of the Jacobins in the club scene, Robespierre and Marat, led the club in an anti-war position, and their schism with the Brissotins became bitter.[18] Brissot began his campaign for war by a foreign policy speech on 20 October 1791, and by 20 April 1792 he had enough of a following that a declaration for war was made.[19]

The Jacobin club suspected that war, for the Brissotins, was a political ploy.[20] The Austrians had traditionally been a target of suspicion for the French, and these suspicions had been increased rather than allayed by the royal marriage of the king to Marie-Antoinette. According to Tim Blanning, there was 'sustained and vocal' opposition to the Austrian alliance, and deputies were convinced that war would be swift and decisive. The decision was helped by the mounting fears of conspiracies being planned by *émigrés* and by foreign monarchs, and it also propelled many national deputies 'well down the republican road'.[21] The army did not, however, make any successful advances in the early weeks of the war, and many generals themselves were losing faith. Radicalism among the Parisians grew as a result.[22] In May 1792, when the king vetoed the decree enacted against the refractories, his decision combined with the fear of retaliation by Austria and Prussia against France increased anxieties in Paris. A war begun because of political ambition and really only expected to be waged against Austria suddenly seemed to have hastened the involvement of the rest of Europe.[23]

In Lyon, there were huge fears about the counter-revolutionary danger of those priests and *émigrés* who would not take the oath, and these fears were increased by anxiety about the safety of the south-east borders close by. Conflict was continuing to be encouraged in many congregations by refractory priests, and this activity was now believed to be linked to Royalist and counter-revolutionary activity and to be more political than religious.[24] The Lyonnais historian Côme Simien suggests the religious issues also became pivotal to the differences between the department of the Rhône-et-Loire and the municipality. The department practised tolerance towards the refractory clergy while the municipal officers tried to repress the riots. As a result, Simien observed that the general population felt increasingly emboldened to attack the administrators, both municipal and departmental, for the lack of action against the priests who ignored the law.[25] The growing conflict about the refractories and the growing parameters of the external war led people to believe that they needed to protect revolutionary advances themselves.

While fears and tensions spread quickly from the national sphere to the local and back again, hope and elation was also still a strong emotion in evidence. A prominent Lyonnais in the national venue at this time was Adrien Lamourette, the new constitutional bishop to Lyon, who had been elected to the Legislative Assembly. On 7 July 1792 Lamourette caused a sensation by suggesting that all the members of the Assembly should put aside factionalism and practise 'fraternity'. He suggested they should all embrace. The king and the deputies did as he suggested and briefly forgot their animosities. They experienced a sense of the wider possibilities of the Revolution for a short time. According to Robert Darnton, there was a renewed enthusiasm and 'conviction that the human condition is malleable, not fixed, and that ordinary people can make history instead of suffering it'.[26] However, these positive feelings were short-lived, as they were shadowed by the encroaching external threats. Fear and dismay soon reasserted themselves as the most powerful emotions of the day.

When the German prince leading the Prussian and Austrian forces, the Duke of Brunswick, put his name to a manifesto of 28 July 1792, this helped to further incense the Parisians.[27] The Duke promised to lead his troops and the armed *émigrés* that supported them to Paris and to destroy the city if the revolutionaries should harm the king. Fear of this credible threat ensured that there was a particularly violent challenge to Louis XVI by the *sans-culottes*. On 10 August 1792, the king and his family were driven from the Tuileries palace. After his Swiss guards continued to fire at the insurgents, some 600 were brutally killed and mutilated by a crowd augmented by members of the National Guard and *fédérés* from the provinces. Soon after, General Lafayette defected to the enemy when the troops he was leading refused to march on Paris. Fears of counter-revolution and invasion once more became high, and the *sans-culottes* remained vigilant.

The rapid growth of popular activism in Paris, impelled by fears of the war going badly, was mirrored in Lyon. The army of the Midi, under General Montesquiou, was at the borders south-east of Lyon as the Central Club of the Jacobins stepped up a campaign for action against refractory priests and 'aristocrats'. Speakers highlighted the great difference in outlook of the Rolandins in municipal office and the common people as well as the obvious dangers of war. While social division in Lyon had always been a feature of the city, the incompatible political and social aspirations of the Rolandins had mostly been masked until the fall of the constitutional monarchy.[28] Dissident voices began to grow even louder from August 1792, when Joseph Chalier returned to Lyon absolved by the Legislative Assembly of any wrongdoing in the way he had pursued his office.

Chalier's time in Paris had done little to curb him of the excesses he was accused of. The months he was out of his position on the bench increased his fervour for vengeance against those other judges who had not supported him. Chalier reclaimed his position on the Tribunal de District, but he continued to believe he was unfairly targeted. This perception then increased his notoriety. George Eynard, his biographer, says 'he exulted with joy at the idea of playing the role of the honest man persecuted for a just cause.'[29] During the months he was resident in the capital, he had met Robespierre, Marat and Desmoulins and had attended Assembly meetings and absorbed the strong feelings of the Parisian clubbists.[30] He also addressed a petition to the Assembly in which he denounced the departmental authorities of the Rhône-et-Loire, describing the sorry history of the Lyonnais consuls and the failed aristocratic plot of 1791. He catalogued the continued failings of the department, including its alleged support for foreign troops against its own people and the suspension of two municipal officers from their function (including himself).[31] His experiences in Paris appear to have radicalised him further.

Chalier's first actions on returning to the city supported an antimonarchical campaign. Alexandrine des Écherolles, a young aristocratic girl, remembers hearing him lecturing people from the steps of the coach that had brought him from Paris. He was enthusiastically relaying the events of 10 August. She said: 'His mouth vomited imprecations and blasphemies.'[32] Most speeches were, however, delivered to the more sympathetic members of the Central Club of the Jacobins, where he had become a favoured orator. He told them it was time that 'citizens rejected lethargy; that the popular societies rose with energy' and took action.[33] Already well known for his tendency to become overwrought, he now adopted the radical rhetoric he had encountered in Paris in his own inimitable style.[34] He told the club he wanted to 'surround the municipality ... and cut off the heads of refractory priests and all aristocrats' because, he said, 'It is only when one sees the impure blood streaming from all sides that we will achieve tranquillity, safety and happiness.'[35] These and similar rousing words ensured he made enemies who were ready to blame him for inciting violent action, even when he was not present at moments of popular protest.

Chalier was, however, only one of the judges and administrators who advocated such radical policies. On the very day of his return from Paris, the equestrian statue of Louis XIV in the central square of Bellecour was ritually destroyed. This action was meant to signify the obliteration of any trace of the abusive monarchy of the *ancien régime*.[36] The pieces were to be melted down to make bullets and cannon for the national army. The ceremony had been suggested while Chalier had been away by the most vocal of the Jacobins, Antoine-Marie Dodieu (later known as Manlius). Dodieu was a printer by trade and president of the radical *section* based around the *quartier* of Rue Juiverie. On 26 August, two days before the return of Chalier, he printed and distributed a circular letter proposing a mass protest.[37] His suggestions included a programme of price fixing and also the replacement of judges by new elections through the popular assemblies. Dodieu's letter ended with the warning that, 'if [taking] the life of a single individual could save the country we have the right to kill him'.[38] Vitet, as mayor, sought legal action against Dodieu for these pronouncements, and it was Ampère who issued Dodieu's arrest warrant on 31 August 1792 for 'writing and signing the circular in quantity'.[39] This case of Dodieu signalled the emergence of a competing revolutionary vision in Lyon that was held in some of the sectional clubs and had at first little to do with Chalier.

Dodieu promptly disappeared. However, he was back in October urging the lower-paid workers and the unemployed to express their own views rather than accept the paternalistic pronouncements of the Rolandins. As he warned his *section* about the hoarders who were making the price of grain rise and the 'aristocratic' judges who were complicit in a conspiracy to make basic foods like bread unaffordable, he also proposed practical methods on how to take action. The most important was a 'taxation' that would impose the Parisian price of bread on the bakers. He advised the silk workers to pursue 'a gradual increase in compensation proportional to the cost of living'.[40] The silk workers then demanded 'a salary which would be commensurate with the growing costs of essentials' and the 'fixation' of a *mode coactive* between the two.[41] They wanted an end to 'humiliating assistance', and the provision of 'true justice (*justice exacte*)'.[42]

When Chalier joined the Jacobins in calling for increased agitation, this had an almost immediate negative effect on many conservatives in the courts and the municipality. It appalled the Rolandins.[43] The negative perception held of him and his allies by the Rolandins in turn curbed his effectiveness in the courts. Roland, dismissed by the king as minister in June 1792, had been reinstated as Minister of the Interior in the provisional government in Paris after 10 August. He was busy re-establishing his position there as well as taking the executive actions required of his position.[44] He had also summoned Champagneux to the capital to help him deal with all the correspondence that came from the provinces; he was especially besieged with letters from his friends in Lyon.[45] The Rolandins remaining in Lyon implored the minister for help in dealing with the growing problem of radical 'agitators' like Chalier.[46] They refused to countersign the petitions of those who advocated fixing prices.[47] Roland was inundated with letters describing how Chalier had become a 'débauché' and allied himself with men and women of unsavoury character.[48] Pressavin, now the *procureur* of Lyon, added that the worst of these characters was Dodieu, 'a dishonorable (*mauvais*) man of the law'.[49] Roland chided the Lyonnais judiciary, saying that they needed to ensure that suspect priests and bad citizens were arrested and punished because 'the most cruel civil war would ensue if individuals were allowed to use violence and put their own will in place of the law'.[50]

Ampère was concerned at the growing political divisions around him, but he was also still impassioned by his new career, and he rose to the challenges he encountered. Although it can be imagined that he shared some of the disillusionment of Rolandins like Vitet and Pressavin and their conviction that the *sans-culottes* were being led astray by the Jacobins, the only evidence we have of any political alignment is contained in a statement of the Jacobin Commissaire National, Hidins. Hidins would be imprisoned after his interrogation by Ampère in 1793, and in his papers he claimed that Ampère was a 'Rolandin-Feuillantin' who had been 'unmasked' and had 'blushed' when it was pointed out to him that he had refused to sign a petition for the death of the king.[51] This was clearly a retrospective accusation to impugn the judge who had helped implicate Hidins in allegations of impropriety in his office. Whether or not there was any substance to the accusation, Ampère, like many others who had been invested emotionally in the monarchy of Louis XVI, now had to adjust to the new state of affairs by the end of the year.[52]

A case that required a more nuanced political decision was that of Benoîte Troncey, heard in August 1792. The case was brought before Ampère by a woman called Grandmaison.[53] She alleged that Troncey had come to her with the sheriff (*huissier*) Jacques Laurent and they both proceeded to terrorise her, threatening to pillage and bomb her home. She appears to have been a relative of the Jacobin commandant of the National Guard of this name and thus the victim of a political crime because of her connection to the Jacobins.[54] Ampère duly wrote up the witness statement in the case, as he was required to do, and the case was sent on appeal to the Tribunal Criminel. Here the officials were exonerated because the crimes they were charged with did not appear in the Code Pénal. The prisoners were released. The case gives an indication of the environment of fear and violence attached to political action around this time in Lyon. It also seemed to vindicate the fears of the Jacobins that enemies of the Revolution would not be punished by conservative judges.

Notes

1. Joseph Chalier, 'Address to the National Assembly', 1792. Trans. M. Abidor. http://www.marxists.org/history/france/revolution/chalier/1792/address.htm (accessed 21 February 2013).
2. T. Tackett, *The Coming of the Terror in the French Revolution* (Cambridge, MA: The Belknap Press of Harvard University Press, 2015), 171.
3. K.F. Taylor, 'Geometries of Power: Royal, Revolutionary and Post-revolutionary French Courtrooms', *Journal of the Society of Architectural Historians* 72 (2013), 440.
4. Taylor, 'Geometries of Power', 443–48.
5. M. Linton, *Choosing Terror: Virtue, Friendship and Authenticity in the French Revolution* (Oxford: Oxford University Press, 2013), 75.
6. For a study of this play and the cosmopolitan ideas of its author: J.P. Johnson, 'Jean-Jacques Ampère and the Translation of Artaxerxes' in P.-Y. Beaurepaire, P. Bourdin and C. Wolff (eds), *Moving Scenes: The Circulation of Music and Theatre in Europe, 1700–1815* (Oxford: Voltaire Foundation, 2018), 289–304. The play itself is preserved in the Archives de l'Académie des Sciences, Paris (Fonds André-Marie Ampère), Chemise 292: 'Artaxerxes ou Le Roi Constitutionnel'.
7. Ampère, *Artaxerxes*, Act 4, Scene 1: ss. '*Quel juge prononça jamais sur l'apparence?*' Mandane argues: '*Les lois sans la rigueur n'ont point d'autorité.*' To which Sémira replies: '*L'autorité des lois n'est rien sans l'équité.*'
8. Johnson, 'Jean-Jacques Ampère', 292–93.
9. M. Wahl, 'Joseph Chalier: Étude sur la Révolution Française à Lyon', *Revue Historique* 34 (1887), 5.
10. Chalier is well known as an animated orator at the local Jacobin club and a contender for the mayoral role, but his role as a judge is often downplayed. He has been the subject of some biographical treatment including: G. Eynard, *Joseph Chalier: Bourreau ou martyr, 1747–1793* (Lyon: Éd. lyonnaises d'art et d'histoire, 1987); an article by Wahl, 'Joseph Chalier' ; a dictionary entry by F. Wartelle, 'Chalier, Joseph/les "Chaliers"', in A. Soboul (ed.), *Dictionnaire Historique de La Révolution Française*) Paris: Presses Universitaires de France, 1989), 200–1.
11. Eynard, *Joseph Chalier*, 10–13.
12. M. Wahl, *Les Premières années de la Révolution à Lyon 1788–1792* (Paris: Armand Colin, 1894), 474.
13. Wahl, 'Joseph Chalier', 5.
14. Eynard, *Joseph Chalier*, 51–52.

15. P. Dawson, *Provincial Magistrates and Revolutionary Politics in France: 1789–1795* (Cambridge, MA: Harvard University Press, 1972), 245–47.
16. AML 1 CM 3, 1 February 1792.
17. T.C.W. Blanning, *The French Revolutionary Wars 1787–1802* (London: Hodder Headline, 1996), 59–63.
18. Tackett, *The Coming of the Terror*, 155–56.
19. T.C.W. Blanning, *The Origins of the French Revolutionary Wars* (London: Longman Group, 1986), 99.
20. C.J. Esdaille, *The Wars of the French Revolution: 1792–1801* (London and NY: Routledge, 2019), 27.
21. Blanning, *The French Revolutionary Wars*, 64.
22. Tackett, *The Coming of the Terror*, 173.
23. Esdaille, *The Wars of the French Revolution*, 27–28.
24. P. Chopelin, *Ville patriote et ville martyre: Lyon, l'église et la Révolution, 1788–1805* (Paris: Letouzey et Ané, 2010), 194–97.
25. C. Simien, *Les Massacres de septembre 1792 à Lyon* (Lyon: Aléas, 2011), 97.
26. R. Darnton, *The Kiss of Lamourette: Reflections in Cultural History* (New York and London: W.W. Norton & Co., 1990), 3–20.
27. Blanning, *The French Revolutionary Wars*, 71–72; Esdaille, *The Wars of the French Revolution*, 79–81.
28. W. Edmonds, *Jacobinism and the Revolt of Lyon, 1789–1793* (New York: Oxford University Press, 1990), 128.
29. Eynard, *Joseph Chalier*, 54.
30. E. Herriot, *Lyon n'est plus: Jacobins et Modérés*, vol. 1 (Paris: Hachette, 1937), 30.
31. Chalier, 'Address to the National Assembly', 1792.
32. A. des Écherolles, *Une Famille noble sour la Terreur* (Paris: Elibron Classics, 2006), 37.
33. As he wrote to Delorme in Lyon in May 1792. Quoted in Edmonds, *Jacobinism*, 117.
34. Eynard, *Joseph Chalier*, 13. From his school years, this 'volcanic' temperament was observed by his acquaintance Chassagnon, who later wrote a plea for him.
35. Eynard, *Joseph Chalier*, 67.
36. Eynard, *Joseph Chalier*, 66.
37. Eynard, *Joseph Chalier*, 66.
38. Eynard, *Joseph Chalier*, 66.
39. AML 2 I 20 Police générale, dossiers particuliers (Dodieu).
40. This advice of October was quoted in Herriot, *Lyon n'est plus*, 96.
41. Herriot, *Lyon n'est plus*, Vol. 1, 96.
42. Herriot, *Lyon n'est plus*, Vol. 1, 96.
43. Eynard, *Joseph Chalier*, 63.
44. S. Reynolds, *Marriage and Revolution: Monsieur and Madame Roland* (Oxford: Oxford University Press, 2012), 183–90, 206.
45. Reynolds, *Marriage and Revolution*, 191, 208.
46. Reynolds, *Marriage and Revolution*, 209.
47. C. Riffaterre, *Le Mouvement antijacobin et antiparisien à Lyon et dans le Rhône-et-Loire en 1793, 29 mai-15 août*, Vol 1 (Lyon: A. Rey, 1912), 11.
48. Eynard, *Joseph Chalier*, 60–61.
49. Letter of 27 August 1792 from Pressavin to Roland quoted in Herriot, *Lyon n'est plus*, 52.
50. See his letter of August 1792 as quoted in Edmonds, *Jacobinism*, 121.
51. See Hidins' statement in a letter to the representatives-on-mission in Lyon in February 1793. He was appealing against his interrogation by Ampère and by what he called the 'royalist' Tribunal Criminel: BML Fonds Cost, Ms 558.

52. See Barry Shapiro for a well-argued case that despite 'a growing intellectual skepticism' there was a centuries-old investment in feelings of love for the king, which 'still carried an emotional charge': 'The Case Against the King' in P. McPhee (ed.), *A Companion to the French Revolution* (Chichester: Wiley Blackwell, 2015), 108.
53. ADR 39 L 23.
54. In November 1793, a certain Grandmaison accused the military commission of not being harsh enough on the rebels. See A. Salomon de la Chapelle, *Documents sur la Révolution: Lyon et ses environs sous la Terreur 1793–1794* (Lyon: Librairie Générale Henri Georg, 1885), 30.

Chapter 8

THE FIRST REPUBLIC

We must be barbarous for the sake of humanity and cut off an arm to save the body.
— Rosalie Jullien, letter 19 August 1792 (as translated by T. Tackett)

Paris was rocked by real fears of invasion as foreign war continued to be waged in August 1792. Prussia, initially thought unlikely to join with Austria, did enter the war, creating a second front that engaged with the French revolutionary forces in the middle of the month.[1] As the frightening prospect of enemy troops arriving in Paris seemed to be growing, so too were fears of conspiracy and betrayal amongst counter-revolutionaries. Rosalie Jullien, a bourgeois wife and mother living in Paris and trying to keep her spread-out family aware of the desperation of the situation in the capital, wrote her worried observation of 19 August (quoted above) acknowledging that the decisive action of the *sans-culottes* in early August against the Swiss Guards was justified and that more may need to be done.[2] The prisons were overflowing with counter-revolutionaries and refractory priests, and most Parisians were aware of how dangerous such traitors could be if released by the Prussians. The city was locked and lit up on the nights of 29 to 31 August while national guards patrolled and searched for traitors.[3]

* * *

An explosion of popular violence took place on 2 September 1792 when incontrovertible evidence arrived that the Duke of Brunswick had laid siege to the French town of Longwy on 24 August and was en route to

Paris. The prisons became a major site of focus for the increasing tensions because they were filled with those suspected of fomenting plots and conspiracies. A group of nineteen counter-revolutionary priests were attacked by a crowd as they were being transferred to a Parisian prison. After this first spontaneous action, various other prisons in the city were then broken into. Prisoners suspected of being counter-revolutionary were summarily tried and executed. Some 1,200 were massacred over a period of days.[4]

A prison massacre also occurred in Lyon a week later. Nine members of the Royal Pologne regiment transiting through the city had been incarcerated in the fortress prison of Pierre-Scize. They had resigned their commissions and were waiting for their resignations to be accepted before they left France. However, the secretive way in which this was managed led to a great deal of local rumour about whether they were now potential counter-revolutionaries. The municipality and the mayor, Vitet, had placed them in the old fortress rather than a regular prison because they were also worried the men in question might become enemies if they were allowed to leave the country.[5] On 9 September, a group of veteran national guards became convinced the former members of the regiment were in fact traitors and were going to join with *émigré* armies outside the borders if they were released. They helped rouse a crowd of around 150 citizens, armed with pikes, to insist that those arrested should be immediately taken to the prison of Roanne. The crowd demanded the keys to the cells from the concierge of the fortress and then seized the prisoners. Vitet, Nivière-Chol and the new commandant of the National Guard attempted to intervene by appealing to the veterans to retire but were unable to stop the abduction of the prisoners.[6]

The captured men were then attacked as they were forced down the steep stone stairs of the fortress leading to the river. Most were killed during the episode, and their heads were then paraded on pikes as the crowd surged across the bridge and into the city square. The threatening group terrorised audiences at the Théâtre des Célestins on the way. Three refractory priests encountered by the crowds in the streets were also massacred. By this time, the conduct of many refractory priests was allied to the counter-revolutionary activity of royalists, and their targeting had become 'more political than religious' according to a leading commentator on the religious conflict in Lyon.[7] The attack against the refractory priests was deliberately linked to the violence of the day, but the major causative factor was the fear of external war in a city situated close to the south-eastern border. As in Paris, fears about the encroaching war, *émigrés* and the plots of refractory clergy had precipitated events.[8]

The rushed recruitment of National Guards from the department by General Montesquiou, following the law of 25 August authorising local recruitment drives, was a significant local circumstance leading to the massacres.[9] Citizens were not only worried about invasion from the Catholic countries of Italy and Spain but also by the prospect of family members going to war. Fears about loss of income from the recruits, a reduction in numbers of workers now being available to work the fields and workshops, and also the vulnerability of the remaining family members to aristocratic or malicious action in their absence were high. Côme Simien credits the hasty recruitment of troops as causing great anguish and a 'paroxysm of feeling of abandonment among the Lyonnais'.[10] Ultimately, the violence of the September episode was, he suggests, not the unthinking terror of a revolutionary crowd but rather an expression of the betrayal and fears of a section of the community when confronted by 'deception, prejudice and danger'.[11]

Those arrested for the massacres in Lyon were put under the protection of Chalier, who described them as modern incarnations of the 'Brutus' who had killed Caesar and were thus saviours of the Revolution and worthy of being crowned by Robespierre.[12] This validation of their violent actions would lead to another, unintended consequence, according to Simien. The *sans-culottes* developed a 'habituation' to violence because there was no significant retributive action against them:

> Blood had already flowed, sometimes very savagely ... these violent moments created a habituation, a passivity to physical violence in the population ... The Lyonnais had integrated, via this passivity the right ... of delivering justice themselves.[13]

Simien observed that the killings then contributed to a 'violent memory', which meant such action could be undertaken again by the *sans-culottes*.[14] While it was initially recognised in Lyon as well as Paris that 'barbarous' measures were needed to deal with compelling circumstances of danger, as Rosalie Jullien had warned, there were many in Lyonnais society who had begun to form a different view, one concerned about the spread of violence. Correspondence directed to Roland from officers like Vitet and Billiemas began to show an increased fear of the contagion of popular violence.[15]

The massacres raised many of the same questions that had been broached in the Poleymieux assassination a year earlier. Popular violence was seen as being antithetical to a society based on the rule of law because it encouraged feelings of fear and instability among the population at large. Alexandrine des Écherolles, in her memoir written sometime after the events, described living nearby the prison when she was a girl of 13. She remembered that 'thousands of people' were impelled to flee during the massacre and hide where they could, some 'in the woods'.[16] Many, she claimed, decided to emigrate after the events. Popular violence was also a huge challenge for the judges, who were, after all, also citizens. Many judicial officers redoubled their commitment to their new role to ensure that judicial order obviated the recourse to violence.

A case heard in the Tribunal Correctionnel at the beginning of September was typical of the crimes heard at the time but also typical of the Rolandin approach to ensuring law and order. Two accused, Filiot and Chavand, were arrested for looting a church.[17] They had been seen kneeling in a church and then caught with sacred items, including a chalice. Ampère was alerted to the circumstances in his *juge de paix* function, and he arrested them. The case went before the judges of the Tribunal Correctionnel, and the accused were found guilty and put in detention. The Tribunal Criminel, to whom they appealed, ratified the decision and ordered that they were to remain in detention until they served six hours in the stocks on the Place Terreaux as punishment. The case showed that the judicial officers involved prioritised the law protecting property and saw their decisions as re-establishing order in accordance with the Code Pénal. Not all judges, however, had the same opinion. In a case such as that brought against Filiot and Chavand, it could have just as easily been argued that church property now belonged to the people and so guilt could not be determined by merely applying the code.

Chalier and the radical Jacobins, who had come to the defence of the perpetrators of the violence of September, were not convinced of such a merely 'legal' idea of guilt. They began to urge instead a greater concern for the disadvantaged, and by such arguments they profited politically in Lyon. The speeches of the local Jacobins in the Central Club during August and September were received well by the populace but awakened new anxieties for the Rolandins. Although it was hoped that popular violence like the murder of the *seigneur* or the prison massacres would not be necessary as the new regime of law and order became more secure, the Rolandins were becoming increasingly intolerant of the *sans-culottes* and the more radical politicians like Chalier, who were seen as encouraging them. The Rolandins, by strictly applying the law without considering extenuating circumstances, were, however, gradually losing the support of the very people who had ensured their political power base.

There were as well continuing cyclical crises that affected the *menu peuple*, particularly women, who had to manage their households and feed their children in a time of increasing shortages and unemployment. Food shortages led inevitably to riots. Such disturbances happened not only because of the Jacobin exhortations to action but because grain supplies were often intercepted before they could reach the urban areas of Lyon. The desperation of those women faced with fluctuating bread supplies caused a particularly intransigent outbreak of rioting, which lasted some days from 14 September.[18] On 15 September 1792, a deputation of the radical club women presented a petition to the municipality demanding that certain subsistence foods should be made available at fixed prices because 'thousands were dying' and mothers were unable to provide basic needs for their children.[19] Without waiting for a reply, the women made up notices themselves, fixing maximum prices on a number of goods that they distributed throughout the city. From 16 to 19 September, they armed themselves with pikes and raided grocery stores to then sell goods at the new low price or *taxation populaire* they had fixed.[20] The women called themselves the 'Female Commissioners of Police' and warned that anyone who opposed them would be regarded as traitors while those who helped them need have no fear because the women would be 'loyal guardians of their property'.[21]

The agitation of women in the markets, coming so soon after the popular violence of the prison massacres, caused some consternation in Lyon. Yet women did have some presence here in the popular Jacobin clubs as they did in Paris. In 1792, during the transition from the constitutional monarchy to the First Republic in September, women were visible in the clubs throughout France with their 'constant, often programmed presence'.[22] In Lyon, a female Jacobin club, known as the 'Citoyennes de Lyon dévouées à la patrie', had formed on 1 August 1791. It encouraged the mothers, daughters and sisters of Lyon, who were members, to go beyond the acts of 'benevolence' that had until then been proposed to more active protest.[23] This was a largely bourgeois club, but more popular women's clubs were also established.[24] Alexandrine des Écherolles had heard of them, and she expressed the worries of her aristocratic family when she spoke of the terrifying Jacobin women whom she called the 'new species of tiger'.[25] Despite the fears their activism aroused, the women rioters did have some success. Both the municipality and local towns did try to ameliorate the causes of the agitation, with the former fixing the price of bread on 23 September and surrounding towns promising to provide more wheat to the city.

News from the capital then, all of a sudden, helped to restore confidence for the future. The first meeting of the National Convention on 21 September 1972 began with a surge of optimism and enthusiasm for the task of creating a new constitution. The historic meeting was buoyed by a French victory at Valmy, when the Prussian army retreated in disarray. The monarchy was now officially abolished, and a solemn proclamation was made of the 'one and indivisible' Republic on 22 September 1792.[26] The war had finally turned around, and details would continue to filter back of the French army defeating the Prussians and Austrians and now advancing on every front into Germany, Belgium and Switzerland.[27] The army of the Midi also successfully invaded Savoy and Piedmont-Sardinia, which lessened the fears of the Lyonnais.[28]

Among those elected to represent Lyon in the National Convention were the mayor Vitet himself and three other municipal officers: Antoine Chasset, Pressavin and Lanthenas.[29] While a number of more conservative delegates were also elected, there were another two deputies who demonstrated a strong radical following. Noel Pointe, a munitions worker, and Cusset, a small-scale silk worker, would speak for the under-represented viewpoint of the *sans-culottes* nationally. They became part of the very small number – no more than half a dozen, according to Alison Patrick – who were elected from the 'genuinely lower-class elements, [and] the *sans-culotterie*'.[30] The most significant effect of the election was that the most popular of the Rolandins were no longer available for local office. Vitet and Pressavin now began to sit on the left side of the Convention with the Montagnards. Adrien Lamourette, the constitutional bishop of Lyon, who had been elected to the previous Legislative Assembly, also remained absent from Lyon, as did Roland.[31] The latter was again given a ministerial post, as Minister of the Interior, by decree of the Convention.[32] The most prominent politicians who had acted as popular moderators were thus in Paris by the end of the month.

The removal of those municipal officers who were elected to the Convention from political life in Lyon meant there were now vacancies on the municipal council. This situation led to some reshuffling. The position of mayor was provisionally taken by Jean-François Perret, who had had a minor role in previous municipalities. Nivière-Chol, who had become a judge in the Tribunal Correctionnel after Chalier, had to vacate this seat when Chalier returned, and he now took on the premier *procureur* position in the municipality.[33] On 28 September Nivière-Chol observed in a private letter describing the reception of the news that 'the decree which abolished royalty has been received by the municipality and the people with joy'.[34] The department of the Rhône-et-Loire signalled its adherence to the proclamation on 6 October and expressed its wholehearted support for liberty and equality.[35] This optimism reflected the widespread feeling that government could now be truly based on the freedoms and equalities that had become fundamentally a part of the language of change.

However, social agitation had intensified political pressures for the Rolandins. Vitet and Roland wanted to make bread more affordable and allay the panic in the markets, but their measures were only short-term strategies. By 9 October, they acted to ensure controlled prices were revoked locally.[36] Edmonds suggests this was a crucial point where the *menu peuple* and the Rolandins diverged. Roland, apparently 'irritated by the fixing of food prices', had privately threatened to cut finances to Lyon if the agitators were not apprehended and dealt with.[37] His reaction to the *taxations populaires* highlighted the differences that had always existed between the Rolandins and popular economics. Fixed prices were anathema to the Rolandins, who wanted to ensure the 'free circulation' of goods such as wheat.[38] Other leaders were then emboldened to ally with the agitators and to challenge the Rolandins, who had demonstrated their loss of control of local politics. Dodieu and the Jacobins argued that the people had a right to expect that subsistence foods should be affordable.[39]

At this point, a guillotine arrived in the city. The Central Club were demanding it be put on public display by October.[40] Chalier was becoming evermore convinced of the intractability of the courts and the possibility of conspiracy. He argued that the time was ripe for the guillotine to 'be exposed to the eyes of the public to hold back the enemies of the country, to frighten off the aristocrats and to make tremble those of the commercial sector'.[41] The municipality, however, refused to put it up. Another provisional mayor, Arnaud-Tison, thought the decision about its use should be for the 'Tribunal Criminel and not for the commune, still less the Central Club whose members were noted for their dangerous intolerance'.[42] A rather gruesome demonstration of the guillotine was attempted by a gathering of protestors on the night of 25–26 October. The machine was stolen from the Hôtel de Ville and erected on a scaffold in the nearby square. Seven prisoners were later taken from the prison of Roanne to be summarily executed by the machine. The operation was intercepted by the National Guard. In the resulting confusion, two prisoners were killed by sabre and thrown into the river.[43] The next day the machine was again removed and transported to Bellecour and placed on the pedestal of the destroyed statue of Louis XIV.[44] Again, the National Guard were called out, but they responded tardily and were unable to restore order.[45]

The municipal authorities feared a reprise of September. Indignant citizens made sure the machine was returned to the prison of Roanne.[46] Two days later, it was decided by the National Convention that Vitet and two other deputies should be sent back to Lyon in November to help calm the situation. On 10 November, Vitet wrote to Roland of his lack of success:

> The Chaliers, the Dodieus, the Laussels and a multitude of other associates keep quiet well enough while we stay in Lyon. But hardly have we left that they provoke disorder, violation of properties, and even individual safety.[47]

Social agitation had again operated to focus attention on difference in the city rather than unity. The Jacobins were suspected of exploiting their growing popularity with the *menu peuple* to advance their inchoate campaign against counter-revolutionary threats. With Chalier at their head, they framed their demands for repression and societal change as the true position of the *sans-culottes* against those who advocated 'aristocratic' – to them, counter-revolutionary – attitudes. Though individual Rolandins had been seen as working for the good of the people, they were also, as a group, now recognised as dismissive of those not sufficiently talented or educated to take on municipal and judicial roles.[48] These differences soon cemented into increased agitation on the one hand and intolerance on the other.

The fear of social disorder meant there was less cooperation within the municipality and also with other local bodies of administration at the departmental level, including the higher courts, where more moderate views were held. Those who feverishly wrote to Roland were beginning to express more concerns about order in society and demanding solutions that would make protest less inevitable. They were becoming less tolerant of social agitation even as they continued to ascribe to the view that problems would resolve if only the rich merchants would 'open their coffers' and 'give to the poor'.[49] Because social demands were becoming more violent, they were dealt with by being increasingly ignored. The poorer social classes, the women of the markets and the ill-paid silk workers soon needed to look elsewhere for support. They were encouraged by the new voices of those like Dodieu, Hidins and the returned Chalier.

Even so, there was not yet a clear divide between factions. Roland was still remembered for his positive contribution to changes in Lyon, particularly the abolition of the *octrois*, and he was still influential. As Minister for the Interior he advised the administrators in Lyon in October 1792:

> When the people see the magistrates are occupying themselves fruitfully with the most pressing interests, those held most dear, they will become calm and more patient of the calamitous circumstances that they well know cannot be prevented.[50]

This advice was heeded by the judges despite the many contrary indications that the 'people' would not remain calm. Municipal and judicial roles were due to be renewed by elections at the end of the year, and the wider franchise legislated in August 1792 meant the possibility of a more socially inclusive representation. The elections were held in Lyon in October 1792, rather than November, because of the troubles that had erupted after the September massacres and the new political voices that were clamouring to be heard in the city at the time.[51] The change to voting eligibility meant previously passive male citizens could now vote, and they were likely to be disconnected from the Rolandin municipality but attracted to those speakers and politicians who they believed shared their own views. According to Trénard, the poorer workers and unemployed were now using the taverns and artisanal organisations to discuss revolutionary events as enthusiastically as the bourgeois had used the Académie des Sciences, the Freemasonry movement and the *cercle social* in earlier years.[52] They were as a result more politically aware.

On 28 October, a number of Jacobins, endorsed by the Central Club, were voted into municipal office. Chalier was not successful in his campaign for the mayoral position, because of a panicked flurry of voting aimed to keep him out, but a number of lesser posts were filled by the Jacobins.[53] The influence of the Central Club was quite pronounced in the poorer areas as predicted.[54] The Rolandins and the representatives from the *quartier* clubs more generally, those who had been politically active since the end of 1791, were now in a minority. Vitet lamented that the inclusion of the Central Club nominees in the municipality presaged the end of 'tranquillity'.[55] The records of the Municipal council immediately after the elections were not so pessimistic. Those newly elected spoke confidently of an expectation that order and stability would soon be achieved in the agitated city. There was a consensus noted that all officers should continue the efforts of the previous administration, which had been characterised by bi-partisan support and less social unrest than had been evident in the first years of the Revolution.[56] Once the administrative tasks related to the election and appointment of officers to various positions had been completed, council meetings and court hearings returned to general business. It was noted at the municipal meeting of 6 December 1792 that a rumour about the 'taxation' of subsistence foods had caused agitation in the marketplace.[57]

All members agreed that the municipal officers should deal with the underlying problems but that there was also a need to address the issue of misinformation, which had the potential to destabilise society. This was addressed by the decision to erect a notice at the markets warning people of attempts to sow discord in society that were intended solely to 'upset (*bouleverser*) the city' at the very moment the newly elected municipality took power.[58] The notice also stated that the new municipality had been occupied with the problem of subsistence foods from their first session. The next day, 7 December, a letter from the administration of L'Hôpital de la Charité was read to members. It asked that help be given to the infants and women whose husbands had been sent to the frontier as volunteer soldiers. This request was followed up in the council session of 26 January 1793, when the municipal officer Sautemouche read out a decree authorising the distribution of money to affected families. A petition was also read on 7 December from the widow of a baker, whose three infant children were suffering after his death at the hands of an angry crowd in October of that year. The baker, by the name of Boeuf, had been charged with making inferior quality bread, but before he could be dealt with for this alleged crime, he died of wounds inflicted by 'the violence of the people'. The municipal council recommended that the woman and her infants should be compensated, if possible, or an indemnity sought for her from the Minister of the Interior. Unanimous decisions were also made about more general matters. On 23 December, it was decided more bronze should be ordered for the fabrication of a cannon and, on 25 December, that residents should sweep the streets on which their apartments fronted to keep the city clean.

A clear majority of Jacobins, this time including Chalier, were also elected to the judiciary, but as tensions were already growing among the judges, the increasingly political selections had a more marked effect. The extremist Jacobin candidates Dodieu, Fernex and Gaillard became judges in the Tribunal Criminel on 27 November. François-Auguste Laussel, also a Jacobin, took on the key judicial role as *procureur* in December.[59] Ampère was re-elected as *juge de paix* with 194 out of a possible 361 voters, and other Rolandins including L'Ange and Billiemas also continued in their roles. Cozon remained President of the Tribunal Criminel.[60] While Ampère, L'Ange and Billiemas continued to form part of the bench of the Tribunal Correctionnel, to which they had been sworn in August 1792, they were now often joined by Jacobin *juges de paix* like Fillion and Jacob, who were also then eligible to sit on the Tribunal Correctionnel.

Chalier had more experience in the judicial role than some of the newer Jacobin incumbents, but he now aspired to a more political role. His dissatisfaction with politics in Lyon appeared to increase when he did not get enough votes to become mayor – a position that went to the Rolandin Antoine Nivière-Chol, who was previously *procureur*. While the municipal sessions of November and December did show numerous attempts to find common ground among those elected to political office in Lyon, there was already a degree of divisiveness amongst the judges, and Chalier appeared determined to take it into the political arena by his increasingly political agitation in the forum of the Central Club of the Jacobins.

Notes

1. T.C.W. Blanning, *The Origins of the French Revolutionary Wars* (London: Longman Group, 1986), 120.
2. The unique viewpoint of Rosalie Ducrollay, widow Jullien, as conveyed in her correspondence formed the basis of the biography by Lindsay A.H. Parker, *Writing the Revolution: A French Woman's History in Letters* (Oxford: Oxford University Press, 2013). She wrote nearly a thousand letters, which were preserved by her son and husband – the former known as Jules and the latter Marc-Antoine. The Jullien family moved from Romans to Paris in 1787. The men of the family quickly joined the Jacobin club, but Marc-Antoine returned to Romans and Jules had a diplomatic post in London, so Rosalie wrote to inform them of events.
3. T. Tackett, *The Coming of the Terror in the French Revolution* (Cambridge, MA: The Belknap Press of Harvard University Press, 2015), 209.
4. T.C.W. Blanning, *The French Revolutionary Wars 1787–1802* (London: Hodder Headline, 1996), 72.
5. C. Simien, *Les Massacres de septembre 1792 à Lyon* (Lyon: Aleas, 2011), 29–39.
6. Simien, *Les Massacres*, 59.
7. P. Chopelin, *Ville patriote et ville martyre: Lyon, l'église et la Révolution, 1788–1805* (Paris: Letouzey et Ané, 2010), 194–97.
8. Simien, *Les Massacres*, 31.
9. Simien, *Les Massacres*, 108.
10. Simien, *Les Massacres*, 119.
11. Simien, *Les Massacres*, 142.
12. A. Raverat, *Lyon sous la Révolution, suivi de la liste des condamnés à mort* (Lyon: La Découvrance, 2006), 57.
13. Simien, *Les Massacres*, 142.
14. Simien, *Les Massacres*, 143.
15. S. Reynolds, *Marriage and Revolution: Monsieur and Madame Roland* (Oxford: Oxford University Press, 2012), 209.
16. A. des Écherolles, *Une Famille noble sour la Terreur*, Vol. 1 (Paris: Elibron Classics, 2006), 57–58.
17. ADR 39 L 59.
18. Maurice Wahl says it reached the point of 'spontaneous anarchy' on 14 September, *Les Premières années de la Révolution à Lyon 1788–1792* (Paris: Armand Colin, 1894), 613.
19. Wahl, *Les Premières années*, 604.
20. See Affiche, 'Les Citoyennes de Lyon', Musée Gadagne, Lyon.
21. Wahl, *Les Premières années*, 606.
22. D.G. Levy and H.B. Applewhite (ed.), *Women and Politics in the Age of the Democratic Revolution* (Ann Arbor: University of Michigan Press, 1990), 81.
23. See 'Institution' and 'Règlements' of the club, BML Fonds Coste, 110945.
24. L. des Combes, *Clubs révolutionnaires des Lyonnaises* (Trévoux: s.n., 1908), 5.
25. Combes, *Clubs révolutionnaires*, 21.
26. A. Patrick, *The Men of the First French Republic: Political Alignments in the National Convention of 1792* (Baltimore, MD: Johns Hopkins University Press, 1972), 3.
27. Tackett, *The Coming of the Terror*, 226, 242.
28. Blanning, *The French Revolutionary Wars*, 88–89.
29. Kuscinski, *Dictionnaire des Conventionnels* (Paris: Librairie Rieder, 1916), 130.
30. Patrick, *The Men of the First French Republic*, 283.
31. Chopelin, *Ville patriote*, 206.

32. M. Linton, *Choosing Terror: Virtue, Friendship and Authenticity in the French Revolution* (Oxford: Oxford University Press, 2013), 138.
33. AML [online] 1217 WP 4, 13–19 Sept.
34. E. Herriot, *Lyon n'est plus: Jacobins et Modérés*, vol. 1 (Paris: Hachette, 1937), 87.
35. Herriot, *Lyon n'est plus*, Vol. 1, 83.
36. Edmonds, *Jacobinism and the Revolt of Lyon, 1789–1793* (New York: Oxford University Press, 1990), 127.
37. Edmonds, *Jacobinism*, 128–29.
38. Vitet in October, when he was in Paris, wrote to the municipality that they should encourage the 'free circulation of wheat'. Roland suggested in September an inquiry was necessary in Lyon because of the 'taxations arbitraire'. See Herriot, *Lyon n'est plus*, 84 and 91.
39. C. Riffaterre, *Le Mouvement antijacobin et antiparisien à Lyon et dans le Rhône-et-Loire en 1793, 29 mai-15 août*, vol 1 (Lyon: A. Rey, 1912), 6.
40. Edmonds, *Jacobinism*, 127.
41. As quoted by G. Eynard, *Joseph Chalier: Bourreau ou martyr, 1747–1793* (Lyon: Éd. lyonnaises d'art et d'histoire, 1987), 73.
42. Eynard, *Joseph Chalier*, 73.
43. Herriot, *Lyon n'est plus*, vol. 1, 93–94.
44. Riffaterre, *Le Mouvement*, 7.
45. Edmonds, *Jacobinism*, 128.
46. Chopelin, *Ville Patriote*, 73.
47. Eynard, *Joseph Chalier*, 735.
48. Edmonds, *Jacobinism*, 133.
49. The words of journalist Louis-Nicolas Carrier, published in the *Journal de Lyon* were quoted by Herriot, *Lyon n'est plus*, vol. 1, 98.
50. Edmonds, *Jacobinism*, 129.
51. Edmonds, *Jacobinism*, 123.
52. L. Trénard, *La Révolution Française dans la région Rhône-Alpes* (Paris: Perrin, 1992), 264–266.
53. Edmonds, *Jacobinism*, 139.
54. Edmonds, *Jacobinism*, 141–42.
55. See his letter to Roland of 15 November 1792, quoted in Edmonds, *Jacobinism*, 136.
56. AML 1 CM 3, especially the session of 6 December 1792.
57. AML 1217 WP 4.
58. AML 1217 WP 4.
59. Edmonds, *Jacobinism*, 131, 314. Laussel, an ex-priest, had been an appointee of Roland, then a radical journalist who denounced those in the Concert Club for being Feuillants and had now joined with the Jacobins.
60. ADR 35 L 19.

Part III

RETRIBUTIONS

Chapter 9

TRIALS AND EMOTIONS

[The nation] must be able to declare: all the general principles of jurisprudence recognized by enlightened men in all lands have been respected ... and when that nation judges a king, then kings themselves, in their inmost hearts, must feel moved to approve the judgment.

—Marquis de Condorcet (Girondin)[1]

Shadowed in darkness, kings persecuted virtue; but we judge kings before the eyes of all ... O you who seem the most severe judges of anarchy, surely you would not have it said of you that your rigor was for the people and that your sympathy was reserved for kings.

—Saint-Just (Jacobin)[2]

The trial of the king began in the National Convention on 10 December 1792 after his arraignment on various crimes, enumerated in thirty-four paragraphs of charges. As a recent commentator has pointed out, the first three of those paragraphs related to June and July 1789, when the king had challenged the sovereignty of the people, the alleged crime explicitly connected to 'the massacres at the Tuileries' of 10 August 1792.[3] The king was permitted to mount a defence, and the decision as to his guilt and the debates about appropriate punishment all took place in the Convention because of the fundamental importance these issues raised for the progress of the Revolution. The elected representatives from the entire nation were then able to put forward their position as part of the final vote, and by a decision of the majority reached on 21 January 1793, he was sent to the guillotine. Factional differences between the newly elected national deputies became sharply etched in the long and harrowing process but also important arguments about how justice could be done in the new modern republic. Was the king to be treated just like any other citizen in terms of his accountability to the law?[4]

* * *

Positions taken by the deputies in the voting, it soon transpired, 'sliced right through the politics of the Republic'.[5] The voting showed that factionalism would again be entrenched in the new Convention, where a greater sense of unity had been optimistically expected. The divisions that had plagued the Legislative Assembly between the Feuillants and the Jacobins now had new forms.[6] Those who sat to the left became the Jacobin faction, sometimes identified as the 'Montagnards', and those sitting to the right were identified as the Girondins or Brissotins, with those in the middle often referred to as the undecided 'Plain'.

The Girondins, although convinced of the king's guilt, suggested an 'appeal to the people' or other alternatives to an immediate sentence of death. Many of them were concerned about the legitimacy of the proceedings in a judicial sense.[7] Condorcet spoke for them when he argued that when Louis ceased to be king by virtue of the constitution, he was then entitled to a trial as would any other citizen.[8] The more radical Jacobin position was that there should not even be a trial, and prolonging one by an 'appeal to the people' was itself treasonous. Saint-Just suggested that the king was not an 'equal citizen' in any sense because kingship had proved to be merely a tyranny. Robespierre went further and reminded those who had legal scruples about the trial procedure that 'the true judgment of the king is the spontaneous and universal movement of a people weary of the tyranny which oppresses it.'[9]

The different opinions delivered during the trial exposed the heart of the dilemma about revolutionary justice. The Girondin position seemed to the Jacobins to be a concern with mere procedural technicalities. It suggested a lack of real commitment to the Revolution. Many Girondins on the other hand saw the Jacobin belief that a trial was not necessary at all as deeply troubling. They felt that real revolutionary justice needed to be demonstrated by fair trials in the new institutions of justice and that the strict application of the law as expressed by the Code Pénal was fundamental to the workings of any judicial system. The different opinions about effecting justice during the trial of the king would thus have enormous ramifications on how institutions of justice would continue to operate more generally.

The debates of the deputies elected from Lyon during the trial of the king mirrored the political animosities that were beginning to appear in Lyon. The Jacobin deputies from Lyon, Pointe and Cusset, with their artisanal background, held more radical opinions than others of those elected from Lyon. While Pressavin and Vitet sat to the left at this early stage, most delegates had been chosen by conservative rural electors and sat on the right of the Convention.[10] While all fifteen of the Lyonnais delegates voted for the king's guilt, only six (Pressavin, Dupuy, Pointe, Du Bouchet, Cusset and Javogues) voted for his death.[11] Lanthenas thought the king should be killed only if his relatives refused to leave France in peace. Others, including Vitet, thought he should be confined or exiled.

The Jacobin judges in Lyon began to freely express their political opinions about the death of the king from this time. Chalier had no doubt that the king should be found guilty, and he led the Central Club in a vehement campaign to ensure a petition with this view was presented to the Convention. *Commissaires* sent from Paris to Lyon in September were 'natural allies' of Chalier and Dodieu, according to Edmonds. They helped further promote the Jacobin position during their stay in the city and, ultimately, helped turn the Central Club against the Rolandins.[12] For many of the undecided, Chalier's inflammatory discourse seemed to confirm that he was a 'vulgar demagogue who flattered the appetites and the vices of the multitudes'. This was a particularly negative view of the man, and there are more considered judgments about him. One historian, Camille Riffaterre, recognised him as a man 'more agitated than dangerous'.[13] Chalier, he pointed out, did not always talk of 'beheadings'. On the contrary, in a warning given to 'aristocrats' on 12 February 1793 at the Central Club, he was noted to have said:

> Do not tremble, do not be scared ... The aristocrats are only incorrigible because we have neglected them too much: it is a matter of re-educating them. One talks of hanging them, of guillotining them; that is soon done; it is a horror. Is there any humanity or good sense in that; throwing a sick person out the window to save you worrying about healing them?[14]

Although Chalier was often compared to Jean-Paul Marat, Riffaterre finds little proof that he in fact demanded, like Marat, great blood lettings as his enemies alleged.[15] It was only at points of great agitation – for instance, when he felt himself to be in mortal danger – that Riffaterre found that his language tended to be extreme. But the Central Club had become, by the end of 1792, the major locus for radical ideas. Riffaterre proposed instead that the 'hate which (Chalier) attracted as a hot-head of the clubs' was because of his egalitarian theories and his criticism of the great merchants, who only offered charity to the poor.[16] For Riffaterre,

Chalier was the most noticeable of the Lyonnais Jacobins (*le plus en vue*) and thus the most demonised.

The Lyonnais Jacobins have often been described as having a cohesive identity at this time, centred around Chalier.[17] One scholar, Takashi Koi, referred to the group as 'Les Chaliers' and suggested they were in fact less like the Jacobins in Paris and more like the group known as the 'Enragés'.[18] However, others, including Edmonds, found this was not the case and that the social solutions the Lyonnais Jacobins proposed were not unique to them. They followed in practice the national Jacobin programme. He also found that some who advocated similar radical agrarian reforms, such as L'Ange, chose not to align with them at all. The Jacobins in Lyon are now accepted to be a much more diverse group than has previously been recognised. The most outspoken of the group was not Chalier but Manlius Dodieu, who had long been critical of the *négociants* and the *maîtres-ouvriers* in the silk industry, accusing them of depriving their own employees of work in times of calamity and crisis.[19]

Dodieu continued to support the radicalism of the *menu peuple* and to propose that bread should be sold at the stable *prix parisien* after October.[20] He was elected to the Tribunal de District shortly after because of his promises to take action against speculators who hoarded grain.[21] Robert Achard, the son of a poor surgeon, represented a similar style of committed social activism, and he deliberately identified as a *sans-culotte* to highlight his concern for the disadvantaged. He became prominent in the security and surveillance initiatives that the Jacobins proposed. The young Rousseau Hidins, who also identified as a *sans-culotte*, became the Commissaire National.[22] In this position, he assisted at council meetings and in judicial decisions. He joined Chalier as speaker in the Central Club, pursuing a 'project' about agrarian reform, borrowing from the *Social Contract* of his adopted namesake Rousseau.[23]

Once the Jacobins had control of the Central Club and the municipality itself, after the elections of late 1792, they tried to advance their initiatives of fixing the price of grain and the establishment of a dedicated revolutionary tribunal. The Jacobins were convinced that 'hoarders' and 'speculators' had caused the food crises, and those elected as judges now advocated for a more rigorous tribunal needed to curtail them.[24] They soon encountered many obstacles, however, when confronted with the hostility of the departmental authorities.[25] Divisions among the republicans in Lyon had been growing stronger since the overthrow of the king on August 10 and the popular violence of September 1792, and the more moderate patriots had long since left the Central Club. The more radical Jacobins, who remained, were strongly connected to the call for regicide, and they continued to focus on the national picture.

At the session of the Municipal Council of Lyon on 26 January, Chalier came with a deputation from the Central Club to 'invite' the municipal officers to attend a civic ceremony to celebrate the death of the king, or as he called him, the 'tyrant Capet'. On this occasion, he asked that *piques* be given to him to bundle around the Liberty tree for the ceremony.[26] When Lepeletier de Saint-Fargeau was killed in the Palais Royale (the arcade in Paris where popular discussion and actions took place), the local Jacobins again reacted strongly because they also felt vulnerable. Saint-Fargeau had been murdered because of his vote to put the king to death. On 5 February, a celebration of his status as revolutionary hero was held in Lyon. The event took place at the pedestal that had previously held the equestrian statue of the king in Bellecour and was attended by many judges of the Tribunals and *juges de paix*. A local journalist parodied Chalier's energetic speech at the ceremony; emphasising the melodrama and his ludicrous imploring of the 'brave *sans-culottes* to swear to exterminate all the tyrants, to purge from the earth of liberty, all those who have given no signs of their *civisme*'.[27] The Jacobin polemic was seen as an awkward attempt to warn those who objected to the death of the king of their wrong thinking. But Hidins, the Jacobin Commissaire National, thought the Jacobins needed to establish the strength of their revolutionary commitment in such vigorous ways because as he said in February 1793 there was 'a price on his head', as there was for Chalier and Gaillard, because of their support for action against the king.[28]

The *quartier* clubs, which represented the neighbourhood *sections* of the city, had at first much less direct political influence than the Central Club, but they grew in size and power as they became an alternative to the more radical Jacobins. They began to operate as a space to express the more conservative fears of disorder and violence and had gradually become an effective oppositional voice. Speakers in many of these clubs, especially in some of the conservative areas of the city like La Croisette, expressed their concerns about extremist Jacobin policies and also about the effect that such oratory had in increasing social disorder. They were worried that violence would negate the gains and the tranquillity that the municipality had thus far achieved.[29] The most trenchant opposition to the radical Jacobins came from their former judicial colleagues, who could not countenance the threats to law and order, to property and to the achievements already made. Rolandin judges like Ampère declared themselves to be republican after September but were not prepared to go further and sign the Jacobin petitions. Hidins would later castigate Ampère as a 'Rolandin-Feuillantin' because of his failure to do so.[30]

Nivière-Chol (the Rolandin Mayor) complained to Roland in a letter of 13 January 1793 of the sheer multiplicity of the Jacobin demands.

They were demanding with 'equal ardour' that a petition be sent to Paris supporting the 'judgment of Louis Capet' and the fixing (*taxation*) of the price of grain.³¹ By conflating their demands about the execution of the king and price fixing, the Jacobin politicians only increased the suspicion of the Rolandins that they were 'rogues' aiming to use social violence to overturn the rule of law. The Jacobins still failed to see that by strictly following national Jacobin perspectives to the detriment of locally achievable aims they were contributing to the alienation of the *sections*. According to Edmonds, they had 'responded like puppets to Parisian impulses', going so far as to publish Parisian criticisms of Roland, harassing those reluctant to sign a petition for the killing of the king and creating friction between the *clubs de quartier*, who still lauded Roland as an early defender of their clubs.³² The Jacobins then found their initiatives of fixing the price of grain and implementing new tribunals too difficult to put in place when the commercial elites also joined the protest through the sectional club movement.

Ideological differences were beginning to cause frictions amongst judges of different political views, but they did not immediately impact on the procedures that were required to be undertaken in the courts of law. The role of the *juge de paix*, in the front line of the judicial system, was little different to other state-paid functions, and although the Jacobins continued to clash with their local opponents over the need for greater surveillance of counter-revolutionary dangers, they did nonetheless contribute to the everyday operation of the courts. Both Chalier and Dodieu were among the Jacobins elected to various judicial positions and welcomed by the mayor on 13 December 1792 at the Municipal Council.³³ Early cases show that the Jacobin judges and *juges de paix* who were elected attempted to work within the established rule of law of which they were part. Ampère appears to have collaborated with Dodieu in spite of the fact that he had ordered the arrest of Dodieu for his 'public agitation' in August. Both performed their public roles earnestly because it was evident that the benefits of the new access to criminal justice were appreciated widely and most of all by the poorer complainants, who had previously had no access to criminal justice.³⁴

Dodieu supported the work of all the cantonal *juges de paix* in his role as director of the jury in the Tribunal de District. The *juges de paix* continued to make preliminary investigations and produce arrest warrants so that Dodieu could then present them to the jury. The case of Jean Tabard, Antoine Richard and Pierrette Ducreux (his wife) was one such case. The originating complaint was brought by a citizen to the canton Halle aux Blés, Ampère's jurisdiction. The case concerned a domestic servant and his wife who had stolen linen, including twenty towels, from their master and then sold them. The case, while fairly minor, demonstrated the grave concerns that both the victims and the perpetrators of such crimes had at a time of revolutionary upheaval. While some citizens felt unsafe in their own homes, others no doubt felt that aristocrats were not being punished and so personal action to redress inequities was justifiable. However, in this case, no regard was had to the particular circumstances of the master/servant relationship. Dodieu presented the questions that had to be determined to the jury as he was required to do in December 1792, and the jury found there was a crime to be judged.[35] No extraneous circumstances could be brought to bear on the punishment because the standard penalty had to be applied. The judges of both political persuasions accepted the rule of law to be applied in such cases. No magistrate could impose a different range of penalty.

The Jacobins continued, however, to rail against the fact that they were unable to punish those they thought culpable of various crimes against 'aristocrats', 'hoarders' and 'speculators' in the courts because the accused regularly evaded prosecution in the absence of very specific laws. They discussed new repressive laws and decided among themselves to investigate tactics in Paris. To this end, the judges Fillion and Gravier were sent to Paris to report on the effectiveness of the guillotine there.[36] In January 1793, the Jacobin judge Gaillard was also sent to Paris to put complaints to the Convention. He was a good speaker, according to Riffaterre, and it was unfortunate he was not available to lead the Jacobins as the Lyon struggle worsened.[37]

The Rolandin *juges de paix*, like Ampère, and the more established judges of the Tribunal Criminel continued to work within the system of justice that had been legislated. Ampère appears to have been relied on more and more to commence matters rather than the more 'democratic' new judges. Gradually, he took on more important cases, not limited to his cantonal area, possibly because of the experience and talent he had displayed in his first year of office. An example is the case heard by the Tribunal Criminel in November 1792 against the Sherriff (*huissier*) of Vienne (a city from the district of Lyon Campagne). The judicial officer Benoît Bonnard and his accomplice, Antoine Poison, were accused of administrative corruption. Ampère helped unravel the facts when in October he summoned witnesses and questioned them about the delivery of counterfeit notes to Bonnard. He took evidence from a certain Jean Michel, who claimed to have been falsely arrested by Bonnard. Michel complained of his arbitrary detention after a search of his premises and the seizure of his belongings, including a sabre, silver, earrings and three *louis* of gold, by the person he described as the 'great thief' and 'rogue' Bonnard. Ampère drew up the arrest warrant on 5 November 1792 against Bonnard.

In the Tribunal Criminel Bonnard was found guilty by a jury of having arrested and imprisoned Michel and another unfortunate on false facts and thus without authorisation. He had done this, it was found, for personal gain from the falsely accused man's property. The accused would later claim he had taken politically justified action against a perceived 'aristocrat'. Part of his argument was that he was the only *patriote* in Vienne and thus a political target.[38] This case thus had a political element even while it suggested a serious dereliction of duty. Ampère dealt with the case initially by addressing the criminality without reference to the underlying motives, which shows a commitment to the rule of law. He was thus prepared to validate the view of the more established magistrates and the Rolandin politicians against someone, like Bonnard, who argued a more radical view. This result would have concerned the new Jacobin judges like Dodieu, who had proclaimed well before their election the need to replace 'the aristocratic and corrupt tribunals', where 'sordid interest' prevailed among complicit judges.[39]

Another case that illustrates the changing judicial and municipal roles in Lyon during 1792 was that of Casati. This case was commenced in August, when Vitet was still mayor and was becoming unnerved by the violence of the *sans-culottes*. He was present on the day set for the destruction of the equestrian statue of Louis XIV in the square of Bellecour. Vitet had hoped that only the figure of the king would be destroyed and that the sculpture of the horse he had been mounted on would be preserved. However, as events continued, Vitet was unable to prevent the total destruction of the statue. He was himself challenged by an Italian artist by the name of Casati for allowing the desecration to take place. In December of 1792, it was again Ampère who was entrusted with drawing up the mandate for arrest of Casati when it was believed he had been conspiring to murder the mayor. The evidence was contained in a letter the accused had written addressed to the Archbishop of Lyon, Lamourette. Ampère collected the evidence, including the complaint from the mayor himself, which enclosed the threatening letter, and testimony from Lamourette.[40] The questions for the jury were then prepared by Judge Dodieu, as required. This was the same man who had been responsible for the destruction of the statue but who was now the director of the jury of the Tribunal de District. Early in the next year, Dodieu would acquit the accused on the grounds of mental instability.[41] Ampère's growing status with the Rolandin politicians would appear to be the reason for his preparation of the case. Being entrusted with such important local matters concerning the deputy and former mayor Vitet and Lamourette, the deputy to the Legislative Assembly, it would seem that Ampère had become more and more part of the decision-making administration even though the Jacobin judge Dodieu would ultimately have to pursue the matter.

These trials, with their political perspectives, were beginning to divide the magistracy. Yet other cases did address counter-revolutionary crimes in a more collegiate manner. An example of successful prosecution was the case of Lescot, which Ampère initiated in February 1793. This case concerned an alleged *émigré* with false papers. Ampère gathered the evidence and sent the papers to Dodieu, who heard the case and presented it to a jury for determination.[42] Ampère, like the other *juges de paix*, regularly heard and made orders in cases concerning false *assignats*.[43] Most of the *juges de paix* were seen to be dealing zealously with cases of forged *assignats* and with the *incivisme* of refractory priests. Carrier, editor of *Journal de Lyon*, noted on 5 February that while they deserved eulogies for their work in the former cases that prevented incalculable harm to the Republic by forgers, they were in fact 'somewhat overzealous' against the refractories. He asked, 'why do such priests need to be arrested in church in the middle of their functions?'[44] Carrier again adopted a tone of irony when he praised Hidins' humanity and respect for the rights of prisoners but went on to criticise Hidins' tendency to fall into diatribes, suggesting that perhaps the burden of office was too much for him.[45] The Jacobin magistrates were incensed by such criticism of their work, and they sought new channels of action.

The Jacobins in Lyon now began to argue for harsher laws against enemies of the new regime. In December 1792, they set up a system of local *comités de surveillance* to identify enemies. When these *comités* began to make arrests, there was a general outcry about their activities among the populace. The Central Club had first established a *comité de surveillance* in July 1792, but this particular group had little impact.[46] The decision to form *comités* in each of the *sections* of the city in December was much more divisive and became one of the core changes that the Jacobins pursued because of their increased electoral support. They signalled their commitment to be vigilant about foreigners and any possible counter-revolutionary threat. The question of the operation of the *comités* became however, according to Chopelin, a continuing motivation for the divergent paths the Jacobins were taking.[47]

A concerted programme to ensure enemies of the Revolution were put in gaol and kept there began to be implemented by the Jacobins on 4 February. It was suggested that pre-emptive domestic searches should be made to find those counter-revolutionaries, refractory priests and enemies who may have been hiding in the city. A deputation sent from the Central Club on this day convinced the municipal council that such visits made during the night would 'purge the city of rogues'. They suggested arrests should begin after 10PM that very night.⁴⁸ When there was alarm at this initiative, despite the gravity of the situation as they saw it, the Jacobins then renewed the debate about a dedicated revolutionary or popular tribunal that could act immediately.

A secret meeting was held on the night of 5 to 6 February in the Central Club. Chalier proposed a vote on Laussel's suggestion of the creation of a revolutionary tribunal.⁴⁹ Laussel was now active in the Jacobin *comité de surveillance*. He wanted to begin a broad campaign for the repression and proscription of all those he described as 'aristocrats'. A number of municipal officers and *notables*, including Carteron, Montfalcon, Revol, Roullot and Judge Fernex, were present at the meeting. They also presented their views about the need for increased repressive action on this night.⁵⁰ Suggestions were made that the guillotine should be installed and activated immediately on the much admired Pont Morand – perhaps this location was deliberately chosen because the recently built bridge had itself been funded by the 'aristocratic' family of Morand.⁵¹

Rumours of the Jacobin plans circulated among the propertied classes, who feared that the Jacobins had vowed to initiate a 'bloody era'.⁵² Herriot described the anxiety this meeting caused the mayor and the departmental authorities, which then 'increased hour by hour'.⁵³ It meant that the Jacobin campaign for action had started in earnest.

Figure 9.1 *Le pont Morand du quai de Retz et les Brotteaux* (The Morand Bridge from the Rhône River). Anon. Watercolour and gouache, inv. 292. © Musée Gadagne (Lyon).

Chalier led his *comité de surveillance* on the night of 5 February in the arrest of hundreds of suspected *émigrés* or aristocrats. Those arrested filled the prisons of the Hôtel de Ville. They included the former mayors Tolozan and Palerne de Savy.[54] Nivière-Chol had managed to forewarn some refractory priests of the pending arrests and many went into hiding. However, five to six were sent to the Pierre-Scize prison and kept there.[55] The next day, departmental authorities ordered that most of those arrested on the night of 5 to 6 February be released because of lack of evidence. At the same time the Jacobin judges were beginning to scrutinise fellow judges for evidence of a lack of revolutionary commitment, the Rolandins began to scrutinise the Jacobins for an excess of *'enthousiasme'*, for fanaticism and for conspiracy and were worried that arrests were unsupported legally.

The Jacobin *comités* were in fact operating well in advance of the national decree of 21 March 1793 authorising *comités de surveillance*. The publication of this national decree was delayed even further in Lyon – until April – by local authorities who thought the Jacobins were already exceeding their authority. The Jacobin *comités* continued to make arrests of suspected *émigrés*, refractory priests and 'aristocrats' and to establish the presence and intention of foreigners being housed in Lyon.[56] On 21 February, the department demanded that the municipality explain their actions and came to the conclusion that 'a simple *comité de surveillance* could not make arrests of citizens on its own authority'.[57] However, thirty-two *comités* were organised by this time and by March had begun to implement a system involving the issuing of certificates of *civisme* and eventually certificates to authorise the purchase of arms and small weapons. The collision over the legality of *comités de surveillance* has been recognised by Chopelin as playing an important role in the development of rival political strategies between the Jacobins and the Rolandins. He suggests that the departmental authorities delayed the formal implementation of the *comités* because of the already heightened fear that the Jacobins were using these groups to ensure that only they could have access to arms. This delay then made the Jacobin activity retrospectively illegal, a situation that would eventually be seized on by their enemies.[58]

The next session of the council after the arrests of 5 February was held on 8 February, and Nivière-Chol did not appear. He was clearly unwilling to validate the Jacobin programme for action. On 9 February, a petition of Jacobins with up to 6,000 signatures declared that the mayor had lost the confidence of 'the people'. The *Journal de Lyon* (whose editor at this time was Fain) suggested there was both growing alarm and disquiet in the city about the new policies of increased domiciliary visits and the setting up of the guillotine, but also about the failing consensus:

Without reading too much into it, we can only tremble at this disastrous split which is dividing both our magistrates and all the city's residents. United, we risk nothing; divided, we have everything to fear.[59]

Fain was reminding his readers of the disastrous consequences that the discord was having amongst the judges, which did not augur well for the future. There was, however, widespread support for the mayor when he resigned from his municipal office in protest at the growing impasse. The Jacobins suspected Nivière-Chol was intent on destabilising local politics even further by his resignation, but few of the sectional clubs of Lyon were now favouring the Jacobins. Many clubs had split, and though the poorer *sections* still supported Chalier, most were now supporting Nivière-Chol.[60] He and other Lyonnais politicians – who had until recently expressed a common cause in protecting the gains of the Revolution against the reactionary elements in Lyon – were objecting to the social and economic initiatives of the Jacobins because they were going much further than the propertied republicans were comfortable with. They began to support the various *quartier* clubs of the *sections* against the Central Club. The municipality had, it would seem, become isolated even from their previously strong social network in the poorer *quartiers*.[61]

From this time, 'the Chaliers isolated themselves even more from their popular base so that they did not achieve any better results in the social terrain than their Girondin predecessors.' They had made an 'under-estimation of the social structures strongly marked by the interdependence of silk-workers and merchants'.[62] Edmonds suggests that the Jacobins were losing their already fragile support because 'rumours of confiscatory taxes and the *partage des biens* spread fear amongst artisans and *boutiquiers*'.[63] Further, he suggested that the Jacobins had unwittingly contributed to their own growing unpopularity because:

> The long-standing tension between the Central Club and the *clubs particuliers* had been increased to breaking-point by the elitism and ideological rigidity of the Robespierrist Jacobins, and their disregard for the independence which the *quartiers* had guarded jealously since 1790.[64]

The violent language the Jacobins used was believed to be inflaming the *sans-culottes* and threatening the lives and property of citizens. In the sectional clubs, there were many who wanted to challenge the views expressed in the Central Club, and they proposed doing so by sitting *en permanence*. This action, however, then served to escalate divisions because the Jacobins suspected the *sections* were becoming 'foyers of intrigue', dominated by bourgeois or 'commercial' concerns.[65] The 'parallel powers' of the Jacobin-dominated Central Club and the more moderate sectional clubs were creating a situation of 'suspicion and mistrust' that Tackett suggests was characteristic of a time of uncertainty when 'breakdown of authority' was imminent.[66] As the power play between the clubs increased, so too did mutual suspicion. Jacobin resistance to sectional independence after this time fed into the growing gulf in local viewpoints.

On 13 February, the *Journal de Lyon* reported that Nivière-Chol had resigned, ostensibly because of his health but in reality so the political situation might calm down. New elections were then required in a city that according to Fain was 'agitated by so many contrary passions'.[67] Divisions reached their climax on 18 February 1793, when Nivière-Chol was re-elected to the position of mayor. He received 8,097 votes of the 10,746 cast and defeated the Jacobin candidate, the judge Fillion.[68] At the close of the day of the election, crowds gathered in the square and went to the home of Nivière-Chol to inform him of the election result. His wife advised that he would not be home until the next day. The crowd continued to grow and some called for Chalier to be held to account. A young man who shouted 'down with Chalier' was arrested by municipal officers.[69] His was not the only arrest of the night. Others were arrested for making threats against the wives of Jacobins.

At some stage, looters broke into the Central Club and desecrated the Jacobin meeting place. Property, including books and registers, was destroyed. Popular agitation continued the next day and night in the Place des Terreaux, in front of the Hôtel de Ville, when the *sections* declared themselves 'in permanence'. News of the pillage led to an immediate reaction by the Jacobin magistrates. Chalier, Dodieu and the Commissaire National Hidins were in the Hôtel de Ville, fronting onto the Place Terreaux, on the evening of the night of 18 to 19 February as events raged around them. They issued and signed a strongly worded decree. They forbade continued popular gatherings and declared themselves to be sitting 'in permanence' until the disorder was stopped.[70] They wrote of the 'seditious gatherings' that were taking place in the square all through the night and how they had been the subject of the 'greatest dangers'. They accused Nivière-Chol of being a 'criminal intriguer' with 'incendiary aristocratic agents', who by his resignation and re-election had purposely engineered a situation of 'counter-revolution.'[71] It was further alleged that 'aristocrats' had taken over the arsenal, where weapons were stored, and the nearby reserves of gunpowder.[72]

The Jacobin authorities thought all 'good citizens' should also be afraid of this circumventing of the power of the elected municipality and its committee.[73] With mounting difficulties put in the way of achieving their reforms, the Jacobins gradually came to the view that only by proposing terror would they 'overcome the contrary forces which stood against them'.[74] This uncompromising position, however, which included their reliance on the national representatives to bolster their powers, meant there was then a consequent increase of local support for the anti-Jacobins and they became as a result even more isolated. The *Journal de Lyon* called for the municipal officers, those who had scrutinised the elections, to acknowledge the result that Nivière-Chol had in fact been fairly elected and should not be impeded in his function as mayor. The editor, Carrier, demanded that Chalier be interrogated for his attempts to silence the will of the people by not working with Nivière-Chol. He described the unwillingness to listen to the mayor and the people who had elected him as a form of 'liberticide'.[75]

The *juges de paix* and magistrates of the Tribunal de District were divided on the question of the legality of the political upheavals that had so spectacularly erupted in the city on the night of 18 to 19 February. The incipient tensions that were evident after the election of the Jacobins to the judiciary with the continuing *juges de paix* and departmental judges continued to grow. Ampère was in many ways caught in the middle because of his commitment to the new laws based on the equality of citizens before the law, but his increasingly influential role at the end of 1792 was based on his desire to see order in the city. His judicial functions had already begun to blur into the political as can be seen in the Casati case, where Ampère was given free rein to undertake all necessary investigations. The Jacobin judges also became increasingly politicised in response to the desecration of the Central Club.

Notes

1. M. Walzer, (ed.) *Regicide and Revolution: Speeches at the Trial of Louis XVI* (New York: Columbia University Press, 1992), 139.
2. Walzer, *Regicide and Revolution*, 167.
3. B.M. Shapiro, 'The Case Against the King', in P. McPhee, *A Companion to the French Revolution* (Chichester: Wiley Blackwell, 2015), 110.
4. R. Steinberg, 'Transitional Justice in the Age of the French Revolution', *The International Journal of Transitional Justice* 7 (2013), 274.
5. Patrick shows how the vote taken on the issue of the death of the king presaged in many ways the Girondin and Jacobin stance on other issues that continued after this time. A. Patrick, *The Men of the First French Republic: Political Alignments in the National Convention of 1792* (Baltimore, MD: Johns Hopkins University Press, 1972), 303.
6. T. Tackett, *The Coming of the Terror in the French Revolution* (Cambridge, MA: The Belknap Press of Harvard University Press, 2015), 228–29.

7. Walzer, *Regicide and Revolution*, 59.
8. Speech of Condorcet, 3 Dec. 1792 in Walzer, *Regicide and Revolution*, 139–58.
9. Speech of Robespierre, 28 Dec. 1792, in Walzer, *Regicide and Revolution*, 178.
10. W. Edmonds, *Jacobinism and the Revolt of Lyon, 1789–1793* (New York: Oxford University Press, 1990), 133.
11. Patrick, *The Men of the First French Republic*, 327–28.
12. Edmonds, *Jacobinism*, 130–31.
13. Edmonds, *Jacobinism*, 304–5.
14. Edmonds, *Jacobinism*, 305.
15. C. Riffaterre, *Le Mouvement antijacobin et antiparisien à Lyon et dans le Rhône-et-Loire en 1793, 29 mai-15 août*, Vol 1 (Lyon: A. Rey, 1912), 306.
16. Riffaterre, *Le Mouvement*, 309.
17. Jean Jaurès claimed the Lyonnais Jacobins formed an advanced and cohesive social grouping that anticipated later social revolutionary theorists. Edmonds, *Jacobinism*, 162–63.
18. See T. Koi, 'Les "Chaliers" et les sans-culottes Lyonnais'. Doctoral thesis, Bibliothèque Diderot de Lyon, 1974KOI.
19. Riffaterre, *Le Mouvement*, fn 9.
20. Riffaterre, *Le Mouvement*, 7.
21. Riffaterre, *Le Mouvement*, 8.
22. Hidins gave his age as 25 in 1793. See *procès-verbal* in the denunciations; ADR 42 L 56.
23. Riffaterre, *Le Mouvement*, 6.
24. Riffaterre, *Le Mouvement*, 6–8.
25. D.L. Longfellow, 'Silk Weavers and the Social Struggle in Lyon during the French Revolution, 1789–94', *French Historical Studies* 12 (1981), 10.
26. AML 1 CM 3.
27. *Journal de Lyon*, 5 February 1793.
28. Hidins Lettre. BML Fonds Coste, Ms 558.
29. Edmonds, *Jacobinism*, 180.
30. Hidins was appealing against his interrogation by Ampère and by what he called the 'royalist' Tribunal Criminel: BML Fonds Coste, Ms 558.
31. Riffaterre, *Le Mouvement*, 9.
32. Edmonds, *Jacobinism*, 148.
33. E. Herriot, *Lyon n'est Plus*, vol. 1, 117.
34. Crubaugh suggests that there was 'lavish praise' for the JP and even after 1794 it was considered 'the greatest institution of the Revolution'. A. Crubaugh, *Balancing the Scales of Justice: Local courts and Rural society in Southwest France, 1750–1800* (University Park, PA: The Pennsylvania State University Press, 2000), 119–20.
35. ADR 39 L 58.
36. Riffaterre, *Le Mouvement*, 16.
37. Riffaterre, *Le Mouvement*, 63.
38. His original case is recorded ADR 39 L 35. His appeal before the Military Tribunal of frimaire An II (3 December 1793) is discussed in A. Salomon de la Chapelle, *Documents sur la Révolution: Lyon et ses environs sous la Terreur 1793–1794* (Lyon: Librairie Générale Henri Georg, 1885), 43.
39. Riffaterre, *Le Mouvement*, 6.
40. ADR 39 L 23.
41. *Journal de Lyon*, 29 January 1793.
42. ADR 39 L 23.
43. ADR 41 L 8 (1793).

44. *Journal de Lyon*, 5 February 1793.
45. *Journal de Lyon*, 5 February 1793.
46. Some of the *quartier* clubs objected to its secrecy and its threats to 'exterminate traitors'; Edmonds, *Jacobinism*, 120.
47. P. Chopelin, 'Un Cancer politique? Vies et morts des comités de surveillance de la ville de Lyon (1792–1795)', in D. Pingué and J.-P. Rothiot (eds), *Les Comités de surveillance: d'une création citoyenne à une institution révolutionnaire* (Paris: Société des études Robespierristes, 2012), 174.
48. AML 1 CM 3.
49. Herriot, *Lyon n'est Plus*, vol.1, 154.
50. Herriot, *Lyon n'est Plus*, vol. 1, 155.
51. The bridge was built in 1774 by Jean-Antoine Morand: Edmonds, *Jacobinism*, 10.
52. See Alexandrine des Écherolles memoire as a young girl, 11 years of age at the time, who describes the terror of the increasingly frequent night visits, the secret meetings of the Jacobins and the threat to eliminate a great number of the inhabitants of the city by guillotine and cannon placed on the bridge. A. des Écherolles, *Une Famille noble sour la Terreur* (Paris: Elibron Classics, 2006), 62–63.
53. Herriot, *Lyon n'est Plus*, vol. 1, 155–60.
54. P. Chopelin, *Ville patriote et ville martyre: Lyon, l'église et la Révolution, 1788–1805* (Paris: Letouzey et Ané, 2010), 211.
55. Ibid.
56. Chopelin, 'Un Cancer politique?', 172–73. Chopelin, *Ville patriote*, 172.
57. Chopelin, *Ville patriote*, 172.
58. Chopelin, *Ville patriote*, 172.
59. ADR 1 L 460 (Presse).
60. W. Edmonds, 'The Rise and Fall of Popular Democracy in Lyon 1789–1795', *Bulletin of the John Rylands Library* (1984), 438.
61. F. Wartelle, 'Chalier, Joseph/les 'Chaliers', in A. Soboul (ed.), *Dictionnaire Historique de La Révolution Française* (Paris: Presses Universitaires de France, 1989), 200–1.
62. Wartelle, 'Chalier, Joseph/les 'Chaliers', 200–1.
63. Edmonds, *Jacobinism*, 155.
64. Edmonds, *Jacobinism*, 153.
65. Riffaterre, *Le Mouvement*, 42.
66. Tackett, *The Coming of the Terror*, 344.
67. *Journal de Lyon*, 13 February 1793.
68. Edmonds, *Jacobinism*, fn 151.
69. This version of events was detailed in a special edition of the *Journal de Lyon*, written by Fain, 19 February.
70. See the Letter Chalier and Dodieu, 19 February 1793. BML Fonds Coste, Ms 549. This letter is reproduced in Appendix 1.
71. Although Nivière-Chol protested his republicanism, there is a persisting question over his possible royalism, but according to Herriot it seems clear he was not opposed to the death of the king. Herriot, *Lyon n'est Plus*, 148.
72. Forty grenadiers remained at the arsenal, declaring they would not leave until prisoners taken the previous night were released. Edmonds, *Jacobinism*, 176.
73. Letter Chalier, Ms 549.
74. Riffaterre, *Le Mouvement*, 12.
75. *Journal de Lyon*, 19 February.

Chapter 10

PRISON WARS

If there is an ecclesiastic in the city whose patriotism could not be suspected, it is me... Be assured of my innocence and the authenticity of my citizenship. I demand nothing more of the citizen commissaires of our august representatives than to be sent the accusations made against me, and that my liberty be completely restored in conformity with the rules as prescribed by the law.

—Jolyclerc, curé constitutionel de Saint-Nizier (upon his arrest for his alleged involvement in unauthorised sectional meetings during the evening of 18 and 19 February 1793)

The tribunal [criminel] ought be destroyed otherwise the people will be forced themselves to deliver justice.
—Letter or 'Decret', signed by Chalier, 19 February 1793

By February 1793, the bi-partisan municipality and judiciary had collapsed. Rolandins and Jacobins were in open conflict, and the courthouse became one of the major sites of active disagreement between republicans in Lyon in 1793.[1] Serious fractures escalated from February of 1793, when many controversial arrests were made and objections to the legality of such arrests were also made. Fundamentally different approaches to the rule of law divided the magistrates from this point, and they contributed to the frictions between the Jacobin municipal officers and the anti-Jacobin movement, which began to grow stronger in the *quartier* clubs. The abiding fear of the Jacobins was that their efforts to ensure change were being impeded by counter-revolutionary conspirators who would stop at nothing to overturn 'popular sovereignty'. Jacobin judges became convinced that revolutionary gains would be lost unless strong retaliatory action was taken against the plots of counter-revolution they had been seeing in the courts. Rolandins became convinced that Jacobin challenges to law and order had to be addressed. Magistrates on both sides began to take political decisions in response to the dangers facing the city.

* * *

Disagreement between the Jacobin and Rolandin magistrates had begun well before the cataclysms of February 1793. A suspicion of pervasive conspiracies was a strong element of pre-revolutionary French thinking, and the same sort of fears soon became evident in the new, supposedly transparent institutions of the Revolutionary state.[2] The case of Étienne Launay, decided initially on 18 January 1793, showed the growing tensions that were emerging between judges of different political persuasions on the question of who should be imprisoned. Launay was acquitted of being involved in a crime involving an alleged assault in the process of stealing the sum of 250 *livres*. Despite his innocence being found unanimously by a jury, he was immediately rearrested by Dodieu for a crime based on the same facts. The President of the Tribunal Criminel again ordered the accused's release some days later, reminding the arresting judge (Dodieu) that the decision of the jury was final and legal facts could not be revisited.[3] The objection of the Tribunal Criminel was that the formal requirements of the law had not been followed because Dodieu had failed to specify any new facts that would show Launay was an 'enemy' of the state, even if he genuinely believed this to be the case. This decision suggests the fundamental incompatibility of those judges who wanted to see a society based on a clear rule of law and those who thought the law should be the means by which the new state was protected from enemies known to be involved in conspiracies. The Jacobin judges were clearly unwilling to let those they considered to be such 'enemies' avoid prosecution for merely legalistic reasons; however, they were stymied by the higher court judges.

On 4 February 1793, another case was brought before Chalier and Dubessey, sitting as judges of the Tribunal de District, which also suggested to the Jacobin judges that there was a conspiracy among the conservative judges to curb their power. The accused, Jean-François Morand, was the former gaoler of the prison of Roanne. It was alleged that he had allowed four prisoners to escape from the prison while he was operating as the concierge there.[4] The case of Morand had been initiated by the arrest warrant of 26 January issued by Ampère, in his role of *juge de paix*. After a preliminary investigation, the papers were then sent to Dodieu, who ordered that the accused be gaoled. Dodieu also sent the papers to the Tribunal de District. He was concerned that the complicity of Morand's wife, the *citoyenne* Besson, and two guards had not been adequately dealt with. Ampère had come to the preliminary conclusion that the crime imputed to all the accused was not to be found in the Code Pénal. In the extract of the minutes of the Tribunal de District meeting held on 4 February, the Jacobin judges Chalier, Fernex, Dodieu and Dubessey noted that the crimes displayed a 'fatal negligence' that merited the censure of the court and punishment despite the fact that it was not explicitly covered by the code. The matter against the wife of Morand and the guards was then sent back to the Police Correctionnelle for hearing. On 5 February, the *Journal de Lyon* noted that Morand was still held at the prison and that 'it appeared his wife had received money to ensure that the prisoners were allowed to escape'.[5] However, on 17 February an appeal to the Tribunal Criminel led to Morand being acquitted.[6] A document submitted in evidence by Morand claimed he was not responsible for the escapes because they had happened when he was no longer living at the prison and when his successor had taken over control.

The Jacobin judges involved in this case were more than ever convinced that the formalities of law were being used to protect enemies of the Revolution. The slow progress of cases through the official court system was becoming increasingly evident to many of them. Hidins, *commissaire national*, complained about the difficulty of getting juries organised to hear the many important cases brought to the *juges de paix*. While the beginning of the process was expedited before these judges, the trial itself was delayed until the *juré de jugement* met. This was usually done on the fifteenth day of each month but only if this had been organised by the fifth. Hidins suggested that this law regarding the juries was 'a vice' and meant in practice that people were held longer in gaol while the necessary time elapsed for the jury to be appointed before their case could be heard.[7] This focus of the judiciary on technical timing issues meant that equality before the law was completely illusory.

The political events on 18 and 19 February surrounding the election of a new mayor upon Nivière-Chol's resignation established new legal quandaries. The Jacobin response to the events of the night of rioting was at first a legal one, using their authority as elected judges and officers to take action against illegal actions. The decree they issued suspending judicial functions, including hearing all criminal cases, until such time as 'public order and calm' were re-established was based on their judicial authority. It was also decreed on that night that all citizens who exercised any profession, especially that of lawyer, and were not in possession of a *carte de civisme* (a document attesting to civic responsibility) were acting illegally. This card would establish a citizen's credentials if he was challenged, and those lawyers who were refusing to carry one – and Nivière-Chol, who was refusing to ratify the decree – were warned by Chalier in an open letter that they would henceforth be considered to be in contravention of the law.[8] Chalier explained that the Jacobin judges had taken these actions because 19 February had awakened them to the dangers that existed even 'amongst those who were closest to them in the exercise of their functions' – that is, among the other judges and *juges de paix* in the administration of justice.[9] The decree made while the Jacobins of the municipality sat *'en permanence'* in the Town Hall through the night was copied and sent to the representatives of the National Convention in Lyon and also to the Comité de Sûreté Générale of the Convention in Paris. It was signed by the authors Chalier, Dodieu and Hidins and also by the judges Dubessey, Fernex and Bussay. This decree of 19 February, subsequently posted throughout the city, was issued with the authority of the elected municipal officials but was also raising the legal authority vested in the representatives of the people.

The Jacobins next used the *comités de surveillance* to arrest twelve rioters over the following two days. These prisoners were kept in the cells of the Hôtel de Ville beyond the 24 hours that had been legislated. Most of the prisoners were, however, soon released for want of evidence by Jean-Joseph Bertholon, who was at this time the substitute *procureur* of the Commune but who had in fact been a former Central Club president.[10] These actions of Bertholon were to become yet another point of fracture among the magistrates. A Jacobin witness, whose signature is indecipherable, declared on the night of 19 February that he had gone to the offices of the Tribunal Correctionnel in the prison of Roanne at 8PM with the purpose of seeing how the perpetrators of the attack on the Central Club were being dealt with. He was able to enter the audience chamber without seeing anyone and then happened upon a room in which a discussion was being held between those who were accused of the 'serious (*grave*)' crimes committed the night before and two *juges de paix*. The group was engaged in a blatant abuse of the law according to the onlooker where no *procès-verbaux* had been taken from the accused, but instead their answers were 'furnished' by the officers, who then cautioned them and let them go. One of the accused had the audacity, the witness claimed, to 'dictate the interrogation' to the court clerk (*greffier*) while Bertholon was present. Although Bertholon had earlier promised to apply the 'rigours of the law' according to the Jacobin witness, he in fact helped 'foster the plot of our enemies'.[11] The divisions between the magistrates had reached their highest point as citizens were imprisoned as a result of the disorder and then released by the opposing factions. Bertholon, despite his high judicial office, was himself arrested that night.

The actions of the Jacobin judges in publishing their document of 19 February and in continuing to hold Bertholon in custody for releasing those arrested after the pillage of the Central Club were the signal for an immediate escalation of the differences among the magistrates. In response to the decree of Chalier and Dodieu and the group of Jacobin administrators who had suspended all court actions, Ampère sent a strongly worded letter to Dodieu. He questioned the unilateral decision Dodieu and other Jacobin 'clubbists' took to suspend administrative functions, take over the mayoralty and impose a new agenda of repression. He expressed his shock and dismay at the disintegration of law and order in the city that he claimed was caused by the Jacobins' action.[12] The letter was dated 20 February and was thus an immediate and strong reaction to the events and a challenge to the Jacobin judges. This document, unlike the Jacobin document, was not widely published. It was addressed to Dodieu, in his function as director of the Jury. The letter interpreted the cascading events and highlighted the dangers to the new system of justice that Ampère had devoted his time to. Ampère first expressed his disquiet to Dodieu about the suspension of the courts of justice and the impugning of an officer of the court (who would appear to have been Bertholon).

Ampère professed himself shocked by the turn of events that threatened the continuing functioning of the legal system. Yet the overall tone of the letter and the observation that he had 'reason to believe in the enlightenment and the honesty (*droiture*)' of Dodieu hint at an understanding between colleagues engaged in similar tasks. This connection made him believe Dodieu could disassociate himself from the proposed actions. His next point was to stress the harm that could come from the judges' unilateral action. According to Ampère, any move to implicate the *juges de paix* and officers of police who had instituted the procedures against those accused on 18 or 19 February would reflect badly on all the magistrates. Ampère thus concentrated on the legality of the arrests occasioned on this night and the fact that those accused had provided sufficient 'clarification' as to the facts to the arresting officer, who was then justified in releasing them. He pointed out that the law stipulated if there was not enough evidence, and there was only the 'suspicion' of a crime having been committed, no accused should be kept under arrest but simply given a warning. This was in fact what Bertholon had sought to do on the night in question.

Just as the appeal court judge Cozon had lectured Dodieu in the case of Launay in January, Ampère a month later was reiterating what the requirements of the law were in the situation. He stated that the action by the relevant officer of the Tribunal Correctionnel was the only possible one because it 'conformed to the requirements of the law'. He took the opportunity to remind Dodieu that 'the diverse tribunals' of law were established to maintain justice and its 'august empire'. He thus made his personal appeal to Dodieu to reconsider the divisive action of the Jacobins in putting Bertholon in gaol, as such an action could only lead to the 'paralysing' of justice and police functions. Ampère's sentiments expressed a widely held view that the actions of Dodieu and other Jacobin magistrates were damaging to the operation of the system of justice in the city and were setting the judges apart.[13] From February, Ampère thus quickly came to a decision about where he stood in these fractious times. It was not with those fellow judges who, he thought, intended to pursue a path that threatened the very institutions of justice. Once this decision was made, he strenuously opposed those he felt were destabilising society in the job in which he was becoming more and more proficient.

While there has been no mention of this particular letter in histories of the period – perhaps because it was in the files of the Tribunal Correctionnel and not the Fonds Coste, where the other letters pertaining to the events of February and March 1793 have been found – it is part of the conversation between the magistrates at the time. It predated and could have precipitated the outpouring of justification and recriminations that followed. The Jacobin judges soon countered with a document that listed the *juges de paix* who were 'patriots' as opposed to those who were 'aristocrats'. Called the *tableaux de réforme* 1793, it was unsigned but is believed to be in the hand of Chalier.[14] Ampère, Revol and L'Ange were ranged on the 'aristocratic' side of the equation as regards *juges de paix* according to Chalier, with Fillion on the patriot side. Cozon was listed as an 'aristocratic' higher judge and Gaillard a patriot.

Dodieu also inveighed against the abuses in the prisons. In a later letter to the *commissaires* from Paris, who were entrusted with investigating the events of 19 February, he noted the starkly different conditions in gaol between those who had money and those who did not; those who still lived the high life with light, heating and food all supplied and the poor who only had a straw bed. There was evidence of 'immoral chaos ... fiery debauchery alongside appalling misery'. Some prisoners had been allowed to escape because those guarding them were often drunk or took bribes and allowed 'files and other instruments' into the prison as tools. He lamented, 'Oh, how far we are still from the wisdom which this sublime institution has dictated.'[15]

Bertholon was held in prison until his case was heard before Judge Dodieu on 5 March. The statement of the witness who had gained access to the Police Correctionelle on the evening in question was used as the basis for the pivotal prosecution against Bertholon, who had been acting as the *substitute procureur* – the chief legal officer of the city at the time. The contentions of the witness were put to him. Bertholon did not deny any of the facts and observed that 'the guilty were interrogated and the innocent given their liberty'. He also asserted that, despite the order that was given that night by the *corps constitué* (the elected authorities), article 7 of the Rights of Man and Citizen required that no citizen should be arrested or detained without due process of law. Because there was no complaint or *procès-verbal* establishing a case for their detention, he reiterated that the law required those arrested on the night of 19 February be released. Bertholon admitted he was in the Police Correctionnelle at the time alleged but claimed he warned the *juges de paix*, who were also there in the following terms: 'You have the habit of simply letting detainees go but if you are considering letting them go the only thing you must do is give a very strong warning.'[16] Bertholon remained in gaol.

Some others kept in gaol at this time included one Baille, the commandant of a battalion of the National Guard who had accolades for his military service. He was imprisoned for eight days for his actions on the night of 18–19 February. The Jacobins denounced him for having taken no action on the night against those who had attacked the club.[17] Baille denied giving any orders on that night but admitted to having suggested a battalion be placed in front of the door of the club when two days later, on 21 February, two young men were beaten up by the Jacobins after trying to gain access. Baille claimed to be 'one of the victims that those with a hateful intention were prepared to sacrifice for vengeance'. He begged the National Convention to intervene and 're-establish order, justice and the execution of law'.[18] His angry wife published an *affiche* that set out the injustice to him. Another of those so kept was François Jolyclerc, the constitutional priest of Ampère's canton, who was suspected of holding sectional meetings 'in permanence' in his church.[19] Jolyclerc was also kept in prison for a number of days and also published his outrage at his treatment, denying his involvement in the inflammatory discussions of those who participated in the *section* meetings held in his church. The case against this 'patriotic' *curé* resulted in a fine and caution being levelled against him.[20]

After the pillage of the Central Club and the issuing of the decree by the Jacobin magistrates, the already high fears and passions felt in Lyon were intensified. These events had resulted in increasingly outrageous political imprisonments and the continued demonising of the Jacobins. Many sectional clubs were anti-Jacobin by the summer of 1793. For their members, the spectre of violence that had re-emerged in September

1792 had only been narrowly defeated, and the Jacobins were conspirators, actively encouraging more violence amongst the *sans-culottes*. The Jacobins felt increasingly threatened by the possibility of armed resistance to the elected municipality and justified in taking the pre-emptive action they did of imprisoning those rioters they thought guilty of illegal action. The court processes in place, however, meant that many of the agitators the Jacobins believed responsible for the attack on the Central Club were allowed to go free. The Jacobins saw this as a deliberate counter-attack in the courts, and they continued to use the *comités de surveillance* to arrest the sectional leaders they thought responsible. On 25 February, they ordered that the next elected mayor, Jean-Emanuel Gilibert, be arrested on the grounds of his involvement in the pillage of the Central Club. He was from the club of La Croisette, which had been opposed to the efforts of the Jacobins to dominate the *quartier* clubs and had become one of the leading anti-Jacobin *sections*.[21] However, Jacobin action against political dissenters like Gilibert in fact encouraged even more comment and reaction in the *quartier* clubs because public opinion was becoming more and more critical of the Jacobins of the Central Club.[22]

Upon the refusal of Nivière-Chol to take up the mayoral role again, and the imprisonment of Gilibert, the decision about who should be mayor was handed over to representatives from the National Convention who had been summoned to help negotiate in the charged atmosphere of Lyon.[23] The first *commissaires* sent from Paris – Rovère, Basire and Legendre – arrived with the mission to 'restore order' on 25 February.[24] They were not as supportive of Chalier as he hoped but neither were they very helpful to Gilibert, who was advised to resign. The *commissaires* held and scrutinised new elections, which returned the Jacobin Bertrand as mayor.[25] They were still there when a religious flashpoint was also reached in the city. Constitutional priests had become more worried about their position, and the refractory priests were becoming bolder. According to Linsolas, an outspoken refractory and memoirist of the period, Nivière-Chol had turned a blind eye to their activities.[26] When Bertrand became mayor, they were still in Lyon but then had to become 'more discreet'.[27] The attempts by the national *commissaires* to restore order meant they addressed both Jacobin and anti-Jacobin concerns but, ultimately, satisfied neither. The most predominant concern for the Rolandins remained the question of the legality of the Jacobin arrests that had taken place on the night of 4–5 February, and the greatest concern of the Jacobins was that those believed guilty of the events of 18–19 February had not been incarcerated.

Again, it was the campaign in the *Journal de Lyon* that squarely put the Rolandin case. In the issue of 2 March 1793, the journalists published the rumours that the Jacobins were letting some cases related to the domiciliary visits of 5 February collapse in the courts on the payment of bribes. Dodieu and Hidins were both alleged to be involved as well as the mother of Hidins, who would later be charged with perpetrating swindles and bribery. It was suggested that Laussel had purposely arrested people of means on this night from whom he believed he could extract money.[28] The *commissaires* acted immediately to cease the operation of the implicated *comités de surveillance*, but they also imprisoned the anti-Jacobin editor of the *Journal de Lyon*, Fain.[29] A new *comité de sûreté et de surveillance général* was set up to direct the work of the sectional *comités*. It was given the legal power to ensure that potential counter-revolutionaries were found if they were hiding in the city and to arrest those who did not hold the correct certificates of *civisme* or permissions to hold arms. The *commissaires* also called for new elections to staff the *comités*, which would take place on 19 May.[30] One of their last actions was to imprison Laussel for exceeding his duties and for a charge of embezzlement.[31]

Hidins was arrested and interrogated by Judge Ampère and Judge Rivolet on 1 March for his actions at this time and for embezzling funds. In response, Hidins tried to impugn these *juges de paix* and other judges in the system. Hidins wrote a number of letters to encourage the *commissaires* to pursue instead those who had let the guilty of 18 and 19 February escape. He exhaustively outlined his revolutionary zeal. He claimed that the President Brochet of the Tribunal Criminel was a 'royalist' known to favour 'conspirators' and that his tribunal was full of 'men of 1788' who did not recognise the new demands of 1793. He positioned Ampère in a less favourable light vis-à-vis himself by claiming the latter did not sign the petition for the death of the king.[32] He also attacked L'Ange for releasing known friends of *émigrés* with only a warning. It is obvious by this time that he was repackaging an interpretation to put his own actions in the best light. However, this letter also attempted to set out the situation from the Jacobin viewpoint. Hidins' long explanation of the legal and political crisis began with his assertion that:

> The law must never be a game for fair and upright men in a Republic ... One cannot abuse it without also compromising public well-being ... [but] in our unfortunate city ... the law is being used in a way that kills its spirit and protects those men who continue to display anti-civic qualities.[33]

In a further letter, Hidins insisted that he had only worked within the law and against those whose *civisme* was suspect. He said he had not 'confused the innocent and guilty'– presumably a response to an implicit criticism of Ampère because these were the actual terms also used in

Ampère's letter of February. Hidins next tried to deflect the criticism of his fellow Jacobins, Chalier and Gaillard. He thought they were trying to blacken his name by falsely accusing him of an excess of ambition in aiming to become mayor.[34] In the end, Hidins did not go to trial. He hanged himself in his cell in early July.[35]

Dodieu was also interrogated on 2 March about his involvement in the arrests and incarcerations of 18 and 19 February and, in addition, a charge of corruption related to the activities of the *veuve* Hidins.[36] Dodieu claimed his innocence here and in a letter to the *commissaires* after his hearing despite the insinuation by Fain in the *Journal de Lyon* that he was the very judge who was taking the bribes from the widow.[37] Dodieu stated in his letter to the *commissaires* that he had been willing to have his case heard in open court because he had nothing to hide. He assured them that no one had worked for the cause of liberty as he did and that he was 'burning with patriotism'.[38] Dodieu also distanced himself from Laussel, who had been imprisoned on 13 March for similar activities. In his letter, Dodieu tried to emphasise his patriotism and the fact that he had 'never been friends with Laussel'. He said he was 'far from having any interest in saving him from the sword of the law'.[39] In his interrogation before Ampère, Dodieu claimed he had only acted in relation to the duties assigned to him as director of the jury on 19 February. Although he admitted helping the *procureur* and his friends on the municipality in composing the document made that evening, his function had only been as 'a scribe with knowledge that he could bring of law and procedure'. He claimed that he had only provided members of the *comités* with information as to the law and thus could not be held accountable for the municipal officers who did not do their duty. This is why he had not instituted any proceedings in his name.[40] He was released.

Marisa Linton has written recently about the public man and the cult of virtue as it was understood by politicians of the revolutionary era.[41] This perspective helps us to understand the experience of the judges in Lyon in 1793, when estrangement became apparent and denunciations of each other began to spiral. She observed that: 'For the Jacobins the *patrie* was the heart of the moral republic, more important even than democracy or equality.'[42] This analysis is as useful in the Lyonnais context as it is in the national context. The question that was important to representatives of the public at the time was whether a man could be said to be truly dedicated to the *patrie* or only appear to conform to the codes of behaviour. Covert activity suggested a lack of virtue or the possibility of conspiratorial action. Using such a concept to measure authenticity meant the political and private lives of those who aspired to political office were ruthlessly scrutinised and their interactions as part of an exclusive group could be used against them. Linton dealt mostly with Robespierre and his interaction with the Parisian militants in their conflict with the Girondins, and later the Dantonists. However, in Lyon there were similar struggles between revolutionary political and judicial leaders who claimed their own motives were determined by virtue and those of their opponents by ambition and dissimulation.

In late March, Ampère pursued a related complaint of corruption against *veuve* (widow) Hidins for a fraud that involved promises to release prisoners arrested by the Jacobin *comités* and the payment of bribes to various judges of the Tribunal de District.[43] On 26 March, he sat as president in the Tribunal Correctionnel with Revol and Corte Jordan and delivered judgement against her and an accomplice, *citoyenne* Barry.[44] The judges found the mother of Hidins had participated in swindles and had compromised certain magistrates, but no particular magistrate was identified. She was fined the 200 *livres* she had extorted and sentenced to eight days in gaol. In this same month, Ampère had an arrest warrant drawn up against Robert Achard (a leading member of the Jacobin *comités*), who, with Charles Sourd (*perruquier*), was alleged to be involved with false certificates of *civisme*.[45] Sourd gave testimony against Achard and was himself acquitted. Dodieu also took this case to the jury, but Achard went into hiding before it could be heard.

The divergences between the magistrates in 1793 were at least as important a factor in the changing balance of power in Lyon as those between the politicians. The Jacobin magistrates found delays, corruption and a general unwillingness to pursue opponents of the Revolution. The magistrates and judges who had been working since the inception of the judicial laws in 1791 suspected the Jacobins of corruption and too much 'enthusiasm' in their methods. The decisions of the Jacobins were questioned repeatedly until finally their conception of the rule of law was discredited, as many of the judges themselves were arrested and interrogated. The judges who remained active in the city were those who thought the law had to be observed to ensure a stable and orderly society and who continued to ascribe to the dominant Rolandin view.

Notes

1. Some of the material in this chapter has been published previously and appears here with permission of the editors. See J.P. Johnson, '"The Law Must Never Be a Game for Fair and Upright Men in a Republic": Revolutionary Justice in Lyon 1792–3', *Oxford Journal of French History* 32(2) (2018), 182–202.

2. P.R. Campbell et al. (eds), *Conspiracy in the French Revolution* (Manchester University Press, 2007).
3. ADR 39 L 60.
4. ADR 36 L 57 and 39 L 27.
5. ADR 1 L 460 *(Presse)*.
6. ADR 39 L 60.
7. Letter Hidins, February 1793; BML Fonds Coste, Ms 558.
8. See Chalier's letter, BML Fonds Coste, Ms 551.
9. Letter Chalier, BML Fonds Coste, Ms 549.
10. Edmonds, *Jacobinism and the Revolt of Lyon*, 132. Bertholon was elected as deputy to Laussel in October 1792.
11. This denunciation was officially presented as evidence in the hearing against Bertholon on 16 April 1793; ADR 36 L 57.
12. This letter appears as part of the scant records of the Tribunal Correctionnel preserved from 1793: ADR 41 L 8.
13. Edmonds notes that at this time the judges of the Tribunal de District, including Chalier, Dodieu, Dubessey, Gaillard, Bussat and the Commissaire National Hidins were considered to be a 'stronghold of the most extreme radicals'. Edmonds, *Jacobinism*, 132.
14. 'Tableaux de Réforme – probablement de la main de Chalier; 1793'. BML Fonds Coste, Ms 609. See the mention of this document in a footnote: Edmonds, *Jacobinism*, 132.
15. BML Fonds Coste, Ms 559.
16. BML Fonds Coste, Ms 559. The interrogation of 5 March, signed on each page by Dodieu and Bertholon, also became part of the court record of 16 April.
17. Edmonds, *Jacobinism*, 176.
18. Lettre Baille, BML Fonds Coste, Ms 602.
19. BML Fonds Coste, Ms 602.
20. Jolyclerc, BML Fonds Coste, Ms 597.
21. Edmonds, *Jacobinism*, 101–2 and 151. This club had also been vociferous against the first *comité de surveillance* in June 1792, 120. It was atypical in its bourgeois and *sans-culottes* mix according to Edmonds (at 88).
22. Riffaterre, *Le Mouvement*, Vol. 1, 37.
23. Edmonds, *Jacobinism*, 168–69.
24. Edmonds, *Jacobinism*, 168.
25. Edmonds, *Jacobinism*, 169.
26. Quoted in P. Chopelin, *Ville patriote et ville martyre: Lyon, l'église et la Révolution, 1788–1805* (Paris: Letouzey et Ané, 2010), 211.
27. Chopelin, *Ville patriote*, 211.
28. *Journal de Lyon*, 2 March 1793. Herriot suggested Fain's campaign showed the strong feelings engaged in the city, and he suggested that 'one cannot contest [the journalist's] talent nor his courage' in his reporting of events. E. Herriot, *Lyon n'est Plus*, vol. 1, 290.
29. Fain was detained for two weeks at this time and was freed after interrogation by the *comité de salut public*. He claimed he only ever wanted the law to punish culprits. He was arrested again after the siege and was brought before the Tribunal Révolutionnaire on 25 October 1793: E. Fayard, *Histoire des tribunaux révolutionnaires de Lyon et de Feurs* (Lyon: H. George, 1888), 93–94.
30. Chopelin, 'Un Cancer politique? Vies et morts des comités de surveillance de la ville de Lyon (1792–1795)', in D. Pingué and J.-P. Rothiot (eds), *Les Comités de surveillance: D'une création citoyenne à une institution révolutionnaire* (Paris: Société des études Robespierristes, 2012), 174–76.

31. Edmonds, *Jacobinism*, 171. Edmonds notes that Laussel's crimes were seen as more serious because he had been involved in denouncing the *procureur* Bertholon for releasing prisoners but without the impropriety that was suggested in his own actions.
32. Herriot, *Lyon n'est Plus*, vol. 1, 197–98.
33. Hidins' letter, 'Aux Citoyens, Les deputés Commissaire de la National Convention, Hôtel de Milan, Place des Terreaux, Lyon'. End of February1793. BML Fonds Coste, Ms 558.
34. Hidins, 'Aux commissaries deputés de la Convention Nacionale (sic), hotel de Milan, Place de Terreaux à Lyon', s.d. BML, Fonds Coste, Ms 558.
35. Fayard, *Histoire des tribunaux*, 31–32.
36. ADR 41 L 7. This case before the Tribunal Correctionnel appears to have been misfiled with the 1792 cases rather than those of 1793.
37. *Courrier de Lyon*, 2 March 1793.
38. See letter, 2 April 1793 (also wrongly dated as 1792) BML Fonds Coste, 615.
39. ADR 41 L 7. In fact, on 3 April the affair of Laussel came before Dodieu and he made sure he went before a jury for his crime: ADR 36 L 57.
40. ADR 41 L 7.
41. M. Linton, *Choosing Terror: Virtue, Friendship and Authenticity in the French Revolution* (Oxford: Oxford University Press, 2013), 32–38.
42. Linton, *Choosing Terror*, 38.
43. ADR 41 L 8.
44. ADR 41 L 8.
45. ADR 39 L 23.

Chapter 11

OUSTING OF THE JACOBINS

> You know, citizens, that the city of Lyon has always been the refuge of counter-revolutionaries ... Lets hurry, citizens, to fly to the aid of the oppressed patriots, to give them the means of slaying the enemies of the Revolution who surround them.
>
> —Tallien, report to the National Convention on the situation in Lyon as of 25 February 1793

> The day of 29 May 1793 opened a noble period of courage [for the Lyonnais]. A sacred crusade where they marched to reclaim their lives and liberty.
>
> —A. des Écherolles, *Une Famille noble sous la terreur*

Living through the Revolutionary period could be an exhilarating but also a fearful experience. At the time, the ultimate outcome of the Revolution was much more tenuous than can be easily imagined. Strong emotions were felt amongst those advancing revolutionary change and those experiencing it. Republicans in Paris were overcome with fatigue and fear about the future by the spring of 1793 in view of the factional rivalries and the hatred that had been unleashed between the deputies in the Convention.[1] The deputies also worried that provincial cities like Lyon and Marseille were about to erupt in violence. At the same time, the external war was proceeding badly.

* * *

The Lyonnais were very aware of the dangerous turn in international affairs by March of 1793. The commercial focus of the city and its proximity to the borders meant that there were continuing fears of the plots of royalists and of invasion from German and Italian cities that supported *émigrés* from revolutionary France, despite French successes in the war at the end of 1792. With the confidence brought by the successes of Valmy and Savoy in September, by the resounding defeat of the Duke of Brunswick and the victory of General Dumouriez over the Austrians at Jemmapes in October 1792, the National Convention had voted to extend the war. On 1 February 1793, in an almost unanimous decision, war was declared against the Dutch Republic and Great Britain. By March, Spain and the Holy Roman Empire were included in a coalition against France. After the retreat from Neerwinden and the defection of Dumouriez on 6 April, the international situation had again quickly become dire.[2] The French general had been negotiating with the Austrian enemies and then threatened to turn his army against Paris. Royalist-led counter-revolution had also begun in the Vendée region of north-western France in March. Rural anxieties at the enormous demands the Revolution was making had increased with the increased levies for armed service. 'Liberty or death' was now a key revolutionary catch-cry, and the focus for 'patriots' was to continue to regenerate the nation and eliminate any potential interference.[3] A number of emergency measures were decreed to cope with internal upheavals, especially those of the Vendée, but they also included the sending of *commissaires* (often now called representatives-on-mission) to other potential trouble spots including Lyon.

The extremist Jacobins in Lyon continued to call for increased repression against 'aristocrats'. They endorsed the national campaign for a purge of counter-revolutionaries.[4] The Rolandins, who had always prioritised law and order, were now actively working to discredit the Jacobins because of the violence they were seen to be preaching. Alexandrine des Écherolles remembered the winter of 1792 to 93 as one of 'high anxiety', where 'sinister rumours abounded; one felt harried by an invisible enemy, and the threats worried even the most courageous'.[5] The intervention of the *commissaires* from Paris convinced neither side of local politics that they should back down. Rolandins and Jacobins remained firmly convinced of their own virtues and deeply suspicious of the motives of others. The changing affiliations of a particularly popular activist, one Denis Monnet, show how fickle the *sans-culottes* of the city could be in their alliance to either side. Monnet was a silk worker who led the strikes of 1787 but who had become seduced by royalists in 1790, then saw through the plot of December that year and informed against the participants. By 1792, he was supporting Chalier but then sided with the Rolandins and modérées in the early months of 1793. Edmonds concluded that Monnet and the working class believed Chalier did not understand their particular viewpoint because their attention had become 'fixed on the machinations of the counterrevolutionary rich, and while they [the Chalier-Jacobins] had no doubt that the virtuous poor could benefit from the eventual triumph of the Republic, economic problems were generally given second place in the meantime'.[6] Monnet's opinion was that the Jacobin obsession with taxing and decrying the rich meant their elected officials were ultimately prepared to ignore the demands of the sectional clubs. Monnet and many of the *sans-culottes* worked from within the *quartier* clubs against the Central Club because they were unimpressed by the focus on repression.

From 18 April, the Jacobin *cartes de civisme* were in operation and being checked by the Jacobin *comités*, but there was now little support for them as the *quartier* clubs prepared for the election of new *comités*, this time under the supervision of the *commissaires*. They had been sent because civil war was becoming increasingly more likely in Lyon as the factions intertwined social issues with the political.[7] There had developed an unbridgeable gap between the Rolandins claiming to speak for the people against the 'anarchists' or 'extremists' and the Jacobins claiming to speak for the people against the 'aristocrats' or the 'counter-revolutionaries' in their midst, and the *sans-culottes* support was crucial.

This local perspective was completely different from the royalist-led eruption that had occurred in March in the Vendée, now a prolonged guerrilla-style war pitted against the republican state. Royalists and *émigrés* were not leading the dissident *sections* in Lyon. However, some royalists and refractories were actively causing troubles, and while this was recognised, it did not halt the rapid deterioration in relations between republicans, even as the successes of the counter-revolutionaries in the north-west and outside the borders of France made the royalists bolder in the local sphere. The *commissaires* still in Lyon were made aware of the danger and tried to find royalist agitators. On 8 April, they thought they had found the meeting place of a 'nest of royalist conspirators', but when they raided the suspected meeting place, where a plot was reportedly being 'brewed', they instead only found a gathering of Lyonnais who went regularly to a tavern to drink a special brew of beer.[8] The *commissaires* returned to Paris at the end of the month with little achieved.

The local differences continued to grow. From March to April 1793, the Jacobins in municipal and judicial office became more concerned about the political opposition in the city and wanted concerted action against those they increasingly accused of being counter-revolutionaries. They continued to demand a popular tribunal to convict those who had threatened them on 18 February, as well as to agitate against the hoarders of grain and the bakers, who made poor quality bread, and the refractories, who were rumoured to be planning an invasion through Switzerland or the Savoy.[9] Chalier led the courts in demanding certificates of *civisme* from those in positions of authority in judgments delivered on 13 March and 25 March. In a judgment of 25 March, he, with Fernex, Dubessey and Dodieu, reiterated that civil rights of citizens should always be subordinate to the 'public interest'.[10] While the Jacobins in municipal office tried to push through some of their economic initiatives to help the poor, managing to establish thirteen ovens to bake bread at a fixed price in some cantons of the city from 14 March until 16 April 1793, the subsidies necessary became impossible. They were unable to extend the programme any further, and it was bedevilled by allegations that the wheat was of poor quality.[11] The Jacobins were losing control of their popular base, becoming increasingly stymied in the courts and more and more convinced of a local convergence of conspiracies.

Although the Jacobin judge Dodieu appears to have made a commitment to continue working with the other magistrates and *juges de paix*, Chalier was less willing to accommodate the different perspectives in the courts. He wrote to the Minister of Justice on 11 March 1793 in his role as president of the Tribunal de District calling for recognition of the rights of a *sans-culotte* by the name of Arcis. His judgment, supporting the worker, had been overturned by the Tribunal Criminel. Chalier complained that the iniquitous judgment of the higher court should be 'promptly destroyed' and that 'truth, virtue and justice be allowed to prevail'.[12] Judge Gaillard and Achard both wrote to the *commissaires* on 14 March 1793 warning of the need for a new 'Société de Jacobins with the character of true *sans-culottes* or republicans'.[13] By early May, it was noted at a combined meeting of the department, municipality and Commune of Lyon that Gaillard and Gravier were still in Paris and advocating before the Convention their view that a Revolutionary Tribunal should be installed in Lyon.[14] They were informed that such a tribunal in Lyon was not going to be allowed.[15] In response to that news, on 9 May, a number of the *sections* still loyal to the Central Club decided to elect new judges despite the ruling. This action was precipitated by the *sans-culottes* of the Le Peletier club, who had most loudly argued that the laws as they stood were insufficient and there was a real need for a revolutionary tribunal locally. A group of candidates for the position of judges and jurors in the proposed revolutionary tribunal assembled on the Place Bellecour for a 'patriotic feast'. They drank a lot of wine, demolished a feudal obelisk but also by their drunken actions lost a great deal of credibility in the eyes of the press and the public.[16]

The next four *commissaires*, Nioche, Gauthier, Albitte and Dubois-Crancé, were sent to the city on 10 May. Their mission was to curb the local rivalries because of the serious risk such dissent posed while there were military threats on the borders. On the same day on which the *commissaires* arrived, the still operating Jacobin *comité* raided the club of La Croisette and arrested its president and secretary.[17] The new deputies tended to ignore the local disputes and proceeded to impose strong measures of their own, which, according to Edmonds, only exacerbated the opposition of locals to the Montagnards in Paris as well as to the Jacobins locally.[18] These measures included increasing the number of conscripts raised for the revolutionary army and sending them to the Vendée, removing arms from those not conscripted and increasing levies on the rich of the city to fund the army, which had to be paid within 24 hours.

The sectional clubs were being revivified by the impending votes for new *comités*, and they were agitating that they be allowed to sit longer hours. They became bolder in challenging the Jacobin actions, as an incident on 18 May against the now Jacobin *comité* of Le Peletier (formerly La Croisette) indicates. The Jacobin members of the *comité* were confronted on this day by a crowd shouting menaces near the Jacobin headquarters.[19] Although nothing serious transpired at this time, the panic about their loss of popular support led Achard and a number of other Jacobin administrative officials and judges to try to address their waning popularity. They began to highlight their continuing support of popular issues by adding the appellation 'sans-culotte' to their name when they signed official documents.[20] Although they were mostly professional men themselves, they wanted to draw attention to their championing of the poorer citizens in a city where there continued to be a great gulf between the poorer workers or unemployed and the rich merchants and ecclesiastics. Achard in a letter to the National Convention on 11 February expressed his view in these terms:

> We sans-culottes of Lyon struggle without ceasing against the successor of Vitet – Nivière-Chol – a mass of ecclesiastics and of émigrés supported by the counter-revolutionary mercantile élite . . . [there will soon be insurrection] if we do not concern ourselves . . . with the subsistence of the unfortunate.[21]

Achard, along with similarly minded Jacobins, actively courted the *sans-culottes* and claimed they were the only politicians with a genuinely revolutionary agenda. They were becoming increasingly aware they needed to strengthen their popular ties.

Another letter was received by the municipality alerting them of the dangers being faced by Jacobins in the community on 16 May. It was sent by Barthélemi Candy, who had been walking with a friend on that day and had recognised Achard at the centre of a disturbance. He knew Achard was a member of the Jacobin *comité* and heard him order a man dressed in red to follow him. It would appear the man was mocking a *sans-culotte*. On the refusal of the man to follow this order, Achard appealed to Candy and his companion that they help arrest him. As Candy went to put his hand out towards the man in red, a large group of young men – allegedly royalist agitators – suddenly appeared and fell on them, releasing the man they wanted to arrest. Candy was knocked to the ground and punched in the face. In his letter, he appealed for justice and complained that, but for his intervention, Achard would have been the victim of the incident.[22] Tempers remained hot.

On 19 May, when the elections were held for the new *comités de surveillance* based in the *sections*, the actions of the Jacobin *comités* then became illegal because they were not authorised. The two overlapping seats of authority in Lyon had clashed over the new *comités* and the control of the arsenal, but it was the departmental authority of Lyon who were ultimately successful over the municipality. The Jacobin municipal officers who wanted to continue conducting surveillance activities through their own *comités* so they could monitor their enemies were unable to do so. The history of the *comités* was thus, as Chopelin has observed, the history of the 'political stakes' of the factions in Lyon.[23] The departmental authorities now ordered that the newly elected *comités de surveillance* replace the Jacobin groups and also denied them the gunpowder and cannon they requested.[24] Their rationale was that the power the Jacobins had been exercising was shrinking the involvement of the moderate *sections* and increasing tensions between the republicans, which then allowed royalist agitators to emerge.[25] The majority of the *sections* encouraged the department's attempts to curb Jacobin initiatives, and they gradually became more active in expressing their views. From this date, many sectional clubs sat in emergency session (*en permanence*).[26] The Jacobins continued to object to the *sections* operating in this way because this meant too great an influence of the department and, in their opinion, the conservative forces.

Edmonds in his account of the growth of the anti-Jacobin movement showed the widespread support for action before the end of May across different classes and ideologies that united the very diverse *sections*. Some clubs had split from the Central Club from early February. Although it is sometimes not clear whether the cause was a disagreement amongst the old *clubbistes* or an influx of new members, the result was a strengthening of the claims of the *sections* to be the new democratic leaders. Edmonds concluded that in Lyon:

Jacobinism was a disastrous failure ... and one of the most important reasons for this was the existence of a well-established popular movement with its own claims, unchallenged by the *patriots* before 1793, to express the people's will.[27]

Many clubs had retained Rolandin sympathies from the partnership with Vitet in 1791 and 1792, and although several clubs did accept the Jacobin view of quick and decisive action, they were mostly those situated in the poorer parts of Lyon like Belle-Cordière and Croix-Rousse. The Jacobins had in fact managed to antagonise many of the *clubs de quartier*.[28]

While some *sections* were clearly supported by activists from among the silk workers, others had royalist perspectives, and yet others still had some sympathy with broader Jacobin initiatives.[29] Yet the Jacobin focus on a more punitive revolutionary tribunal and repression of 'aristocrats' was increasingly seen to be estranged from the most basic demands of the populace. On 24 May, a group of women broke into a warehouse and sold off butter and were not deflected by the mayor Bertrand, who was trying to dissuade them.[30] Not all *sans-culottes* thus accepted that the Jacobins still spoke for them. By 26 May 1793, the municipality had lost control of the majority of *sections* in the city and was relying on the deputies from Paris to support them locally. But the most recent *commissaires* from Paris were by now viewed suspiciously by many of the *sections* because of their connection with the nearby Armée des Alpes. Dubois-Crancé was stationed in Grenoble, but his arrival back in Lyon with some of the troops was believed to be imminent. A report by the *commissaire* Nioche confirmed that this was possible. Some of the Lyonnais *sections* then approached Nioche and Gauthier to countermand such an order.[31] The departmental administrators were also expressing concern about threats to the city, and they called out the National Guard. These fears led to even more suspicion of the Jacobin municipality.[32]

The Jacobins in both judicial and municipal roles were being roundly challenged by the end of May even though they had been the challengers at the beginning of February. The stage was being set for a reassertion of control by the anti-Jacobin faction. Herriot, Edmonds and Chopelin all highlight the renewed political power of the *sections* after the Jacobin *comités* were declared illegal, and these historians see a direct connection between the Jacobin loss of power and the transference of control of surveillance activities to the departmental and anti-Jacobin politicians. The events of February were, for Edmonds particularly, fundamental in the development of the polarised views that had enabled this political change by encouraging the propertied classes to unite and regain the support of the *quartier* clubs.[33] Another historian who looked at the local political situation was Antonino de Francesco. He found evidence that the activist workers and *sectionnaires* accepted the reality of their interdependence with the Rolandins and preferred the promises of this group to maintain social and political order to the perceived disorder of the Jacobins.[34] Thus the Rolandin mayors Vitet and Nivière-Chol and the more politically astute *sectionnaires* who exploited this belief among the poorer *sections* were ultimately able to mobilise the people against Chalier and the Jacobin mayor Bertrand, who were unsuccessful in the new political atmosphere.[35] These various analyses help explain the growing opposition to the local Jacobins among different social and economic groups. Despite the social divisions of the city it was the anti-Jacobins who now managed to harness the popular support of the sectional clubs and thus gain ascendency.

The revolt of 29 May 1793 then ousted the elected municipality. That morning, 6,000 protestors led by the dissenting sectional clubs gathered in the city centre calling for the municipality to resign.[36] Some *sections* had already taken the pre-emptive action of seizing the arsenal earlier that morning. By the afternoon, two cannons positioned outside the headquarters of the municipality by the Jacobins were fired into the crowd, which included the battalion of National Guard ordered to congregate there by the departmental authorities. Few of the battalions on the day were supporting the Jacobins, possibly because the battalions in the richer areas of the city were closer to hand. After this, a coalition of armed *sectionnaires* suddenly decided to act. With the support of the National Guard, they overcame a Jacobin counter-offensive from the Hôtel de Ville within two hours and surrounded them. The deputies Nioche and Gauthier were trapped in the arsenal where they had tried to regain control of the situation. The next day they ruled that the troops of the Armée des Alpes should be returned to Grenoble and that the municipality should be suspended.[37] Although figures are uncertain, the most reliable sources agree that up to 115 people were wounded and 43 died, mostly amongst the *sectionnaires*.[38] This figure would encompass the 26 corroborated deaths found by the Surgeon-General of the Lyon military hospital to have been occasioned by shots fired from the Hôtel de Ville, further injuries caused by cannon shot, and also the deaths of a number of fleeing insurgents (anti-Jacobins) who were attacked by the *menu peuple* of the poorer *quartiers*.

Notices soon began to appear in the city, printed by various *sections*. On 31 May, the new *section* of Fraternité (previously Rue Neuve) declared its support for the actions taken against the 'tyrants'.[39] The *section Terraille* called for subscriptions to help the wounded and those left widowed by the events.[40] By 6 June, two *sections*, Vaise and Croix-Rousse, joined forces to print an account giving an opposing view of what had transpired on

29 May and warning of false rumours.[41] Also on this day, the Jacobins printed a notice accusing the insurgents of having ignited a civil war. This notice was signed by Mallan (president) and Achard (secretary).[42] However, the Jacobins were in an invidious position, their *comités* ruled illegal and the authority of their defensive actions on 29 May now being questioned. Most of the Jacobin municipal officers and their judges were imprisoned.

Rather than make fears in Lyon recede, re-establishing the institutions of politics and of justice meant there was an even greater emphasis by the anti-Jacobins on the dangers that were believed to have been so narrowly averted and those new ones that now threatened. The reaction against the Jacobins locally that continued after the revolt of May began to be reinforced by a particular interpretation of the 'rule of law' by those judges who now remained in office. A project devised by a sculptor called Joseph Chinard called 'La Liberté et l'Égalité' helped in this task. Chinard had proposed a sculptural work to be placed on the front panel of the Hôtel de Ville in the place of the statue of Louis XIV that had been removed when the republic was declared in 1792. A plaster model of his new work was presented to the municipal council on 5 June and seemed to indeed encapsulate the essential relationship between the 'Droits de L'Homme' (the rights of man) and the 'Loix Républicaines' (The Republican Laws) that was now acceptable, and the decoration was enthusiastically endorsed by the departmental authorities.

While Chinard wanted an emblem that would speak to 'patriots' about the new republican spirit in the city, and he used the classical lines of the figures to highlight the Phrygian cap on the top of the bundle of sticks or 'baguettes' representing the citizens of Lyon, he was also careful to represent the spirit of equality as 'equality before the law' and not the more divisive Jacobin idea of social equality, which called for property to be shared equally. Chinard's plaster was put in place in September, but it would later be criticised for its ambiguities, including the 'aristocratic sensuousness' of the figures and the position of Liberty's crown to the side of the statue.[43]

The anti-Jacobin 'rule of law' began with the arrests of the former municipal and judicial officers who were associated with the Jacobins, of whom eighty-three were charged to stand trial on 15 July.[44] The *juges de paix* and magistrates needed to legitimate proceedings by connecting the Jacobins to the various crimes related to the crisis, especially the firing on the *sectionnaires* on 29 May.[45] There was an initial period of uncertainty as to what to do with the prisoners because the National Convention did not immediately rule on this question, despite requests to do so.[46] The deputies, Nioche and Gauthier, were still in Lyon and helping to calm the

Figure 11.1 *La Liberté et l'Egalité* (Liberty and Equality), 1793. J. Chinard, inv. B1359. Bibliothéque et documentation, Musée des Beaux-Arts Lyon.

turbulence after the revolt. They recognised, according to Edmonds, that the previous municipality had had few defenders and that the majority of *sections* were indifferent to the fate of the Jacobin leaders. The *menu peuple* were not engaged with the Jacobins as they had been in earlier revolts. Gauthier observed on the morning of 29 May that 'the bulk of the population' were unmoved by the 'rhetoric' of the Jacobins and had remained fairly passive when the *sections* gained control of the arsenal.[47] He cautioned the Convention against precipitate action in a letter of 3 June because he and the deputy Nioche believed there was no reason to fear counter-revolution in Lyon.[48] The Armée des Alpes was, however, still watching from its position on the border near Grenoble, and the deputy who had gone to join the troops there, Dubois-Crancé, was urging Paris to take decisive action to support the arrested Jacobins. The Convention, after hearing from Nioche and Gauthier, now ordered Dubois-Crancé to only act with 'extreme prudence' in dealing with Lyon. They also sent Robert Lindet to find out what was going on.[49] After his return, Lindet also advised against armed intervention, instead supporting a policy of negotiation.[50] Although he had tried to participate in official discussions from 8 to 15 June while he was in Lyon, his overtures were rejected by the departmental authorities because there were suspicions that he was influenced by the Jacobin judge Gaillard, who had travelled from Paris with him.[51]

The sectional clubs of Lyon acted quickly to normalise the political situation as best they could from this time. However, the provisional municipality was hindered in its operation by its lack of legal status, not having been elected directly but only from amongst the presidents and secretaries of the *sections*. The *sectionnaire* Bémani took on the role of mayor in the first hours after the insurrection when, according to Riffaterre, only half of the *sections* had appeared. He was from a royalist *section*.[52] By the time the rest of the *sections* began to participate in June, a more representative provisional mayor, Jean-Jacques Coindre, was elected and he stayed in this role for the next few months. Again, however, he was not elected through the primary assemblies but from amongst the *sections*. The municipality remained fairly indecisive because it relied so heavily on ratification and discussion of actions and decrees with the *sections*.[53] The sectional *comités de surveillance* elected in May continued in operation and also encouraged the reliance on the power base of the *sections* to which they were attached.

Three of the 32 *sections* in the city were composed of poorer members and were still Jacobin oriented: Saint-Georges, La Grande-Côte and Saint-Vincent. In some others, there were rumoured to be royalist affiliations. Most of the *sections* had now changed their names after the insurrection. The new names they took on included La Paix, Fraternité, La Bonnefoi and L'Unité. The citizens of Bon-Rencontre preceded their name with 'd'Amis des Lois [Friends of the law]'.[54] Many professional and educated Lyonnais were ready to take leadership of the various *sections*. They included the constitutional priest of Saint-Nizier, Jolyclerc and the surgeon and eventually president of the Commission Populaire of the *sections* Jean-Emanuel Gilibert.⁵⁵ Fain, who wrote for Carrier's *Journal de Lyon*, continued to support the motives of such leaders. He had been instrumental in calling for the sectional committees to take action as they did on 29 May against those who supposedly used the name of *sans-culotte* as 'a licence to kill [*brevet de massacreur*]'. He did this at the same time as warning the rich *négociants* of the danger of their ignoring the needs of the poor by their *égoisme*.⁵⁶ Gilibert and Jolyclerc, because they had been imprisoned by the Jacobins after the events of February, were highly motivated to act after the revolt in support of the protection of the rule of law and the stability of the republic in Lyon.

While those Rolandins who had been active in the previous year now had influence again, they were wary about taking control in a way that would make them appear to be as ignorant of the protocols and the rule of law as the Jacobins had been. They were also concerned about how the actions of the *sections* would be viewed in Paris. These tensions helped continue the climate of indecision following the uprising that was exacerbated by the proximity of the Armée des Alpes. Called upon to make decisions, such as disarming suspects, the provisional municipality did not act decisively but only used delaying tactics.⁵⁷ The *sections* supported the need to send a delegation to the Convention to present the facts of what had happened to the previous municipality but in fact only funded a small delegation. The journalist Fain also went to attempt to present the actions of the Lyonnais in the best possible way.⁵⁸ However, the Lyonnais had little opportunity to talk to the Convention. When they returned, they brought news that the Girondins had been expelled from the Convention by the *sans-culottes* in Paris on 2 June and the Montagnards were in the ascendant.

Events had favoured the Rolandins against the Jacobins in the provinces at the same time as the opposite had happened in the capital; the Girondin deputies had been ejected from the National Convention. After the defection of General Dumouriez in March 1793 and the attempted impeachment of Marat in April, suspicion of the Girondins had been increasing in Paris. The Paris Commune with a militia of 20,000 *sans-culottes* surrounded the Convention in May and precipitated the crisis by calling for the arrest of the Girondin deputies on 2 June.⁵⁹ Lyon was now seen to be part of the more general revolt known as 'federalism' because of its ongoing rebellion. The attitude of the anti-Jacobins now in power in Lyon was one of protest against the dismissal of the Girondins. Paul Hanson has identified a 'federalist program . . . [though] not a truly "federalist" vision' amongst four principal cities, including Lyon, in reaction to what they presumed to be evidence of 'anarchists' in Paris.

However, Hanson hastened to add that these opponents: 'did not advocate a federated republic'.⁶⁰ The real question for him was not whether a provincial city advocated taking the directional lead of the Revolution but rather whether the so-called 'federalist' cities were part of a more general questioning of where political sovereignty in the country actually lay. Indeed, it has been recognised that there were many exchanges of correspondence and visits from the fleeing Girondin representatives and discussion with other provincial cities, like Marseille, worried about the seemingly 'anarchistic' events in Paris.⁶¹

As a result of the developments in Paris, the provisional administrators of Lyon were anxious to appeal to the National Convention for their right to contest the radical policies of the Jacobin municipal officers, but they were unsure how to put their case when there was still a great deal of uncertainty about what would happen in the national sphere.⁶² Without waiting for official sanction, the *sections* voted for continued rebellion. They affirmed their:

> Horror of anarchy, royalism, feudalism, despotism.... [and continued their pledge] to defend to the death the unity, the indivisibility of the republic, respect for persons and their property, their acquiescence to the law and to the constituted authority.⁶³

The sectional leaders by this pledge wanted to reiterate their innocence of counter-revolutionary intention by showing their continuing support for the 'indivisible republic'. Yet they also had to accommodate the views of the different *sections* and those leaders who were now also worried about what was happening in Paris. Many of them suspected that a temporary chaos had been unleashed in the capital because the Parisian *sans-culottes* had gained inordinate power. The *sectionnaires* in Lyon and the other rebellious provincial cities argued that the *sections*, which had been created in 1789, were still the most basic and thus legitimate forums for discussion. They decided to wait on developments.⁶⁴ In Marseille the *sections*, which had been dominated by Jacobins since the time the Popular Tribunal was created there in 1792, were also determined to manage their own city's affairs, but they never sought permission from the Convention for their initiatives as the Lyonnais did attempt to do.⁶⁵

While Parisians at the time, and many historians since, have suggested Lyon was taking the lead in a 'federalist' challenge to Paris, others are more inclined to see events as a bourgeois reaction to the local threat of social activism that then slowly escalated into resistance. The historian Riffaterre was one of the first to highlight the local nature of the revolt in Lyon and also the fact that it was not in opposition to the National Convention. Riffaterre proposed that it was the local Jacobins who convinced Paris of the royalist nature of the revolt and that this then led to the intervention of the republican troops. Because this reaction was disproportionate to the initial revolt by the Lyonnais it led to 'the frightening prospect of terrible reprisal which explained the resistance of the insurgents'.[66] The printed notices posted in Lyon, including those from the National Convention, do show the intense feelings gripping the city. Gilibert was president of the anti-Jacobin *comité*, and his explosive notice in July warned of the 'anarchists' in Paris, who were 'arming the poor against the rich' and 'crime against virtue'. He hastened to assure citizens that tranquillity would be restored in Lyon and civil war averted.[67]

Reactions to events in Paris had become increasingly negative as the southern cities heard more from the Girondin politicians who had fled. These proscribed deputies, in fear of their lives, increased fears about the alleged anarchy and terror that the Jacobins appeared to be unleashing. Notices were printed and posted in Lyon by Chasset, the Lyonnais Girondin delegate and also by Birotteau.[68] The cities of Lyon and Marseille, where actions had been taken against local Jacobin municipalities, became even more worried about how their own actions would be viewed in this fearful climate. Their respective insurrections, as Hanson observed, thus 'fed on each other – each gathered force and confidence from reports of the other, and they fed into the federalist revolt in each city as well'.[69] The cities of Caen, Bordeaux and Toulon had also experienced similar anxieties about what was happening in the capital. They were also conscious of the need to distinguish themselves from the insurgents of the Vendée. However, the rebels of Marseille and Toulon went further than the other provincial cities in actually refusing to vote on the decree relating to the Constitution of June 1793 on the grounds that they regarded any legislation emanating from the Convention after the purge of 2 June as illegal.[70] Toulon's intransigence in fact led to their collaboration with the external enemy, when the English invested the port in August.[71] From Caen, in Normandy, an army of volunteers, incensed by the plight of the Girondins, set off towards Paris. They were soon dispersed when they encountered resistance from the national army.[72] Despite the planning by the Marseillais of a combined departmental force with the mission of marching to Paris, their armed resistance was also short lived. They only got as far as Avignon and so did not even reach Lyon.[73] The insurrection in Lyon, while focused on local issues, nevertheless began to be regarded as a serious internal threat by the National Convention.

Notes

1. T. Tackett, *The Coming of the Terror in the French Revolution* (Cambridge, MA: The Belknap Press of Harvard University Press, 2015), 246–47.
2. T.C.W. Blanning, *The Origins of the French Revolutionary Wars* (London: Longman Group, 1986), 60.
3. P. McPhee, *Liberty or Death: The French Revolution* (New Haven, CT and London: Yale University Press, 2016), 204.
4. W. Edmonds, *Jacobinism and the Revolt of Lyon, 1789–1793* (New York: Oxford University Press, 1990), 175.
5. A. des Écherolles, *Une Famille noble sour la Terreur* (Paris: Elibron Classics, 2006), 61–62.
6. W. Edmonds, 'A Study in Popular Anti-Jacobinism: The career of Denis Monnet', *French Historical Studies* 13 (1983), 215–51.
7. Edmonds, 'A Study in Popular Anti-Jacobinism', 240.
8. G. Eynard, *Joseph Chalier: Bourreau ou martyr, 1747–1793* (Lyon: Éd. lyonnaises d'art et d'histoire, 1987), 105–6.
9. See C. Riffaterre, *Le Mouvement antijacobin et antiparisien à Lyon et dans le Rhône-et-Loire en 1793, 29 mai-15 août*, Vol. 1 (Lyon: A. Rey, 1912), 14–16.
10. E. Herriot, *Lyon n'est Plus*, 'Le Siège', Vol. 4 (Paris: Hachette, 1940), 208–9.
11. Edmonds, *Jacobinism*, 145.
12. ADR 39 L 59.
13. Riffaterre, *Le Mouvement*, 48.
14. ADR 1 L 375.
15. The Lyonnais Deputy from Lyon, Chasset, had objected to it. Riffaterre, *Le Mouvement*, 50–55.
16. Edmonds, *Jacobinism*, 161; E. Herriot, *Lyon n'est Plus: Jacobins et modérés* (Paris: Hachette, 1937), 326.
17. Edmonds, *Jacobinism*, 175. This *comité* was headed by Achard and appears to have been the active arm of the Jacobin sections.
18. Edmonds, *Jacobinism*, 173.
19. Letter, Bertelet and others, 18 May 1793, AML 1 (2) 3.
20. See the letters of Hidins and Dodieu: BML Fonds Coste, Ms 558.
21. Letter of Achard and Gaillard, 19 February, BML Fonds Coste, Ms 545.
22. Letter, Candy, 16 May 1793. AML 1 (2) 3.
23. P. Chopelin, 'Un Cancer politique? Vies et morts des comités de surveillance de la ville de Lyon (1792–1795)', in D. Pingué and J.-P. Rothiot (eds), *Les Comités de surveillance: D'une création citoyenne à une institution révolutionnaire* (Paris: Société des études Robespierristes, 2012), 179.
24. Herriot suggested that this decision led to the 'grave *dissentiment*' between the Municipal officers and their opponents and thus ultimately to the insurrection of 29 May. *Lyon n'est Plus*, Vol. 4, 296.
25. Herriot, *Lyon n'est Plus*, Vol. 4, 176–77.
26. Riffaterre, *Le Mouvement*, 58–59.
27. Edmonds, *Jacobinism*, 153.
28. Edmonds, *Jacobinism*, 154.
29. Edmonds, *Jacobinism*, 190.
30. Edmonds, *Jacobinism*, 156.
31. Edmonds, *Jacobinism*, 188.
32. Edmonds, *Jacobinism*, 188.
33. Edmonds, *Jacobinism*, 181–82.

34. A. de Francesco, 'Les Rapports entre administrateurs et administrés à Lyon dans les premières années révolutionnaires (1789–1793)', in B. Benoît (ed.), *Ville et Révolution française: Actes du colloque international, Lyon, Mars 1993* (Lyon: Presses universitaires de Lyon, 1994), 218–20.
35. Francesco, 'Les Rapports', 218.
36. According to the patriot Gonchon, Letter of Varlet Gonchon, 14 June. Quoted in Riffaterre, *Le Mouvement*, 84.
37. Edmonds, *Jacobinism*, 188–89.
38. Riffaterre, *Le Mouvement*, 89.
39. AML 936 W 60.
40. AML 936 W 61.
41. AML 936 W 56.
42. AML 936 W 64.
43. P. Bordes, 'L'Invention d'une iconographe Révolutionnaire: Joseph Chinard (1756–1813), *Studi neoclassici* 4 (2016), 48.
44. Riffaterre, *Le movement* 95–98 and 198–201, established much of the framework of the events leading to the revolt and siege of 1793 in Lyon on which later studies, including my own, depend. Riffaterre did also highlight the arrest of the six Jacobin judges demanded by the *sections* between 29 and 30 May and the resulting legal impasse when they were in gaol. He then made some mention of Ampère and his actions in the case of Chalier. Although Riffaterre hinted at the lack of real evidence to support the detention of the judges, he really only concentrated on the case of Chalier.
45. Riffaterre, *Le movement*, 182.
46. It was more than a week after the events that the image of the city as 'counter-revolutionary' began to form even amongst the Montagnards, but a decree ordering a report of the status of counter-revolution in Lyon was not voted until 3 July: M. Biard, *1793 Le Siège de Lyon: Entre mythes et réalités* (Clermont-Ferrand: Lemme, 2013), 11.
47. Edmonds, *Jacobinism*, 194.
48. Edmonds, *Jacobinism*, 205.
49. Edmonds, *Jacobinism*, 206–7.
50. According to Hanson, Lindet countermanded an order for armed intervention made by Dubois-Crancé: P.R. Hanson, *Jacobin Republic under Fire: The Federalist Revolt in the French Revolution* (University Park, PA: Pennsylvania State University Press, 2003), 27, 73.
51. Hanson, *Jacobin Republic under Fire*, 72. On this question, Edmonds suggested the authorities were playing for time, by questioning Lindet's credentials and refusing to share with him crucial documents. Edmonds, *Jacobinism*, 206.
52. Riffaterre, *Le mouvement*, 174–75.
53. Riffaterre, *Le mouvement*, 229.
54. Riffaterre, *Le mouvement*, 179–80.
55. Hanson, *Jacobin Republic under Fire*, 181–82.
56. Herriot, *Lyon n'est Plus*, 290.
57. Riffaterre, *Le mouvement*, 235.
58. Fain said he left on 2 June with three others to take the news of what had happened in Lyon on 29 May to the National Convention. E. Fayard, *Histoire des tribunaux révolutionnaires de Lyon et de Feurs* (Lyon: H. George, 1888), 94.
59. McPhee, *Liberty or Death*, 184–85.
60. Hanson, *The Jacobin Republic under Fire*, 11, 34.
61. Tackett, *The Coming of the Terror*, 283.
62. Biard, *1793*, 20–25.

63. Hanson, *The Jacobin Republic under Fire*, 14.
64. M. Crook, 'Les révoltes "fédéralistes" et les origines de la Terreur en 1793', in M. Biard and H. Leuwers (eds), *Visages de la Terreur* (Paris: Armand Colin, 2014), 21.
65. W. Scott, *Terror and Repression in Revolutionary Marseille* (London: The MacMillan Press, 1973), 39.
66. Riffaterre, *Le Mouvement*, 4–5.
67. AML 936 W 83.
68. AML 936 W 86 and 936 W 87.
69. Hanson, *The Jacobin Republic under Fire*, 87.
70. Hanson, *The Jacobin Republic under Fire*, 15.
71. M. Crook, *Toulon in War and Revolution* (Manchester: Manchester University Press, 1991), 129–39.
72. For an account of Bordeaux see A. Forrest, *Society and Politics in Revolutionary Bordeaux* (Oxford: Clarendon Press, 1975).
73. Hanson, *The Jacobin Republic under Fire*, 90.

Chapter 12

BASTILLE DAY, 1793

> The cortege ... began to move at 11.30. The proceedings were simple, but imposing; there were no signs of the transient sumptuousness of times past, procured by the sweat of an unhappy people; citizens participated with even greater pleasure than in those days in the reunion of all their magistrates, the defenders of their rights.
> —Description of the civic festival that took place at Lyon on 14 July 1793 by the *section* Droits de l'Homme

The fourth anniversary of the taking of the Bastille, 14 July 1793, was celebrated in Lyon with great ceremony. The officials of the Department of the Rhône-et-Loire, including all the magistrates, came from the mayoral offices and descended into an amphitheatre specially constructed on the main square of Bellecour. The rousing ceremony included music and salvos of artillery from 'valiant' soldiers, and a speech by the mayor, Coindre, was full of 'virtuous principles', which led to cries of 'vive la République!' from the watching public. There were no disputes observed, only 'generosity', 'patriotism' and everywhere 'republican songs and dances spread throughout the day in the squares around the trees of Liberty'. In fact, all the hallmarks were noted of a successful revolutionary festival: unity, harmony, celebration and virtue. According to the *comité de surveillance* of the *section*, Droits-de-l'Homme, all was well for its 'good citizens'.[1]

* * *

In reality, all was far from well. A new general, Citizen (formerly Count) Perrin-Précy, was also being sworn in to lead the battalions of departmental armed forces. Although he protested his 'devotion to the Republic and the execution of law', the local press entertained suspicions that he was still a royalist.² The reference to the 'law' he pledged to observe was a little equivocal, according to historian Michel Biard, considering the laws had been rendered obsolete by the decision of the Lyonnais on 12 July not to recognise any of the decrees of the National Convention that came to them after 31 May.³ A contrasting view of the celebration of Bastille Day in 1793 was contained in the annotation added in 1847 by Marie-Pierre Gonon in his 'official' preface to the surviving sectional records. He suggested that it was a stage-managed 'imposture which had been given reception by a partisan group'. By denying the memory of the opposition constituents, who were in gaol at the time, he warned that historians could be misled.⁴ The provisional municipality now established in Lyon was far from achieving peace and harmony despite their claim to be celebrating the ideals exemplified by the first Bastille Day.

The fall of the Bastille represented the hard-won battle of the people against the mighty fortress of absolute power in Paris, and the annual event now also celebrated the 'one and indivisible' republic. It was a powerful trope for the Lyonnais as it was for the rest of France. As we have seen, Chalier proudly kept a piece of the actual Bastille fortification as a keepsake from 1789.⁵ Ampère wrote of it in his play about the good king Artaxerxes in 1792.⁶ The magistrates and *sectionnaires* of the sectional clubs and assemblies who were at the celebration in Lyon in 1793 now used the occasion in a flagrantly propagandistic way. National observers as well as those Jacobin magistrates and politicians who were still in prison after the overthrow of the municipality on 29 May would not have been impressed, as Gonon observed.

The month before the celebration of Bastille Day, decisions had been made to convoke the primary assemblies to elect a new municipality based on the sectional assemblies of the *quartiers*.⁷ Three provisional bodies were then established to administer local government after the uprising. Delegates had been elected to a new Commission Populaire on 24 June, and this group numbered some 210 members, including, according to Takashi Koi, some 17.4 per cent of those who were ex-nobles and ex-priests. The administrative body of the department had twenty-six members, and the provisional municipality comprised some ninety people elected from amongst the *sections*.⁸ The elections of 24 and 25 June had only attracted a small number of voters but still claimed to be democratically based.⁹ The result meant a difficult balancing act for those Lyonnais who took up the reins of power because they had ejected a legitimately elected municipality, and there were now enemies on both the left side of politics (there were still *sections* with Jacobin affiliations) and the right side (the royalists were attempting to gain from the situation).

Dubois-Crancé continued to urge a negative view of the situation in Lyon, and he was still a threat because of his proximity with his battalions in nearby Grenoble, ready to attack if orders came from Paris to do so. He urged the Convention by letter of 2 June, which was read in the Convention on 6 June, to consider the fact that: 'This city, for so long the refuge for counter-revolutionaries of the Midi, would ultimately pay to the criminals they hosted the price of their complaisance.'[10] By 21 June, Marat was urging the Convention to action because he feared that Chalier would soon be subjected to the 'ferocity of the aristocrats of Lyon'.[11]

To understand how the legality of the situation was now rationalised in Lyon, we need to go back to the arrests of the Jacobin judicial officers. The operation of the courts had been severely disrupted by the arrest or threatened arrest of the director of the jury, Dodieu, various *juges de paix* and some judges of the Tribunal de District, including the former president Chalier and judge Gaillard (who had been arrested when he returned to Lyon from Paris on 8 June). Those not in gaol were in hiding. Cozon, now president of the Tribunal de District, was at first unwilling to undertake any prosecutions against those arrested because of the risk this action could be seen as unauthorised, even though there was some pressure to do so from the *sections*. He warned that prosecutions could only be done in a 'legal manner' and not attempted in the absence of a director of the jury. He was clearly worried that Dodieu's position would have to be filled before any prosecutions could commence. In fact, Cozon was so concerned that he offered to resign his position on 30 June so this principle would not be compromised. The departmental authorities hastened to encourage him and the remaining judges not to resign and to help bring the judicial administration back into operation.[12]

The *juges de paix*, who had not been identified as Jacobins, were the only magistrates available to validate the imprisonments while questions of procedure were being debated. These magistrates were still operating in their offices and in the Police Correctionnelle and had been ever since the Jacobin magistrates had been unseated or had fled. Ampère was one of the working judges called on to help untangle the legal problems faced by the sectional leaders. He seems to have been convinced that judicial operations should soon be re-established and came to have a major role in how this would be done. While before February 1793 there is nothing in the records to suggest Ampère had seen the radical judges who worked with him as enemies, he was worried about their commitment to the maintenance of law and order as we have seen in his communication to Judge Dodieu about the events of February. Ampère's alienation from the Jacobin judges grew from that time. Until then, he had been open to the quite radical ideas proposed by the municipal officer Pressavin (whose books were in his library) and the fellow *juges de paix* like L'Ange and Billiemas, who came from quite different social backgrounds but were equally hard-working in the service of the new courts.[13] He certainly cooperated in an official manner throughout 1792 with Dodieu and Hidins, who identified as *sans-culottes*. It was not until the threat to 'paralyse the institutions of justice' – as he characterised Dodieu's actions in February 1793 – that Ampère saw how irreconcilable was the different vision they had. His decision was no doubt reinforced by the proven corrupt dealings of Hidins and Laussel also coming to light in February and March. After the revolt of May, Ampère readily made himself available to help challenge those he now believed were attempting to compromise the judicial apparatus that had been in place since 1791.

Chalier was the first Jacobin judge to be dealt with legally after the uprising in early June. By 30 June – the same day that Cozon was expressing his concerns about the legality of acting at all – Ampère was signing documents as President of the Police Correctionnelle, taking on the premier role that had been held by Chalier a year earlier.[14] Although Ampère did not live in the canton in which Chalier resided, and thus did not have any authority to pursue the action against him, Ampère appears to have ignored this technicality.[15] He was the only *juge de paix* immediately willing to commence the task of gathering evidence against Chalier. This point was raised against him by Chalier in a letter written from prison. Chalier alleged that he was treated 'like a prisoner of war' and asked how there could be another judge 'so barbarous and so dismissive of his oath to uphold the unity and indivisibility of the Republic as to pronounce upon him . . . a battle veteran (*cheval de bataille*)'.[16] Ampère nevertheless continued to gather evidence. On 1 June 1793, a 'packet of papers concerning Citizen Chalier' was found in his house at 3AM that morning by a member of the *comité de surveillance*.[17] Ampère prepared the documentation to begin the prosecution.[18] On 7 June, his mandate of arrest ordered Chalier to be taken into custody and taken before the *juré d'accusation*. Louis Renard had now been appointed director of the jury by a vote of the *sections* on 8 June.[19] Renard was to protest later that he was not fully responsible for the work that this position usually entailed. As a 'simple silk worker' he did not know how to draw up the necessary documents. He only admitted to signing the documents given to him by the Commissaire National in this case.[20]

In reality, Ampère dealt with much of the evidence that would be presented on 13 July against Chalier to the final jury, as Chalier attested.

Chalier complained also about the 'biased nature' of Ampère's reporting in what he labelled the 'extravagant' allegations drawn up.[21] Chalier suggested if Ampère was truly acting with probity, with the 'least ability to look him in the eye (*blanc d'oeil*), the least principles of justice', he would have straight away recused himself from the case against his fellow judge.[22] The *acte d'accusation* detailed the critical actions taken at the secret meeting of 6 February of the Central Club – that is, the proposal of the Tribunal Révolutionnaire and participation in the formulation of a plot to 'slit the throats of many citizens'.[23] Ampère was also sent a letter collected from the distribution centre of the postal service that suggested Chalier had engaged in a counter-revolutionary plot with a noblewoman across the border. This letter never appeared in the evidence against Chalier, and it would appear to have been lost or recognised as a forgery by Ampère and thus not included.[24] By the time the case reached the Tribunal de District, there was no mention of 'treason' in regard to Chalier; only the question of whether he had 'provoked murder' on 29 May by his 'writings and discourse'.[25]

In his long letter of 16 June, Chalier continued to rail about the case against him: 'Of all the prisoners who moan about the frightful weight of their irons, there is perhaps none more unfortunate, more innocent, none who has more to complain of the oppression of their horrible captivity' than he. He was concerned about the rumoured false letter and was tormented that the 'real conspirators', the 'real traitors', the 'real enemies of liberty' were free while he was being brought before the courts. The overwhelming impatience and suspicion that the Jacobin judges had felt while they were in power and their conviction that counter-revolutionaries were being allowed to evade justice and continue to threaten the state by means of the so-called 'legal processes' in place were again detailed. Chalier also wrote to Gaillard, the former Jacobin judge, observing that the gaols were still 'more like taverns than prisons', 'favouring those who had money'.[26] Gaillard, also in gaol, tried a different approach, appealing to Ampère for recognition of his plight in the spirit of fraternity between former co-workers.[27]

The beliefs of the judges who remained in power about the culpability of the former Jacobin judges only grew more rigid and legalistic as the provisional municipality continued to hold Jacobin officials to account for the troubles of 29 May.[28] The departmental records of 29 and 30 May summed up the official view of the situation. These claimed that there had been evidence from February of the formation of a 'Tribunal of blood' – a Jacobin plot 'which the Convention had prohibited "with horror"' – and finally of 'the most intolerable despotism ever to exist in Lyon'.[29] Ampère was involved in the many cases that dealt with this 'plot' alleged against the imprisoned Jacobins. He ordered that the Jacobin Carteron be detained on 6 June because of his attendance at the secret meeting of the Jacobins at the Central Club on 6 February.[30] On 26 June 1793, Ampère then interrogated this accused man as to the death threats he had made to those who had attended the secret meeting of 6 February and who might be tempted to divulge anything that had been discussed there.[31] Carteron denied being in attendance himself, but a packet of papers found on him was opened in front of him and revealed political notices and instructions made on 14 May discussing the issue of the *sections* sitting 'in permanence'. He was further accused of presenting himself as a judge in an illegal 'Tribunal Populaire'. The facts in both interrogations were written up in Ampère's own hand.

By the end of the month of June, Ampère delivered to the director of the jury, Renard, the accusations against fifteen Jacobins including the former mayor, Bertrand, held in gaol after the popular uprising of 29 May. Although the task of writing up the accusations was usually completed by the director himself before going to the jury, it would appear the work was largely undertaken by Ampère. The document was produced in the form of a printed notice, which made it easier to inform the populace of the proceedings against the accused and to help establish the legality of what the city had done. It is thus difficult to be absolutely confident about who was responsible for its contents, but Ampère's name was clearly appended, and he did not try later to deny his involvement in its production as Renard did. In view of the work Ampère had done up to this point in the case of Chalier and Carteron, and in view of Renard's claim that he did not have the education to draw up such accusations, it is more than likely that the setting out of all the cases against the Jacobins, as well as the warrants, were prepared by Ampère. Ampère agreed at his later trial that he was responsible for 'many instructions' against the municipal officers from 29 May, and he had dealt with those matters required to go before the director of the jury 'according to the law in the case of all accused'.[32]

The primary action against the fifteen Jacobins, which commenced on 30 June, was based on the allegation that they had been planning an attack 'against the sovereignty and the liberty of the people', which was put into action on the day the *sectionnaires* had decided to protest.[33] This allegation was contained in a composite document against all the accused, designed to draw attention away from the fact that the Jacobins were responding to an uprising by the *sectionnaires* calling for the dismissal of the elected municipality on the day of 29 May. As well as the mayor, the other accused were Jean Roullot (*dessinateur*), Jean Richard, Gilbert Roch, Louis Dubois, Charles Turin, Pierre Chazot, Jean-Baptiste Carteron, Vincent

Noël (*comédien*), Pierre Bourchenu, Didier Fillon (*perruquier*), Jacques Montfalcon, Jean-Claude-Etienne Jacob (*tailleur*) and Jean-Baptiste Foret and Jean-Pierre Revoux (both silk workers).[34] The document described a conspiracy involving these 'former municipal officers and *notables*', as well as the 'former judges of the district court' of the city and other 'anarchists' who allegedly commenced the violence on the day. The facts outlined an attempted seizure of power by the Jacobins from 6 February, including the publishing of 'incendiary placards', which had 'provoked murder and pillage'.

The accusation document was intended to clearly outline the conspiracy to the public of Lyon and ultimately to the nation. The document identified those members of the Jacobin municipality who were alleged to have been involved in events culminating on the day of the uprising whether or not they were at the Hôtel de Ville at that point. Although those who were present did claim to be exercising their authoritative positions and so to have had a legitimate defence, they were nonetheless held responsible for the deaths and woundings of *sectionnaires* who had gathered outside to protest on 29 May. The actions of the Jacobins on the day in question were seen as the culmination of a conspiracy against the 'liberty, the lives and fortune of citizens' of Lyon, an argument that could well have been expected to raise some alarm because of its wide ambit. The cases were then remitted to the higher courts for judgment.[35]

The document, by its characterisation of the crimes that allegedly occurred, supported the narrative that readers of the *Journal de Lyon* would have easily recognised: the supposed Jacobin attempt to retain power by violent rather than democratic means. The narrative began with the 'secret' meeting of the Jacobins in the Central Club and the proposals about a Tribunal Révolutionnaire and the use of the guillotine on aristocrats. The numerous allegations of 'pillage' and 'incitement to pillage' were basically the same for most of the Jacobins. Those who were in charge of the defence of the Hôtel de Ville and had ordered the use of the cannon against the rebels were charged with murder. While there were no prosecutions for the *sectionnaires* who had broken into the arsenal to obtain arms used against the municipality, those Jacobins who had distributed gunpowder to their supporters were also to be charged with murder, and so too were those National Guard battalions who responded to the calls of the municipality for military support. They were accused of firing on the insurgents and of murder.

By casting the imputations against the Jacobins in this way, the document was intended to legitimise the opposing actions of the rebels. It framed as crimes what had been until then contested interpretations of events leading up to and following the pillage of the Central Club and thus presented an interpretation that accorded with the new view of the rule of law. These facts could then be inserted into the evolving 'plot' theory and validate retrospectively the reactions of the Rolandin faction. In this way, what the Jacobins had seen as the cause of disorder, the pillage of the club on the night of 18–19 February, was dismissed as having any real significance. By using the confrontational language of 'murder' and 'pillage' in the context of a conspiracy, the Jacobin actions were those deemed to be criminal. The excess of revolutionary enthusiasm they had displayed now made them 'anarchists', not capable of holding the measured and selfless virtues that their roles as judges and administrators required and liable for prosecution as 'conspirators'.

This interpretation of the law then supported the claim that the new municipality made and continued to make: the Rolandins did have the required virtues to participate in public office, and their actions had re-established the rule of law. By setting out the justification for the attack on the former municipality in this seemingly legalistic and unemotional way, Ampère was instrumental in the process of presenting a reformulation by the victorious faction of the rule of law. The legitimacy of the actions taken by the rebels on 29 May was assumed. Although they had attacked an elected government, they did so only because it had become illegitimate. By blaming the Jacobins for the 'murder' of the citizens who had in fact been amongst the original attackers, this document had set out a firm framework for continued action against the Jacobins. Ampère had thus become one of the most relentless of the *juges de paix* in the process of having the suspect judges unseated and the power of their *comités* broken.

The powers of the *juges de paix* to initiate functions of arrest and interrogation were again used in the case of Duperret, which was ultimately decided by the Tribunal Criminel.[36] Duperret was a member of the National Guard who had been arrested at the Hôtel de Ville on 29 May but who claimed that he was not involved in the armed resistance. He said he had sheltered there for eight hours but had done nothing. This evidence was taken by Ampère in June of 1793 but was not tested until July. The case against the *juge de paix* Pierre Fillion of the canton of L'Hôtel-Dieu was another such case. It came before the Tribunal de District on 18 July, on appeal, to establish whether the magistrate's actions actually constituted a crime based on the Code Pénal.[37] He was accused of being complicit in the assassinations of 29 May by not helping a wounded person and being heard to encourage the Jacobin actions. He was initially investigated by the *juge de paix* Boivin and sent before the Tribunal de District, where it was decided that his case was covered by the Code Pénal and should be remitted to be heard by the Tribunal Correctionnel. He was imprisoned for six months and fined the sum of 200 *livres*.

Ampère was careful to show due respect for the Code Pénal and the rights of individuals. As the register of the Saint-Joseph prison indicates, he continued to visit and advocate for the needs of the prisoners.[38] Ampère also interviewed one of the municipal officers known as 'Sautemouche' on 27 June with a view to making sure he was in fact guilty of a crime recognised in the Code Pénal. The complaint against Sautemouche was that he had so frightened a woman when he arrived at her house brandishing a sabre and demanding the payment of a tax levy that she later died.[39] The result of this questioning was that Ampère could not find sufficient facts to keep the prisoner incarcerated and so he refused to remit the case against this former municipal officer to the higher court. The *Journal de Lyon* of 30 June described the sequelae of this decision:

> The *Police Correctionnelle*, by an excess of indulgence that one can hardly believe, absolved ... Sautemouche ... Someone recognised him, in a moment numerous citizens gathered; he was arrested, some wanted to take him to prison, others to throw him in the Saône; the crowd grew ... cries of à la lanterne were heard ... [preparations were made to string him up] when a blow from a sabre hit him on the left side, and he was killed; he was then thrown straight into the Saône.[40]

In this particular instance, Ampère patently held more concerns about the requirements of the law and the functioning of justice than the journalist appeared to have. Ampère stresses that he had found Sautemouche innocent of the charge, and it was his haste to get out of his 'irons' that led to his demise.[41] In his discussion of this case at his trial in November 1793, Ampère pointed out that as a result of his decision, 'most of the *sections* loudly demanded my own arrest, because I had obeyed my conscience and my opinion in freeing an innocent'.[42] The murder showed a continuing popular recourse to violence that persuaded the authorities to in fact hasten the action against the rest of the Jacobins in gaol.[43] Sautemouche had appealed for refuge to the *section* of Porte-Froc, which was sitting as an assembly at the time of his release, but he had been promptly ejected into the anti-Jacobin crowd.[44] It was the violence the *sans-culottes* visited on Sautemouche and the refusal of the *sections* to stop this violence that then helped strengthen the resolve of the municipality to curb the increasing threat of popular violence in Lyon. The mayor, Coindre, arranged for a notice to be printed and exhibited on 29 June that said that only the authorities should be 'the sword of the law' and warned that uncontrolled vengeance would not be tolerated.[45]

From this point, a more active response of the provisional municipality of Lyon to sectional violence also ensued. On 2 July, the municipality made the decision to disarm the troublesome Jacobin-influenced *sections* in Lyon. This followed a riot at the Saint-Georges *section*, where 2,000 women invaded an evening meeting and demanded that Chalier be released. They continued their demonstration outside his prison cell on the evening of 2 July. In response, the municipality took action the next day against Saint-Georges and another worker-dominated *section* called Gourguillon. The sectional gatherings in these two areas were confronted by troops and a cannon and ordered to deliver up their guns. The leaders of the suspected insurrection were taken to the Police Correctionnelle.[46]

Misunderstandings then escalated between Lyon and representatives of the National Convention, with both seemingly blinded to the disastrous effect of their different viewpoints on the other.[47] The Convention, after hearing reports from the *commissaires* Lindet and Couthon decreed on 3 July that the newly constituted authorities in Lyon would henceforth be responsible for the fate of those arrested, and they would 'answer individually, on their own heads, for attacks made against the safety of those arrested'.[48] On 4 July, the provisional municipality decided to ignore this strongly worded decree and reiterated the judicial listing of Chalier's crimes; his involvement in the secret meeting of 6 February and in the destabilising threats to use the guillotine and his responsibility for inciting those who had fired on the crowd of rebels in May 1793. They were unrepentant about the procedures begun against the incarcerated Jacobins and only sorry that some Jacobins, like the administrator Achard, had 'alone escaped the rage against rogues' so keenly felt by the city.[49] A speech on this same day presented by the Girondin Birotteau, claiming the new regime in Paris was illegitimate, was instrumental in the decision made by the Lyonnais that they would not recognise decrees made after this date. Birotteau had also called into Lyon while fleeing from house arrest in Paris after being dismissed from the Convention on 2 June and helped inflame passions, but even more influential was the arrival on 8 July of Chasset, the elected local deputy to the Convention, also fleeing from house arrest in Paris. Like Birotteau, he exaggerated the 'curse of anarchy and despotism' afflicting the city, claiming that some 250 Montagnards now in power were counter-revolutionary and were planning to 're-establish the *dîme*, feudal rights, all imposts and all the markers of the slavery of the *ancien regime*'.[50] There were in fact only fifty deputies identifying as Montagnards and many more who remained with the *'plaine'* or the middle ground, but by now Lyon was convinced that anarchy was indeed rife in the capital.[51]

The decision not to recognise decrees from Paris after 12 July meant the city disregarded the definitive order made in July to send the imprisoned Jacobins to Paris for their cases to be heard by the Revolutionary

Tribunal. An older law was found to support the Lyonnais position legally. It stated that those accused should be tried where the crimes had taken place.[52] A decision was made by the local administration that trials would commence against the Jacobins on 15 July before the juries and judges of the Tribunal Criminel and the much depleted Tribunal de District. New supplementary judges had been augmented, with judges from other districts of the Rhône-et-Loire replacing those Jacobins who had fled or were imprisoned.[53]

Ampère continued to issue warrants and interrogate those who were allegedly involved in the Jacobin resistance. He began investigating Achard because of his intention (as suspected by the provisional municipality) 'to arm the *sans-culottes* (the *canaille*), complete the formation of the revolutionary army, seize the arsenal and the store of gunpowder, to form a revolutionary tribunal and establish the guillotine in permanence'.[54] Achard – previously a surgeon – had been a leading member of the Jacobin *comités* and was alleged to have called the Armée des Alpes to Lyon. Ampère gathered evidence on 17 and 18 July from neighbours and on 19 July searched the premises of Achard with his assistants and an armed force. Inside the premises, Ampère came across Achard's domestic servant, Françoise Perris (aged 26), who agreed to open his desk and cupboards. Ampère extracted some letters, including one he kept as evidence of Achard's association with the judges, Chalier, Gaillard, Fillon and Gravier. In the letter, the 'friends' were reminded to never mention to anyone outside themselves their 'stormy' and 'scandalous' gatherings.[55] Ampère also searched the cellars and interrogated the domestic servant, Françoise Perris, about her master's absence. Although Achard was not found, Perris, despite her help in the search of the premises, was arrested for disturbing the peace in a neighbourhood of law-abiding citizens and their families and taken into custody.

When interviewed by Ampère, Perris was asked about secret correspondence with her master and about her knowledge of the 'massacres' of citizens that had taken place on 29 May and the arrests Achard had made as a member of the local Jacobin *comite*. The most damning evidence against her was the testimony of the neighbours who claimed she was, with her master, 'organising gatherings of men and women to protest about the events of 29 May'.[56] She had also been accused of indulging in 'grimaces', 'threats' and 'obscene remarks' since that date.[57] The choices Ampère made when confronted by the sort of social unrest that Perris and Achard represented were at best a triumph of conservatism and at worst a validation of the reactionary justice, which would eventually lead to the first use of the guillotine in the city.

Notes

1. M.-P. Gonon, *Lyon en 1793: Procès-verbaux authentiques et inédits du Comité de Surveillance de la section des Droits de l'Homm; l'une des 32 sections de cette commune pendant le siège* (Lyon: A. Mothon, 1847), 18.
2. Biard, *1793, Le siège de Lyon: Entre mythes et réalités* (Clermont-Ferrand: Lemme, 2013), 30.
3. Ibid.
4. Gonon presents the neo-Jacobin view that Chalier was the subject of slander and false claims including the fact that he wanted a 'Tribunal Révolutionnaire', fears of which led to the 'deplorable division' between Lyonnais. Gonon was writing some sixty years after the events he was annotating. See Gonon, *Lyon en 1793*, 5–8, 17.
5. Edmonds, *Jacobinism*, 116.
6. This play has been preserved in the Fonds Ampère of the Archives de l'Académie des Sciences [AAS] Chemise 292. One of the stage directions in Act IV suggests that a prison should be constructed in the background 'sur le plan de la Bastille'.
7. Edmonds, *Jacobinism*, 219–30. Edmonds recognised that the *sections* even in the poorer areas where popular democracy was stronger supported the decision to close down the clubs.
8. T. Koi, 'Réflexion sur la Révolution Français à Lyon', *La Révolution et nous – Blogue de historien Claude Guillon*. Retrieved 1 August 2018 from https://unsansculotte.wordpress.com/2018.
9. E. Herriot, *Lyon n'est plus*, Vol. 4, 85.
10. Quoted by Biard, *1793*, 10.
11. Biard, *1793*, 11.
12. Riffaterre, *Le Mouvement*, Vol. 1, 275–76.
13. Both these *juges de paix* were to be executed in the aftermath of the siege because of their proscription of the Jacobins. Edmonds, *Jacobinism*, 164, 302.
14. Amongst the documents gathered for his trial subsequent to the siege, there is a signed letter of 30 June 1793, where he advises of the risk to health of a contagion spreading to the community, first noted among the prisoners by the resident doctor. ADL 42 L 62.
15. Ampère's canton of Halle aux Blés did adjoin the canton of Chalier and was in fact in 1795 renamed as the Canton Chalier. The fact that he did not technically operate in the same canton meant he should not have been the relevant *juge de paix* as Chalier noted in his complaint from prison of 16 June. This letter is included in the archives with the papers used to establish the crime of Ampère: ADR 42 L 56.
16. ADR 42 L 56.
17. ADR 42 L 56.
18. See Chalier's allegation that he had prepared the *acte d'accusation* also contained in the letter of 16 June.
19. Riffaterre, *Le Mouvement*, 275–76.
20. E. Fayard, *Histoire des tribunaux* révolutionnaires de Lyon et de Feurs (Lyon: H. George, 1888), 112.
21. Chalier, Letter 16 June. ADR 42 L 56.
22. ADR 42 L 56.
23. Fayard, *Histoire des tribunaux*, 31.
24. Commissaire Gonchon wrote an inexact copy of the letter and sent it to the Minister of the Interior. He claimed the original had gone to Ampère. See Riffaterre, *Le Mouvement*, 196.
25. Riffaterre, *Le Mouvement*, 201–2.
26. Riffaterre, *Le Mouvement*, 258.

27. Gaillard managed to escape to Paris again, where he described his terrible experiences in gaol after he was arrested on 8 June. He then returned to Lyon after the siege with Collot d'Herbois and appointed to the *comité de surveillance*. In 1795, he resigned from this position and killed himself while in a depressed state. See A. Salomon de la Chapelle, *Documents sur la Révolution: Lyon et ses environs sous la Terreur 1793–1794* (Lyon: Librairie Générale Henri Georg, 1885), vii–viii.
28. ADR 1 L 375.
29. ADR 1 L 375.
30. ADR 42 L 62.
31. ADR 42 L 62.
32. Interrogatoire de J-J. Ampère ADR 42 L 62. The original documents in the Carteron case both appear only in the file of Ampère as evidence against the *juge de paix* in his own appearance before the Tribunal Révolutionnaire in November 1793, which leads to the conclusion that many other original documents were also not retained in the relevant Tribunal records.
33. This *acte d'accusation* is held in the Gadagne museum, an old hotel once owned by the Gadagne family and an important resource for the history of Lyon with its many rooms of objects, documents and engravings. Two rooms are dedicated to the revolutionary period.
34. On 10 October, Couthon declared that all these officers who had been 'thrown into cells by the aristocracy' were to be established in their previous municipal functions. See Fayard, *Histoire des tribunaux*, 52–53.
35. 'Acte d'accusation contre des officiers municipaux', 30 June 1793, from the collection of the Musée Gadagne.
36. ADR 36 L 57.
37. ADR 1 L 375.
38. Register of St Joseph prison, ADR 1 L 1202.
39. Riffaterre, *Le Mouvement*, 276–67.
40. C. Cave, *1793: L'Esprit des journaux* (Saint-Étienne: Publications de l'Université de Saint-Etienne, 1993), 174.
41. J-J. Ampère, 'Exposé', 9 October 1793. AAS, Fonds Ampère.
42. Fayard, *Histoire des Tribunaux*, 115.
43. Riffaterre, *Le Mouvement*, 275.
44. Edmonds, *Jacobinism*, 200.
45. AML 1 CM 3.
46. Eynard, *Joseph Chalier*, 145.
47. See the thesis of Michel Biard that there was a double blindness in Lyon as to what was happening in Paris and in Paris as to what was happening in Lyon and that these misconceptions grew over the course of the crisis. Biard, *1793*, 7.
48. Biard, *1793*, 11.
49. Extract of the register of the *Conseil Général de la commune provisoire de Lyon*, BML Fonds Coste, Ms 110960.
50. Biard, *1793*, 18.
51. Biard, *1793*, 18–19.
52. Fayard, *Histoire des tribunaux*, 30–31.
53. Riffaterre, *Le Mouvement*, 256.
54. Extract of the register of the Conseil Général, Fonds Coste, Ms 110960.
55. ADR 42 L 56.
56. Testimony of Sebastien Cochet, ADR, 42 L 62.
57. *Interrogatoire*, ADR 42 L 62.

Chapter 13

TERROR IN LYON

All individuals who fulfilled the function of juge de paix at the moment of the siege and who continued to do so to the moment of the expulsion of the rebels, are all deposed, with the exception of Citizen Fillion, one of them, who remains honourably exempted.

—Decree printed on 14 October 1793, signed by Couthon, representative-on-mission to Lyon

The town of Lyon will be destroyed: everything belonging to the rich will be destroyed. Only the houses of the poor will be left, those of patriots slaughtered and repressed, buildings used by industry, and monuments to humanity and education.

—Barère to the National Convention (as translated by P. McPhee)

Chalier was the first Jacobin to come to trial after the revolt against the municipality and was duly found guilty by the jury of having 'provoked murder and pillage by his writings and discourse' and for 'contributing to the massacre of 29 May'.[1] He was condemned to death the next day, on 16 July, by the Tribunal Criminel. The first official use of the guillotine was then necessitated but, because the machine had been damaged the previous year, it did not run smoothly. It took three drops of the blade to kill Chalier. The trial of the Jacobin Joseph Julliard, who had been elected to the position of *commandant-général* of the National Guard, was also held on the 15th and led to his acquittal. Several days later, on 22 July, Riard-Beauvernais, a battalion commander involved in the shooting on 29 May, was the second Jacobin to be convicted and executed by guillotine.

Those now in leadership roles, however, continued to proclaim their innocence of counter-revolutionary intention. The provisional municipality continued to try to convince the National Convention to withdraw its decrees, which suggested the city was counter-revolutionary. The Lyonnais also sent news to Paris that the majority of *sections* had voted for the acceptance of the new constitution on 28 July. On 30 July, they addressed a proclamation to neighbouring departments. In this proclamation, Lyon denied they were rebels or royalists. They reiterated that they had examined and accepted the new constitution, the *tricolore* flag flew above them and they offered the 'olive branch of peace'. Their arms would only be used against those who wanted to 'enslave them'.[2] But events had gone too far. Armed forces of the Convention were marching against Lyon.

The siege of Lyon began on 10 August 1793 when Republican troops began to encircle the city. From 22 August, bombardment commenced. During September, waves of bombing continued, largely to the peninsula area between the Saône and Rhône rivers, held by the rebel Lyonnais.

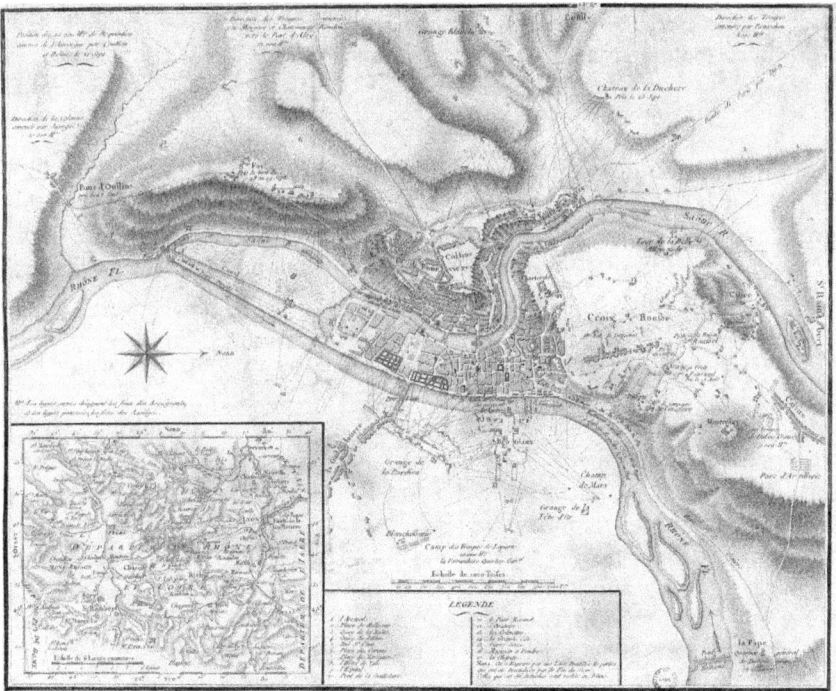

Figure 13.1 *Carte Siege de Lyon* (Map of Siege of Lyon). Bibliothèque Municipale de Lyon.

Amongst the notes General Doppet, leader of the republican forces, had collected about the conduct of the siege were the following observations: from 23 August until 29 September the national army exploded cannons and bombs almost daily 'as much during the night as the day'. Some 16,000 bombs or shells were thrown at the city, 800,000 rifle shots loosed, and 300,000 packets of gunpowder utilised. The anonymous writer noted there were cries of 'Vive la République' from both the besiegers and those under siege: 'the tricolour flag was in combat against the same colours . . . it was an explicable problem that hate had caused to happen, despite an apparent conformity of feelings.'[3]

Yet there were aristocrats and royalists in the city. Alexandrine des Écherolles, the young memoirist from an aristocratic family still in hiding in the city, remembered being part of a group enduring bombing in August:

> I did not sleep the first night of the bombardment: fear and curiosity even kept me awake for several more nights, as it did for everyone in the building. Several of them gathered in our apartment to spend the night . . . Everyone shared their doubts, their alarms; one would approach the window curiously only to withdraw in fright, when a bomb, exploding, sounded its thunderbolt. If death did not come with them, the bombs offered a pleasant spectacle . . . these trembling stars described an immense arc in the air and dropped with a whistle, to burst with a crash.[4]

Ampère, like other magistrates still working during the siege, had time to ponder his position as the political realities of the failed insurrection grew clearer, but the question remains unclear whether he knew about or wilfully ignored the evidence of the participation of counter-revolutionaries and *émigrés* in the battle during the closing weeks of the siege. What is clear is that he continued hearing cases; perhaps returning to the legalistic side of his work dulled his reaction to the dangers swirling around him.

Citizens continued to present complaints of criminal actions against their person or property to their local *juge de paix* and denunciations against those they considered responsible for criminal action against the nation. Ampère continued receiving such complaints and making decisions on the spot in smaller cases, or assessing their suitability to be passed on to a higher court when required.[5] The Citizeness Claudine Henriette Archimbaud was brought before him on 10 September. She was a seamstress suspected of having passed forged *assignats* and to have evaded prosecution. She claimed to have absconded because she had been 'bombarded for the first time and was seized with fright'.[6] Ampère accepted her explanation and found her not guilty. Another matter heard on 19 September 1793 was more cause for concern. Ampère was informed of a death impacting the life of one of the prisoners under his responsibility. The former home of Citizen Binard, an inmate of the Roanne prison, had been hit by a bomb on the previous evening. His wife had been killed, their furniture had been left unprotected, and arrangements were urgently needed for the care of their very young children.[7] When these facts were made known to him, Ampère ordered the man be taken immediately by two National Guard members to his former domicile to make the necessary arrangements. Binard, according to the Register of Denunciations made after the siege of Lyon, was one of the 'patriots' incarcerated before the siege had commenced.[8] The *juge de paix* must have felt some horror at the fact that the man was unable to protect his family because of his imprisonment on a political charge.

After two months of siege, the encirclement by national forces became more complete, food supplies dwindled and the commander of the rebels, Précy, escaped the city. The city surrendered, and General Doppet entered at the head of the national army on 8 October. He soon after released the 'honourable victims of patriotism' as he called the imprisoned Jacobins and posted troops throughout the city while the representatives-on-mission reinstalled the municipality of 29 May.[9] Between 9 and 16 October 1793, Georges Couthon, representing the national Comité du Salut Public, was personally charged with imposing punishment on the city of Lyon. The Lyonnais were starving, and their insurrectionary army under the leadership of Count Précy had fled. Couthon noted that the city was affected both by the inward looking 'character of isolation' it had pursued since it had expelled the Jacobins from municipal office in June and by the terrible mists of the two rivers, the Saone and the Rhône, which flowed around the city, to which he attributed their otherwise inconceivable actions.[10] He caused extracts of the minutes of the National Convention to be affixed to the walls of the city, proclaiming: 'Lyon made war against the forces of liberty; Lyon is no more'.[11] Henceforth it was to be called Ville Affranchi or 'Liberated City'.

Couthon was then deputised by the National Convention to find the 'conspirators' responsible for attempting to 'overturn the Republic and re-establish Royalty'. The first decisions of culpability were made by Couthon under the authority of a military commission and soon after by the *commission populaire* presided over by Philippe Antoine Dorfeuille. By 27 November, a local Revolutionary Tribunal was organised.[12] Those elected judges who had been so devoted to the new institutions of justice but who had remained in the city during the siege were immediately indicted. Those who had been imprisoned by their fellow judges at the height of the crisis in May 1793 were released and reinstated to their previous positions. Their former inquisitors were as a result some of the first Lyonnais to be convicted of counter-revolutionary activity. The assemblies of the *sections* of the city who had supported the popular uprising and had formed the backbone of the provisional government were also imprisoned. The military commission began to charge those who were found in possession of arms, which was in contravention of the national decrees.[13]

Dorfeuille proclaimed that the death of Chalier would be morally avenged in a public ceremony on 28 October held in the Place des Terreaux. He told the Lyonnais:

> In this regenerated city and within these purified walls we wanted to enact this ceremony of a renewed people using the heavenly skies as a dome, with the stars for lamps and liberty as the Pontiff... he was assassinated, him for whom we shed our tears, assassinated judicially... Monsters! Those who have committed this infamy... Chalier, I promise you here, in the name of the French people... [those] Aristocrates, fanatics, snakes of the courts, executioners who have accused and condemned you... brigands... Cry, cry everyone and let your tears today be our sole eloquence.[14]

Dorfeuille used the language of fanaticism against those who had condemned the Jacobins. He reasserted the moral authority of the law against them. Just as Ampère had called the Jacobin judges to account in May and June 1793 for the 'conspiracy' of February–May of that year, so by November he was called to account for his own infamous actions but mostly for his role in the indictment of Chalier. Ampère was in his turn driven to write of his ignominious treatment; he had been manhandled by a young gunner of the republican army who held two fingers to his temple like a mock pistol and pointed him out to the rest of the army as if he were a 'chief of the Vendée'.[15] While imprisoned, Ampère was given the regulation diet of bread and water and slept on the regulation amount of straw in his cell.

Because of his active involvement in the judicial administration of the city during the siege, it was inevitable that Ampère would be identified and arrested as a key rebel. In his exposé written while in prison, he accepted that he had commenced many proceedings against the Jacobins but denied that he had sentenced them. He claimed to have only dealt with those citizens who had tried to 'inflame' the population on the day of 29 May 1793 and stated that he did no more than he was required to do by the law. He was also keen to remind his captors that he had seen his duty as 'comforting many of those who were in prison who were unable to be interrogated because of the multitude of cases waiting to be heard', and he had hastened to set the patriot Sautemouche free when he found there was no evidence to hold him. This action itself led to the death of the former municipal officer but through no fault of his own because the former prisoner 'succumbed to the blows of those intent on malicious action (*malveillants*)'. It was for this reason he said that he counselled the other patriots in gaol not to take the same risk. He said that he 'preferred that they stay in prison' rather than their lives be similarly put in danger. Ampère claimed that he had been constantly attempting to deal equally as much with the agitation of counter-revolutionaries in his work.[16] Ampère did not address the political nature of his actions, his disquiet at the arrests and prosecutions that the Jacobin judges had effected and his efforts to enable their prosecution because of his fear that their articulation of the 'rule of law' was plainly wrong.

At his trial on 22 November, Ampère was accused of being involved in a 'conspiracy' against the Jacobins. He was not permitted to elaborate on his motivation for the actions he had taken but only to answer the points that were put to him to support his prosecution. They were, first, that he had stayed in Lyon during the period of the siege, which he admitted; and that he had set up the preliminary inquiries of patriots, including the 'virtuous Chalier', as president of the Tribunal Correctionnel. Ampère agreed he had set up the preliminary inquiries, as he was required to do, but added that he had played no part in the judgments made against the accused in the higher courts – again, a clear attempt to exculpate himself from any political agenda. He reminded the questioners that he had let Sautemouche free because he 'obeyed his conscience and his opinion in not detaining an innocent'.[17] Ampère was asked whether he had had any correspondence with the provisional authorities during the siege, which he denied. As to whether he had sent a retraction of his actions, as required by the National Convention, he said he had no retraction to give. When he was asked whether he had prepared the mandate of arrest against Chalier, he agreed that he had done so. This crime was considered one of the most serious because Chalier was now widely seen as a martyr, and Ampère's acknowledgment of his involvement in the execution, however it was characterised, was more than enough to justify his indictment. At this stage, the interrogation and any further opportunity to reply was stopped. A further witness was called for the prosecution. He was Gilbert Roch, one of the municipal officers arrested by Ampère by the 31 May *acte d'accusation*. Roch confirmed that Ampère had interrogated and commenced proceedings against patriots. In a final ironic twist, Roch alleged that Ampère had forced those Jacobins who he had accused to confess and had truncated their questioning once they did so.[18]

Ampère was then taken before the Tribunal Révolutionnaire, where he was found guilty of having begun vexatious proceedings against

Figure 13.2 *Tribunal révolutionnaire de Lyon* (Revolutionary Tribunal of Lyon), woodcut inv. N 3188 © Musée Gadagne (Lyon).

patriots (especially those who were 'clubbistes'); of enabling the projects of the counter-revolutionaries and participating in the revolt; of sitting as President of the Tribunal Correctionnel during the siege; of not having made a retraction; and, finally, of having prepared the arrest warrant against Chalier.[19] He was condemned to death and his belongings were confiscated. Ampère was again humiliated with a placard on his back, calling attention to his role as '*juge de paix* responsible for the arrest warrant against Chalier' as he was led to the guillotine the next day.[20]

Collot d'Herbois and Joseph Fouché were next appointed by the National Convention as *représentants en mission* to address the administrative issues in Lyon after the siege. They were not inclined to be lenient on those who had taken such drastic action against local Jacobins. They had orders to punish and continue to stabilise Ville Affranchie.[21] They set up a temporary *comité de surveillance républicaine* to punish those guilty of insurgency, and on 16 November they published a notice setting out the crimes of the rebel Lyonnais and the changes that would now take place. This document articulated five main goals. The first was to revitalise the *esprit révolutionnaire*, which was interpreted as the well-being of the *sans-culottes*, founded on the concept of 'free men'. The second was the arrest of suspects – those who had shown contempt for the *sans-culottes*. A 'total revolution' was required to be directed against the infamous rich, who had subverted the values of the revolution. All good republicans were exhorted to rise up against the rich oppressors to help arrest suspects, traitors (*les Dumouriez*). The third goal was a revolutionary tax to cover the expenses of war. The fourth goal was the provisioning of the markets and making food available for the people. The final goal was that all priests and 'fanatics' needed to be extirpated and the crimes of the rebels dealt with.[22] The Jacobins who had been languishing in gaol were put back into their administrative positions and manned new *comités de surveillance* in charge of deciding which goods would be confiscated from the rebels.[23]

The new authorities proposed a horrendous punishment that involved the firing of a cannon at a line of chained prisoners in the fields of Brotteaux. This punishment was envisaged as a powerful, almost allegorical statement to terrify those who would threaten the unity of the nation.[24] It was

Figure 13.3 *Mitraillade des Lyonnais aux Brotteaux* (Massacre of Lyonnais at Brotteaux). Engraving by Paul Constant Soyer after Paul-Jean Flandrin, 1845, inv. N 1945.16. © Musées Gadagne (Lyon).

a theatrical example of the 'terrible justice' the nation needed to impose.[25] This brutal but ineffective method of killing declared enemies, however, quickly became soul destroying for those who witnessed it and those who had to enact the punishment. Many prisoners were only wounded and had to be individually bludgeoned or shot by troops on hand, and this method was soon discontinued. The remaining accused were killed by firing squad or guillotine.

Notes

1. Judgment of Cozon in the trial of Chalier, Fonds Coste, Ms 625.
2. Quoted in E. Fayard, *Histoire des tribunaux révolutionnaires de Lyon et de Feurs* (Lyon: H. George, 1888), 36.
3. M.P. Gonon, *Lyon en 1793: Procès-verbaux authentiques et inédits du Comité de Surveillance de la section des Droits de l'Homme; L'une des 32 sections de cette commune pendant le siege* (Lyon: A. Mothon, 1847), 179–80.
4. A. des Écherolles, *Une famille noble sour la Terreur*, vol. 1, 78.
5. The case of Adier and Lachaux concerned the stealing of a silver watch. The accused was interviewed by Ampère and found not guilty by the jury of the Tribunal District on 15 August: ADR 39 L 59.
6. ADR 41 L 8.
7. ADR 1 L 982.
8. ADR 42 L 62.
9. 'Rapport' by Doppet, in Gonon, *Lyon en 1793*, 177.
10. Georges Couthon, Letter, October 1793, trans. by Mitch Abidor at Marxists.org., accessed 19 December 2016, http://www.marxists.org/history/france/revolution/1793/wretched-city.htm.
11. E. Herriot, *Lyon n'est plus: La repression*, Vol. 3 (Paris: Hachette, 1939), 27.
12. P. Mansfield, 'The Management of Terror in Montgnard Lyon, Year II', *European History Quarterly* 20 (1990), 467.
13. E. Herriot, *Lyon n'est plus*, Vol. 3, 5–12.
14. BML Fonds Coste, 114667.
15. Jean-Jacques Ampère, 'Exposé', 9 October 1793. ADR 42 L 62.
16. 'Exposé', ADR 42 L 62.
17. See the trial transcript in Fayard, *Histoire des tribunaux*, 114–15.
18. Ibid.
19. Fayard, *Histoire des tribunaux*, 116.
20. G. Eynard, *Joseph Chalier: Bourreau ou martyr, 1747–1793* (Lyon: Éd. lyonnaises d'art et d'histoire, 1987), 181.
21. See Paul Mansfield for a discussion of the centralist Montagnard control behind the policies of repression. 'The Management of Terror in Montagnard Lyon, Year II', 465–96.
22. A. Salomon de la Chapelle, *Documents sur la Révolution: Lyon et ses environs sous la Terreur 1793–1794* (Lyon: Librairie Générale Henri Georg, 1885), 27–30.

23. P. Chopelin, *Un Cancer politique? Vies et morts des comités de surveillance de la ville de Lyon (1792–1795)'*, in D. Pingué and J.-P. Rothiot, *Les Comités de surveillance: D'une création citoyenne à une institution révolutionnaire* (Paris: Société des études Robespierristes, 2012), 197.
24. W. Edmonds, *Jacobinism and the Revolt of Lyon, 1789–1793* (New York: Oxford University Press, 1990), 287–88. Edmonds described the 'thunderbolt' of national revenge as quickly seen as a 'bloody shambles'.
25. Mansfield, 'The Management of Terror', 465–96.

Conclusion

The judicial feud in Lyon had begun with disagreements among the elected magistrates about how to effect revolutionary justice as early as 1792. Judges had slowly developed different political agendas by force of their very different revolutionary experiences and expectations. Most of the new men of law in Lyon elected in 1791–92 were bourgeois property owners and tended to identify with the Rolandin viewpoint. Even some of those elected, like Billiemas and L'Ange, who professed quite advanced social ideas accepted the political leadership of the Rolandins as to how law and order should be used to defeat 'fanaticism' and 'anarchy'. They believed that social violence would be lessened in their city because of their strong advocacy for a clear 'rule of law'. Yet when a wider franchise was achieved in 1792, more judges came to challenge the world view of the Rolandin judges. The relatively early appearance of ultra-democratic judges in the elections at the end of this year made the political divisions in the magistracy sharper in the city and the question of what constituted the 'rule of law' a fiercely contested one.

Chalier found allies among the working-class leaders like Dodieu and Hidins, who thought, as he did, that the judiciary should become more concerned about the indictment and conviction of enemies of the Revolution. From September 1792 and into the new year, these judges were at the coalface as the Republic navigated growing threats of internal and external war. They had to deal with crimes unanticipated by the Code Pénal, with the machinations and plots of *émigrés* and refractory clergy. The Jacobins by early 1793 came to the conclusion there was a need for the operation of new revolutionary tribunals. The Rolandins, however, continued to assert that the already established courts should only address the questions of culpability and punishment of any accused by reference to the uniform Code Pénal, and they refused to acknowledge the need for exceptional tribunals. If there was no crime found by the evidence that related to a crime described in the code, the judges had to dismiss the case, which they did on a number of occasions.[1] They argued that the courts were not empowered to hold people on suspicion of counter-revolutionary intention or to excuse them because of political reasons. The Jacobins challenged the view that convictions of guilt could only be made in cases where the crimes were clearly established by the new transparent code without any attempt to mediate the needs of the revolutionary state in a time of crisis.

These arguments and counter-arguments were expressed frequently in the judgments delivered in the courts of Lyon during the early part of 1793. The factionalism affecting the magistrates, which became more evident during the trial of the king, increased locally until there were clearly opposed groups who viewed the decisions of the 'other' to be infected by deeply suspicious motives. Angry accusations were then made about the existence of plots and conspiracies, and the virtues (or lack of them) of legal practitioners were regularly called into question. The Rolandins accused the Jacobins of corruption, and some important cases, including that pursued against the family of the Jacobin Commissaire National Hidins, were found to have some substance. The Jacobin judges, led by Chalier, remained convinced that 'aristocratic' judges were trying to subvert the Revolution itself by their legalistic manipulation of the legal process they observed taking place after the Jacobin headquarters were pillaged in February of 1793. It was believed that one particular Judge, Bertholon, had actually let guilty prisoners go free before trial.

These divergent viewpoints played out before the various criminal tribunals of the city. Judicial feuding was a very real and observable phenomenon, and it finally culminated in the dramatic arrest of Chalier in June 1793 by his fellow judge Ampère, who had become convinced that the Jacobins were guilty of a wide-ranging conspiracy. They had begun by ignoring the provisions of the Code Pénal in their haste to prosecute and imprison innocent people, pushing for illegal tribunals and arrests as part of a plot that led to the deaths of citizens. Finally Ampère was himself found guilty of conspiracy and fanaticism by his framing of these alleged crimes against those whose virtues were subsequently rehabilitated. Strong emotions and language reinforced the convictions of the legal practitioners in Lyon and caused them to question the revolutionary virtue and conduct of their counterparts. The split among the magistrates thus played a big part in the uprising against the Jacobin municipality of 1793 and the imprisonment thereafter of elected judicial and political officials. The rival conceptions of the 'rule of law' held by the magistrates had led directly to the Jacobin judge Chalier being sentenced to death and indirectly to his status as a martyr when the city was taken by national forces after the subsequent siege. The rage felt by the Montagnards in

Paris at his treatment sealed the fate of those Lyonnais eventually held responsible. The magistrates remained divided politically as the city plunged into civil war and their competing interpretations of the 'rule of law' justified an otherwise inexplicable turn to violence.

Looking at the history of Lyon and the Revolution, we can thus see how the factional divides that were so noticeable in Paris at the time of the king's trial also affected the local magistracy. The notion of 'conspiracy' was widely used by the Rolandins and the Jacobins in Lyon to describe the treachery of their political opponents, but it also became a common suspicion used against fellow magistrates. The term 'fanaticism' had a similar power to inspire outrage and fear as did 'conspiracy' and 'terror'. The failure of politicians and justices to live up to their original ideal of revolutionary 'virtue', as explained by Marisa Linton, does help explain these continuing denunciations and the eventual recourse to violence of both judicial and political adversaries.[2] By the time of the repression of Lyon, the nation through its representative Couthon then felt justified in using 'terror' against the 'traitors' and 'brigands'. According to a commentator on contemporary events, Rosalie Jullien, even to come from Lyon now appeared to be a crime, a situation she was prepared to accept in spite of the injustice to some individuals.[3]

Looking back to the early stages of the Revolution, neither Ampère nor Chalier could have envisaged the situation they found themselves in as they faced the guillotine in 1793. As they separately contemplated the end of their lives, they were also forced to contemplate how their actions would be perceived in historical terms. Both had come from similar careers in the silk industry and were elected as magistrates in the new institutions of justice set up by the Revolution after 1791. However, despite their championing of the progressive reforms in revolutionary justice, they came to represent the different sides of the republican debate in this jurisdiction. By February 1793, they had become implacable enemies and were expressing incompatible ideas of how revolutionary justice should be exercised and to what ends. Both also died before the full tragic consequences of their schism were unleashed on the general population. Their last letters prior to execution mirror similar sentiments and show how they both still felt themselves to be at the centre of the drama. Chalier's declaration to his loved ones ran as follows:

> I have loved all humanity and liberty, and my enemies, my executioners who are my judges have sent me to my death. I am going to return to the bosom of eternity ... if the sacrifice of my life could suffice for all my enemies, who are those of liberty, I die innocent of all the crimes that are alleged against me.[4]

Figure 14.1 *Chalier partant de sa prison* (Chalier leaving his prison). Bibliothèque Municipale de Lyon.

His last words to the Abbé La Sausse, who accompanied him to the guillotine, were the following: 'I have only one favour to ask of the people of Lyon, it is that I be the only victim and that they will pardon all the others.'[5]

Ampère in his instructions for his wife also expressed his love of his country and said:

> I regret nothing but the misfortune of being misunderstood [by my country], for to be condemned by my enemies or those who are envious of me affects me less than my astonishment. I have never had anything other than the aptitude for and the passion of my duty. I have neither repented nor expressed remorse and am always worthy of your esteem.[6]

Before going to the guillotine, Ampère wrote these last words:

> I hope that my death will be the seal of a general reconciliation between all our people [*frères*]. I pardon those who rejoice at it, those who have caused it, and those who ordered it. I have reason to believe that the national vengeance, of which I am one of the most innocent victims, will not extend to our meagre belongings.[7]

Both men appeared to be genuinely amazed at how their motives were misconstrued, how their attachment to their civic duty was lost in the recriminations brought against them. Yet their actions had directly led to the repression of Lyon when thousands of citizens were killed by guillotine, by hangings and the fusillades carried out on the fields of the Brotteaux, and by the firing of a cannon. Events in Lyon had profoundly tipped the scale for considering the use of the salutary laws of 'terror', and the new judicial systems inaugurated by the Revolution would forever be tarnished as a result.

Notes

1. E.H. Lemay and A. Patrick, *Revolutionaries at Work: The Constituent Assembly 1789-1791* (Oxford, 1996), 87.
2. P. Campbell, T. Kaiser and M. Linton focused on the fear of 'conspiracy' in the new 'transparent political system' of elected government. P.R. Campbell et al. (eds), *Conspiracy in the French Revolution* (Manchester University Press, 2007). Linton's later work on virtue and denunciation among the revolutionaries went further and suggested that public officials claiming the 'moral legitimacy' of 'political virtue' interpreted the actions of their fellow officers as motivated by ambition and dissimulation and were then able to justify policies of 'Terror'. M. Linton, *Choosing Terror: Virtue, Friendship and Authenticity in the French Revolution* (Oxford, 2013), 7–8, 48, 75.
3. T. Tackett, *The Coming of the Terror in the French Revolution* (Cambridge, MA: The Belknap Press of Harvard University Press, 2015), 303.
4. Tackett, *The Coming of the Terror*, 167.
5. Tackett, *The Coming of the Terror*, 168–69.
6. Ampère, 'Instructions pour ma femme', 17 October 1793. ADR 42 L 62.
7. Ampère, Letter, 23 November 1793. ADR 42 L 62.

GLOSSARY OF TERMS

Active citizens: Those who had the necessary property qualification to allow them to vote in primary assemblies; those who paid direct taxes.

Ancien régime: Term used by revolutionaries to refer to the old order of absolute monarchy in France and Europe before 1789.

Assignats: Credit bonds used in payment for *biens nationaux* (the former property of the churches). Their use as paper money contributed to growing inflation.

Biens nationaux: Nationalised property previously owned by the church or *émigrés* used to raise revenue.

Cahiers de doléances: Notices of grievances prepared before the meeting of the Estates-General.

Canton: Administrative divisions within the districts of France, which were in turn part of the eighty departments.

Chalier-Jacobins: The name sometimes given to those members of the Central Club in Lyon who followed Joseph Chalier.

Commissaires: Delegates or envoys sent out by the Convention to the provinces or the army as representatives-on-mission.

Constitutional clergy: The reforming clergy who swore an oath to uphold the Constitution and were thence paid a state salary.

Consulate: The name for regions ruled by local consuls and an Intendant appointed by the king.

Curé: The parish priest in charge of 'curing the souls' of his parishioners.

Émigrés: Those who decided to leave France at the time of the Revolution for political reasons, often of noble families.

Estates-General: An assembly meeting that included representatives from the Three Estates of France.

Feuillant: Staunch constitutional monarchs who resigned from the Jacobin club after the flight of the king in June 1791.

Jacobins: The name given to the early revolutionaries who met in the convent of the Jacobin friars. It became more closely associated with those who sought radical changes after August and September of 1792.

Juge de paix: Elected justice of the peace who was paid by the state to assist the people of his canton in civil and criminal jurisdictions. He was responsible for the initiation of all matters before the courts and a number of police functions.

Menu peuple: The groups of poorer people of the towns.

Modérées: The moderate patriots who distinguished themselves from extremist Jacobins after 1792.

Négociants: The grand merchants who negotiated contracts.

Octrois: Internal tax paid on goods entering past the city customs barriers.

Parlements: The independent courts of appeal in the *ancien régime*, who claimed political rights and registered royal edicts. They were replaced in 1791 by the new judicial structures.

Patriots: The name given to those who identified with the new ideas associated with revolutionary changes from 1788–89 and which was still in use at the time of the First Republic in 1792.

Procureur: Magistrate at the heart of the system of justice, who had a prosecution role.

Procureur fiscal: Tax official.

Quartiers: The neighbourhood groupings that became the basis for the political *sections*.

Refractory priests: Those priests who refused to take the oath to the Constitution, preferring to remain faithful to the Pope.

Revolutionary tribunals: Exceptional courts that followed emergency procedures during periods of revolutionary crises.

Rolandins: Originally a derogatory term that came to mean the political group who followed Roland in advocating revolutionary change but also usually desirous of maintaining internal free trade and the law of the market.

Sans-culottes: The French term meaning literally those who were 'without breeches'. It referred to those who wore trousers and not the breeches of the upper classes.

Sections: Electoral units based on the districts.

Seigneur: The lord or principal landowner of the feudal regime.

Taxation Populaire: A fixed but fair price imposed on goods by social activists.

Third Estate: The Third Estate was the social group comprised of all those not in a religious order (the First Estate) or who did not hold a noble title (the Second Estate).

Traboules: Covered passageways that allowed people to pass directly through buildings to avoid the winding streets in Lyon and reach the river.

Glossary of Names

Ampère, Jean-Jacques. *Négociant*, father of André-Marie (the savant who wrote about electromagnetic theory), elected *juge de paix*, President of the Tribunal Correctionnel.

Chalier, Joseph. *Négociant*, member of the Commission of Commerce and Industry, became a judge of the Tribunal de conservation (Tribunal de commerce) and the Tribunal de District as well as President of the Tribunal Correctionnel.

Cusset, Joseph-Marie. Silk industry. Elected as a deputy to the National Convention, where he sat with the 'Mountain'.

Delandine, François. Librarian and academician who wrote the *Tableaux des prisons de Lyon* after having himself been incarcerated.

Dodieu, Antoine-Marie (later known as Manlius). A printer by trade and president of the radical *section* based around the *quartier* of Rue Juiverie. Became 'Director' of the jury.

Gilibert, Jean-Emanuel. President La Croisette *section*. Elected mayor after resignation of Nivière-Chol but was imprisoned by the Jacobins and later resigned.

Hidins, Rousseau. Jacobin Commissaire National.

Imbert-Colomès, Jacones. The last Consul of the city.

L'Ange, François-Joseph. An 'artiste' of the silk industry, driven by a concern for social justice, *juge de paix*.

Nivière-Chol, Antoine. Rolandin, Judge on the Tribunal Correctionel, Mayor of Lyon.

Perisse-Duluc, Jean-Andre. From a family of booksellers. Freemason. Elected a deputy for the Third Estate to the Estates-General Member of the National Assembly.

Pressavin, Jean-Baptiste. Surgeon, substitute *procureur*, Deputy to the National Convention.

Soufflot, Jacques-Germaine. Architect.

Vitet, Louis. Mayor of Lyon, deputy to the National Convention (excluded 31 May 1793).

Bibliography

Archival Sources

Archives départementales du Rhône

La Série L: Documents de la période révolutionnaire 1790-AN VIII.

Sous-série 1 L: Département du Rhône (et Loire):
  1 L 336, 1 L 375, 1 L 378, 1 L 469, 1 L 981–6, 1 L 1080, 1 L 1095, 1 L 1202, 34 L 23.
Sous-série 35 L: Justice révolutionnaire:
  35 L 14, 35 L 18, 35 L 19, 35 L 27, 35 L 28.
Sous-série 36 L: Tribunal de district (Lyon-Ville):
  36 L 57, 36 L 60, 36 L 96 /97, 36 L 105.
Sous-série 37 L: Tribunal de district (Lyon-Campagne):
  37 L 35.
Sous-série 39 L: Tribunal criminel du Rhône:
  39 L 5, 39 L 22–39, 39 L 58/59/60, 39 L 105.
Sous-série 41 L: Tribunaux correctionnels:
  41 L 6 (1791), 41 L 7 (1792), 41 L 8 (1793).
Sous-série 42 L: Tribunaux révolutionnaires:
  42 L 56, 42 L 59, 42 L 60, 42 L 62.
Sous-série 44 L: Tribunaux de Paix:
  44 L 89, 44 L 109 (1791), 44 L 110/111 (1792–3).

Archives Communales, État Civil (Poleymieux)

EDEPOT 153

Archives municipales de Lyon

1 (2) 3, 1 (2) 4.
2 I 2, 2 I 20.

Séances Municipaux

1 CM 1 (1790), 1 CM 2, 1 CM 3. Archives en ligne: URL: http://www.archives-lyon.fr/.
Affiches. Archives en ligne: URL: http://www.archives-lyon.fr/.
Registres paroissiaux et d'état civil. Archives en ligne: URL: http://www.archives-lyon.fr/.
La Grande Fabrique de Soie. Archives en ligne: URL: http://www.archives-lyon.fr/.

Archives nationales

D/XXIX/65.
2 B 348, 2 B 114.

Archives parlementaires

Cahiers des doléances pour les États-Généraux de 1789.
Archives en ligne: URL: gallica.bnf.fr/.

Archives de l'Académie des Sciences Paris (Fonds André-Marie Ampère)

Ampère, Jean-Jacques. *Artaxerce et Pièces diverses concernant Jean-Jacques Ampère*, Chemise 292.
Autobiographie, André-Marie Ampère, Chemise 326. Archives en ligne: URL: http://www.ampere.cnrs.fr/manuscrits/catalogueAS.pdf.
Correspondance. Chemise 323–372. URL: http://www.ampere.cnrs.fr/.

Bibliothèque municipale de Lyon (Fonds Coste, Desvernay et Molinier)

Achard: Ms 110957, 110960, 534, 545.
Baille: Ms 601.
Bertrand: Ms 592.
Chalier: Ms 289, 549, 551, 565, 589, 609, 620, 622, 625.
Dodieu: Ms 559, 615.
Grégoire: Ms 569.
Hidins: Ms 558, 582, 608.
Jacobins: Ms 560.
Jolyclerc: Ms 597.
L'Ange: Ms 984.

Primary Printed Sources

Newspapers

Courrier de Lyon 1790–91.
La Feuille Villageoise
Journal de Lyon 1791–93.

Printed and Electronic Sources

Aulard, F. (ed.). *La Société des Jacobins: recueil de documents pour l'histoire de club des Jacobins de Paris*. Tome V. Paris: 1889–97.
Cahier des doléances du Beaujolais par les États-Généraux de 1789. Lyon: Imprimerie Nouvelle Lyonnaise, 1939.
Cave, C. *1793: l'esprit des journaux*. Saint-Étienne: Publications de l'Université de Saint-Étienne, 1993.
Chevreux, H. *Journal et Correspondance de André-Marie Ampère*. Paris: Hetzel, 1872.
Couthon, G. Affiche, 14.10.1793, ADR I L 981.
_____. 'Letter to National Convention 1793'. Translated by Mitchell Abidor at Marxists.org. Retrieved 19 December 2016 from: http://www.marxists.org/history/france/revolution/1793/wretched-city.htm.

Delandine, A.F. *Tableau des prisons de Lyon, pour server à l'histoire de la tyrannie de 1792 et 1793*. Lyon: Daval, 1797.
Dwyer, P. and P. McPhee (eds). *The French Revolution and Napoleon: A Sourcebook*. Hoboken: Taylor and Francis, 2002.
Écherolles, A. des. *Une Famille noble sous la Terreur*. Vols I and II. Paris: Librairie Plon, 1879 [and Paris: Elibron Classics, 2006].
Gonon, M.-P. *Lyon en 1793: Procès-verbaux authentiques et inédits du Comité de Surveillance de la section des Droits de l'Homme; L'une des 32 sections de cette commune pendant le siège*. Lyon: A. Mothon, 1847.
Guillon, A. *Histoire du siège de Lyon, des événements qui l'ont précédé et des désastres qui l'ont suivi, ainsi que de leurs causes secrètes, générales et* particulières, 2 vols. Paris: Le Clère, an V, 1797.
L'Ange, F.-J. *Adresse à mille Français de Lyon*. Lyon: Louis Cutty, 1792.
Laukhard, F.-C. *Un Allemand en France sous la terreur: souvenirs de Frédéric-Christian Laukhard. 1792–1794*. Paris: Perrin, 1915.
Launay, L. de. *Correspondance du Grand Ampère*. Paris: Librairie Gauthier-Villars, 1936.
Metastasio, P. *Oeuvres de L'Abbé Metastase, trad. de l'italien par Bonnet de Chemlin*. Paris: Delormel, 1749.
Pressavin, J.-B. 'Rapport fait au Conseil du District de Lyon; par M. Pressavin, un de ses membres', in *Divers écrits de Lyon sur la Révolution* (Canberra: National Library of Australia, n.d.), 1–18.
_____. *Nouveau traité des vapeurs ou traité des maladies des nerfs*. Lyon, 1770.
Reichardt, J.F. *Un Prussien en France en 1792: Lettres intimes de J.F. Reichardt*. Paris: Perrin, 1892.
Roland de la Platière, J.-M. *An Appeal to Impartial Posterity by Citizenness Roland*. Oxford and New York: Woodstock Books, 1990.
Rousseau, J.-J. *Émile*. London: Everyman's Library, 1974.
Salomon de la Chapelle, A. (ed.). *Documents sur la Révolution: Lyon et ses environs sous la Terreur 1793–1794*. Lyon: Librairie Générale Henri Georg, 1885.
Stewart, J.H. (ed.). *A Documentary Survey of the French Revolution*. New York: MacMillan Company, 1951.
Vurpas, A.-M. and J. Filleul (eds.). *Les chansons Lyonnaises à l'époque Révolutionnaire*. Lyon: Editions lyonnaises d'art et d'histoire, 1987.

Secondary Sources

Ado, A. *Paysans en Révolution: Terre, pouvoir et jacquerie, 1789–1794*. Paris: Société des études Robespierristes, 1996.
Allen, R. *Les Tribunaux criminels sous la Révolution et l'Empire 1792–1811*. Translated by James Steven Bryant. Rennes: Presses Universitaires de Rennes, 2005.
Andress, D. *The Terror: The Merciless War for Freedom in Revolutionary France*. New York: Farrar, Straus and Giroux, 2007.
_____. (ed.). *The Oxford Handbook of the French Revolution*. Oxford: Oxford University Press, 2015.
Angleraud B. et al., *Femmes de Lyon*. Lyon: Editions Lyonnaises d'Art et d'Histoire, 2016.
Audin, A. *La Conspiration Lyonnaise de 1790 et le drame de Poleymieux*. Lyon: Éd. Lyonnaises d'art et d'histoire, 1984.

Balleydier, A. *Histoire politique et militaire du people de Lyon pendant la Révolution Française, 1789–1795*. Paris, 1816.
Beaurepaire, P.-Y. *Le Mythe de l'Europe française au XVIIIe siècle: Diplomatie, culture et sociabilités au temps des Lumières*. Paris: Éd. Autrement, 2007.
Benoît, B. 'Assassinat d'un soldat Suisse à Lyon le 19 juillet 1790', in *Actes du 112e Congrès National des Sociétés Savantes* (Paris: Éditions du CTHS, 1987), 91–98.
———. 'Analyse des violences urbaines à l'époque révolutionnaire: l'exemple Lyonnais', in B. Benoît (ed.), *Ville et Révolution Française: Actes du Colloque International, Lyon, Mars 1993* (Lyon: Presses universitaires de Lyon, 1994), 147–62.
———. 'Histoire, mémoire et identité politique: L'exemple de la Révolution à Lyon'. *Annales historiques de la Révolution Française* 305 (1996).
———. *L'Identité politique de Lyon: Entre violences collectives et mémoire des élites, 1786–1905*. Paris: L'Harmattan, 2000.
———. 'Lyon rouge ou/et blanc 1789–1799: Approche historique et historiographique des minorités politiques Lyonnais', in C. Peyrard (ed.), *Minorités politiques en Révolution (1789–1799)* (Aix-en-Provence: Publications de l'Université de Provence, 2007), 181–96.
———. (ed.). *1793*. Lyon: Presse universitaire de Lyon, 1993.
Benoît, B. and R. Saussac. *Guide Historique de la Révolution à Lyon, 1789–1799*. Lyon: Éditions de Trévoux, 1988.
Bernardin, É. *Jean-Marie Roland et le Ministère de l'Intérieur 1792–1793*. Paris: SÉR, 1964.
Biard, M. *Collot d'Herbois: Légendes noires et Révolution*. Lyon: Presses universitaires de Lyon, 1995.
———. *1793 Le siège de Lyon: Entre mythes et réalités*. Clermont-Ferrand: Lemme, 2013.
Biard, M., H. Leuwers, M. Linton, P. McPhee and T. Tackett. 'Analyser "la Terreur" dans l'historiographie Anglophone'. *Annales Historiques de la Révolution Française* 2 (2018), 141–65.
Bittard des Portes, R. *Contre la Terreur: L'insurrection de Lyon en 1793: Le siege, l'expédition du Forez, d'après des documents inédits*. Paris: E. Paul, 1906.
Blanning, T.C.W. *The Origins of the French Revolutionary Wars*. London: Longman Group, 1986.
———. *The French Revolutionary Wars 1787–1802*. London: Hodder Headline, 1996.
Bordes, P. 'L'Invention d'une iconographe Révolutionnaire: Joseph Chinard (1756–1813)'. *Studi neoclassici* 4 (2016), 41–50.
Campbell, P.R. *The Origins of the French Revolution*. Hampshire: Palgrave MacMillan, 2006.
Campbell, P.R, T.E. Kaiser and M. Linton. *Conspiracy in the French Revolution*. Manchester University Press, 2007.
Caradonna, J.L. *The Enlightenment in Practice: Academic Prize Contests and Intellectual Culture in France 1670–1794*. Ithaca: Cornell University Press, 2012.
Champdor, A. *Lyon pendant la Révolution 1789–1793*. Lyon: Librairie Albert Guillot, 1983.
Chopelin, P. *Ville patriote et ville martyre: Lyon, l'église et la Révolution, 1788–1805*. Paris: Letouzey et Ané, 2010.
———. 'Un Cancer politique? Vies et morts des comités de surveillance de la ville de Lyon (1792–1795)', in D. Pingué et J.-P. Rothiot (eds), *Les Comités de surveillance: D'une création citoyenne à une institution révolutionnaire* (Paris: Société des études Robespierristes, 2012), 170–97.
Coller, 'Turbans of Liberty: Revolutionary Emotions and Global Emotions', Conference talk, *Society of French Historical Studies*. 10 May 2018.
Combes, L. de. *Clubs révolutionnaires des Lyonnaises*. Trévoux: s.n., 1908.
Crook, M. *Toulon in War and Revolution*. Manchester: Manchester University Press, 1991.

_____. *Elections in the French Revolution: An Apprenticeship in Democracy, 1789–1799.* Cambridge and NY: Cambridge University Press, 1996.

_____. 'Les Révoltes "fédéralistes" et les origines de la Terreur en 1793', in M. Biard and H. Leuwers (eds), *Visages de la Terreur* (Paris: Armand Colin, 2014), 15–26.

Crubaugh, A. *Balancing the Scales of Justice: Local Courts and Rural Society in Southwest France, 1750–1800.* University Park, PA: The Pennsylvania State University Press, 2000.

_____. 'The Peasant at the Gates of Heaven: La Feuille Villageoise, Religion, and the French Revolution, 1790–1791'. *Journal of the Illinois State Historical Society* 38 (2010).

Darnton, R. *The Kiss of Lamourette: Reflections in Cultural History.* New York and London: W.W. Norton & Co., 1990.

Dawson, P. *Provincial Magistrates and Revolutionary Politics in France: 1789–1795.* Cambridge, MA: Harvard University Press, 1972.

Doyle, W. *The French Revolution: A Very Short Introduction.* Oxford: Oxford University Press, 2001.

_____. *The Oxford History of the French Revolution.* Oxford and New York: Oxford University Press, 2002.

Dumas, J.-B. *Histoire de l'Académie des sciences, belles-lettres et arts de Lyon.* Lyon: s.n., 1839.

Dupré-Latour, L. 'Historical Note on the Poleymieux House'. *Bulletin de la Société des Amis d'André-Marie Ampère* 56 (Oct. 2012), 58.

Edelstein, M. 'La Feuille Villageoise, the Revolutionary Press, and the Question of Rural Political Participation'. *French Historical Studies* 7 (1971), 175–203.

_____. *The French Revolution and the Birth of Electoral Democracy.* Farnham and Burlington, UT: Ashgate, 2014.

Edmonds, W. 'A Study in Popular Anti-Jacobinism: The Career of Denis Monnet'. *French Historical Studies* 13 (1983), 215–51.

_____. 'The Rise and Fall of Popular Democracy in Lyon 1789–1795'. *Bulletin of the John Rylands Library* (1984), 408–49.

_____. *Jacobinism and the Revolt of Lyon, 1789–1793.* New York: Oxford University Press, 1990.

Ellis, D. *Literary Lives: Biography and the Search for Understanding.* London: Routledge, 2001.

Elster, J. *Closing the Books: Transitional Justice in Historical Perspective.* Cambridge: Cambridge University Press, 2004.

Esdaille, C.J. *The Wars of the French Revolution: 1792–1801.* London and New York: Routledge, 2019.

Etèvenaux, J. *Lyon 1793: Révolte et écrasement.* Lyon: Éditions Horvath, 1993.

Eynard, G. *Joseph Chalier: Bourreau ou martyr, 1747–1793.* Lyon: Éd. lyonnaises d'art et d'histoire, 1987.

Fayard, E. *Histoire des tribunaux révolutionnaires de Lyon et de Feurs.* Lyon: H. George, 1888.

Feilla, C. *The Sentimental Theater of the French Revolution.* Farnham and Burlington, VT: Ashgate, 2013.

Feyel, G. *Dictionnaire de la presse française pendant la Révolution 1789–1799.* Paris: Centre International d'étude du XVIIIe siècle, 2005.

Forrest, A. *Society and Politics in Revolutionary Bordeaux.* Oxford: Clarendon Press, 1975.

Francesco, A. de. 'Les Rapports entre administrateurs et administrés à Lyon dans les premières années révolutionnaires (1789–1793)', in B. Benoît (ed.), *Ville et Révolution française: Actes du colloque international, Lyon, Mars 1993* (Lyon: Presses universitaires de Lyon, 1994), 217–28.

Furet, F. 'Review of *Jacobinism and the Revolt of Lyon, 1789–1793*, by W.D. Edmonds'. *The Journal of Modern History* 64 (1992), 136–38.

Garden, M. 'La Révolution et l'Empire', in A. Latreille (ed.), *Histoire de Lyon et du Lyonnais* (Toulouse: Privat, 1975), 255–78.

———. *Lyon et les Lyonnais au 18e siècle*. Paris: Les Belles Lettres, 1975.

Garrioch, D. *Neighbourhood and Community in Paris, 1740–1790*. Cambridge: Cambridge University Press, 1986.

———. 'The Everyday Lives of Parisian Women and the October Days of 1789'. *Social History* 24(3) (Oct. 1999), 231–49.

Godfrey, J.L. *Revolutionary Justice: A Study of the Organization, Personnel, and Procedure of the Paris Tribunal 1793–1795*. Chapel Hill, NC: University of North Carolina Press, 1951.

Gueniffey, P. *La politique de la Terreur: Essai sur la violence révolutionnaire 1789–1794*. Paris, 2000.

Habermas, J. *The Structural Transformation of the Public Sphere*. Cambridge, MA, 1989.

Halperin, J.L. 'Justice', in A. Soboul (ed.), *Dictionnaire Historique de La Révolution Française* (Paris: Presses universitaires de France, 1989), 610–14.

Hanson, P.R. *The Jacobin Republic Under Fire: The Federalist Revolt in the French Revolution*. University Park, PA: Pennsylvania State University Press, 2003.

Heller, H. *The Bourgeois Revolution in France, 1789–1815*. Oxford: Berghahn Books, 2006.

Hemmings, F.W.J. *Theatre and State in France, 1760–1905*. Cambridge: Cambridge University Press, 1994.

Herriot, E. *Lyon n'est Plus*, 4 vols. Paris: Hachette, 1937–1940.

Heylen, R. *Translation, Poetics, and the Stage: Six French Hamlets*. London: Routledge, 1993.

Higonnet, P. *Goodness Beyond Virtue: Jacobins during the French Revolution*. Cambridge, MA: Harvard University Press, 1998.

Hoffman, J.R. *André-Marie Ampère*. Oxford: Blackwell, 1995.

Hufton, O. *Women and the Limits of Citizenship in the French Revolution*. Toronto: University of Toronto Press, 1994.

Hunt, L. 'The Experience of Revolution'. *French Historical Studies* 32 (2009), 671–72.

Johnson, J.P. 'Jean-Jacques Ampère and the Translation of Artaxerxes', in P.-Y. Beaurepaire, P. Bourdin and C. Wolff (eds.), *Moving Scenes: The Circulation of Music and Theatre in Europe, 1700–1815* (Oxford: Voltaire Foundation, 2018), 289–304.

———. '"The Law Must Never Be a Game for Fair and Upright Men in a Republic": Revolutionary Justice in Lyon 1792–3'. *Oxford Journal of French History* 32(2) (2018), 182–202.

Joly, A. *Un Mystique Lyonnais et les secrets de la franc-maçonnerie: Jean-Baptiste Willermoz 1730–1824*. Paris: Éd. Télètos, 1938.

Kates, G. *The 'Cercle Social', the Girondins, and the French Revolution*. Princeton, NJ: Princeton University Press, 1985.

———. (ed.). *The French Revolution: Recent Debates and New Controversies*. London: Routledge, 1998.

Kennedy, E. *A Cultural History of the French Revolution*. New Haven, CT and London: Yale University Press, 1989.

Kennedy, M. *The Jacobin Clubs in the French Revolution: The First Years*. Princeton, NJ: Princeton University Press, 1982.

———. *The Jacobin Clubs in the French Revolution: The Middle Years*. Princeton, NJ: Princeton University Press, 1988.

———. *The Jacobin Clubs in the French Revolution, 1793–1795*. New York: Berghahn Books, 2000.

Koi, T. 'Les Chalier et les sans-culottes Lyonnais'. Thèse de troisième cycle, Université Lyon 2, 1974.

_____. 'Réflexion sur la Révolution Français à Lyon', La Révolution et nous – Blogue de historien Claude Guillon. Retrieved 1 August 2018 from https://unsansculotte.wordpress.com/2018.
Kradraoui, C. *Au Théâtre à Lyon de 1789 à 1799*. Lyon: Éditions lyonnaises d'art et d'histoire, 1988.
Kuscinski, A. *Dictionnaire des Conventionnels*. Paris: Librairie Rieder, 1916.
Landes, J. *Women and the Public Sphere in the Age of the French Revolution*. Ithaca, NY: Cornell University Press, 1988.
Lemay, E.H. *Dictionnaire des constituants, 1789–1791*. Paris: Universitas, 1991.
Lemay, E.H. and A. Patrick. *Revolutionaries at Work: The Constituent Assembly 1789–1791*. Oxford, 1996.
Levy, D.G. and H.B. Applewhite (ed.). *Women and Politics in the Age of the Democratic Revolution*. Ann Arbor: University of Michigan Press, 1990.
Linton, M. *Choosing Terror: Virtue, Friendship and Authenticity in the French Revolution*. Oxford: Oxford University Press, 2013.
Longfellow, D.L. 'Silk Weavers and the Social Struggle in Lyon during the French Revolution, 1789–94'. *French Historical Studies* 12 (1981), 1–40.
Mansfield, P. 'The Management of Terror in Montgnard Lyon, Year II'. *European History Quarterly* 20 (1990), 467.
Marion, B. 'Le Collège de la Trinité: Histoire d'une Bibliotheque de son Cabinet de Curiosités'. Mémoire de Masters, Université de Lyon, 2014.
Marion, P. *Le genial bonhomme Ampère*. Lyon: Mémoire des Arts, 1999.
McManners, J. *The French Revolution and the Church*. London: SPCK, 1969.
McPhee, P. (ed.). *The French Revolution 1789–1799*. New York: Oxford University Press, 2002.
_____. *Robespierre: A Revolutionary Life*. New Haven, CT: Yale University Press, 2012.
_____. *A Companion to the French Revolution*. Chichester: Wiley Blackwell Publishing, 2015.
_____. *Liberty or Death: The French Revolution*. New Haven, CT and London: Yale University Press, 2016.
Mornet, D. *French Thought in the Eighteenth Century*. Hamden, CT: Archon Books, 1969.
Noyer-Ohlmann, N. *Rue Juiverie; rue aux blazons, rue des artisans d'art*. Lyon: Broché, 1995.
Oates, J.L. 'The Influence of the French Revolution on Legal and Judicial Reform'. MA Dissertation, Simon Fraser University, Feb. 1980.
Palmer, R.R. *The Improvement of Humanity: Education and the French Revolution*. Princeton, NJ: Princeton University Press, 1985.
Parker, A.H., *Writing the Revolution: A French Woman's History in Letters*. Oxford: Oxford University Press, 2013.
Patrick, A. *The Men of the First French Republic: Political Alignments in the National Convention of 1792*. Baltimore, MD: Johns Hopkins University Press, 1972.
Perrat, C. 'Un Lyonnais à la veille de la Révolution: "Pierre Poivre, Ancien Intendant des Iles de France et de Bourbon"'. *Annuaire-Bulletin de la Société de l'histoire de France* 74(1) (1938), 99–116.
Plumtre, A. 'A Narrative of a Three Year's Residence in France', Vols 5–7 (1810) in S. Bending and S. Bygrave (eds), *Women's Travel Writings in Revolutionary France* London: Routledge, 2008.
Raverat, A. *Lyon sous la Révolution, suivi de la liste des condamnés à mort*. Lyon: La Découvrance, 2006.
Reddy, W. *The Navigation of Feeling: A Framework for the History of Emotions*. Cambridge: Cambridge University Press, 2001.

Reynolds, S. *Marriage and Revolution: Monsieur and Madame Roland*. Oxford: Oxford University Press, 2012.
Riffaterre, C. *Le Mouvement antijacobin et antiparisien à Lyon et dans le Rhône-et-Loire en 1793, 29 mai-15 août*, 2 vols. Lyon: A. Rey, 1912, 1928.
Ronald, S. *A Genealogy of Terror in Eighteenth Century France*. Chicago and London: University of Chicago Press, 2018.
Rudé, G. *The Crowd in the French Revolution*. Oxford: Oxford University Press, 1959.
Scott, W. *Terror and Repression in Revolutionary Marseilles*. London: The MacMillan Press, 1973.
Shapiro, G. and J. Markoff. *Revolutionary Demands: A Content Analysis of the Cahiers de Doléances of 1789*. Stanford, CA: Stanford University Press, 1998.
Simien, C. *Les Massacres de septembre 1792 à Lyon*. Lyon: Aléas, 2011.
Soboul, A. *The French Revolution, 1787–1799; from the Storming of the Bastille to Napoleon*. New York: Random House, 1975.
_____. (ed.). *Dictionnaire historique de la Révolution Française*. Paris: PUF, 1989.
Steinberg, R. 'Transitional Justice in the Age of the French Revolution'. *The International Journal of Transitional Justice* 7 (2013), 267–85.
Storobinski, J. *Jean-Jacques Rousseau: La transparence et l'obstacle*. Paris, 1971.
Tackett, T. *Becoming a Revolutionary: The Deputies of the French National Assembly and the Emergence of a Revolutionary Culture (1789–1790)*. Princeton, NJ: Princeton University Press, 1996.
_____. *When the King Took Flight*. Cambridge, MA: Harvard University Press, 2003.
_____. *The Coming of the Terror in the French Revolution*. Cambridge, MA: The Belknap Press of Harvard University Press, 2015.
Taylor, K.F. *In the Theater of Criminal Justice: The Palais de Justice in Second Empire Paris*. Princeton, NJ: Princeton University Press, 1993.
_____. 'Geometries of Power: Royal, Revolutionary and Post-Revolutionary French Courtrooms'. *Journal of the Society of Architectural Historians* 72 (2013), 434–74.
Thomas, C. and D.F. Bell. 'Terror in Lyon'. *SubStance* 27 (1998), 33–42.
Thomas, D.A. *Aesthetics of Opera in the Ancien Régime, 1647–1785*. New York: Cambridge University Press, 2002.
Trénard, L. 'La Crise sociale Lyonnaise à la veille de la Révolution'. *Revue d'histoire moderne et contemporaine* 2 (1955), 5–45.
_____. 'Un Notable Lyonnais pendant la crise Révolutionnaire: Pierre-Toussaint Dechazelle'. *Revue d'histoire moderne et contemporaine* 3 (July 1958).
_____. 'Lyon, Capitale d'une "seconde Vendée"?' in *Actes du 112e Congrès National des Sociétés Savantes* (Lyon: Éditions du CTHS, 1987).
_____. *La Révolution Française dans la région Rhône-Alpes*. Paris: Perrin, 1992.
Uglow, N. *The Historian's Two Bodies: The Reception of Historical Texts in France, 1701–1790*. Aldershot: Ashgate, 2001.
Van Damme, S. 'Sociabilité et culture urbaines'. *Histoire de l'éducation* 90 (2001), 79–100.
Varnet, F.A. *Géographie du département du Rhône*. Lyon: Gallica, 1897.
Viola, P. 'The Rites of Cannibalism and the French Revolution'. Retrieved December 2015 from www.library.vanderbilt.edu/Quaderno/Quaderno3/Q3.C10.Viola.
Wahl, M. 'Joseph Chalier: *Étude sur la Révolution* Française à Lyon'. *Revue Historique* 34 (1887), 1–30.
_____. *Les Premières années de la Révolution à Lyon 1788–1792*. Paris: Armand Colin, 1894.
Wahnich, S. *Des Objets qui racontent l'histoire: Collections du Musée Gadagne*. Lyon: ÉMCC, 2003.

Walzer, M. (ed.). *Regicide and Revolution: Speeches at the Trial of Louis XVI*. New York: Columbia University Press, 1992.
Wartelle, F. 'Chalier, Joseph/les "Chaliers"', in A. Soboul (ed.), *Dictionnaire Historique de La Révolution Française* (Paris: Presses Universitaires de France, 1989), 200–1.
Woloch, I. *The New Regime Transformation of the French Civic Order, 1789–1820*. New York: W.W. Norton and Co., 1994.

INDEX

Académie Royale des Sciences, Belles-Lettres et Arts de Lyon (Academy of Lyon) 17, 18, 33, 122
Achard, Robert, 132, 155, 161–63, 166, 184–85
Acte d'accusation (Accusations), 179, 193
active citizens, 48, 57, 84, 87, 88, 203
Affiches de Lyon, 53
Albigny-sur-Saône, 27
Albitte, 161
Americas, 18
Ampère, André-Marie, 1, 30–31, 33, 42
Ampère, Jean-Jacques, 1–2, 5, 14, 21, 25–27, 30–33, 47, 55, 58–59, 87–93, 102–3, 109, 110, 117, 123, 133, 135–7, 142, 146–7, 149–55, 176–80, 182–3, 190–94, 199–201, 206
  trial of, 192–4
anarchists, 160, 19, 171, 181, 182
anarchy, 129, 170, 171, 184, 198
Ancien régime (Former or Old Regime), 37, 48, 49, 52, 59, 66, 68, 74, 76, 84, 90, 95, 109, 184, 203
anti-Jacobin(s), 142, 145, 151, 152, 153, 163, 164–65, 166, 169, 171, 183
Appeal to the people, 130
arsenal, 41, 48, 141, 163, 165, 168, 181, 185
Archimbaud, Claudine Henriette, 190
Arcis, 16
aristocrat(s), 1, 15, 56, 58, 71, 78, 107, 120, 131, 135, 138–39, 141, 150, 159, 160, 164, 177, 181, 190
Armée des Alpes, 164–65, 168, 169, 185

Arnaud-Tison, 120
Artaxerxes, 102, 176
assignat, 53, 69, 92, 100, 105, 137, 190, 203
August decrees (4 August 1789), 65
Austria, 70, 106, 115
Austrian(s), 106, 119, 159
  alliance, 106
  forces, 107

Baille, 151
Basire, 152
Barrollière, Marite de la, 25
Barry (citoyenne), 155
Bastille, 41–2, 48, 49
Batelière, 13
Beccaria, Cesare, 103
Belgium, 119
Belle-Cordière, 164
Bellecour (Place), 3, 13, 109, 120, 133, 136, 161, 175
Bémani, 168
Berthet, 91
Berthier, Abbé, 70, 92
Bertrand (mayor), 152, 164–65, 180
Besson (citoyenne), 147
Biens nationaux, 57, 69, 203
Billiemas, François, 50, 68, 70, 84, 86, 90, 91, 92, 116, 123, 178, 198
Binard, Jean-Joseph, 191
Birotteau, 171, 184
Boeuf (baker), 123
Boivin (*juge de paix*), 182
Bonaparte, Napoleon, 18

Bonnard, Benoît, 105, 135–36
Bonnet, 93
Bon-Rencontre, 168
Bordeaux, 171
bread
   affordability of, 50, 83, 90, 94, 109, 181–20, 132, 161
   quality of, 123, 160
   shortages, 48
   supplies, 118
Brissot, Jacques-Pierre, 25, 53, 75, 106, 130
Brissotin(s), 106
   ministry, 96
Brochet, (Pres.), 153
Brunet (*châtelain*), 28, 32, 57–58
Brunswick (Duke of), 107, 114, 159
Buisson (*Curé*), 69
Bureaux de paix (office of the JP), 85, 87
Bussay, 148

Caen, 171
Cahiers de doléances, 37, 38–41, 66, 203
Candy, Barthelemi, 162–3
Cannibalism, 73
cannon, 109, 123, 144n, 163, 165, 181, 184, 190, 195, 202
canton, 20, 47, 67–69, 76, 80n, 86–89, 91, 95, 98n, 105, 134, 151, 161, 178, 182, 186n, 203, 204
canuts, 15
Capet, 133–4
Carte(s) de civisme, 148, 160
Carrier, Louis-Nicolas, 125n, 137, 142, 169
Carron, Claude, 84
   family, Poleymieux, 36n
Carteron, Jean-Baptiste, 138, 180, 187n
Casati, 136, 142
Central Club, 50, 52, 100, 107, 108, 117, 120, 122–23, 131–3, 137, 140, 148, 152, 160, 161, 163, 203
   pillage of, 141, 142, 148–152
Cercle social, 122
Chalier-Jacobins, 52, 132, 140, 160, 184, 203

Chalier, Joseph, 2, 5, 14, 52, 66, 68, 84, 100, 103–10, 111n, 116, 117, 119, 120–3, 131, 132–33, 132, 138–42, 152, 154, 156n, 159, 161, 165, 176, 177, 184, 185, 186n, 193, 194, 198, 199, 200–1, 206
   death of, 188, 200
   trial of, 178–80, 188, 189
Chalon, Jean-François, 84
Champagneux, Luc-Antoine, 52, 66, 68, 85, 90, 105, 110
   Courrier and, 53–54, 61n, 79n
Chanoines-comtes, 20
Chasselay, 25, 58, 71, 75
Chasset, Antoine, 119, 171, 172n, 184
Chénier, Marie-Joseph, 95
church(es), 1, 13, 20, 26, 29, 32, 70, 72, 94, 117, 137, 151
   Catholic, 20–21, 40, 43, 54, 55, 69
   Constitutional, 69, 70, 93, 117
   hierarchies, 43, 53, 57, 68–69, 94
   non-conforming, 93–94
   property–selling of, 68–69, 94, 117, 203
   reformed, 54, 55, 69
   refractory, 94
   See also Cordeliers, Poleymieux, Saint-Nizier
civic
   ceremony, 133, 175
   duties, 84, 202
   rights, 67
   virtues, 95, 155
Civil Constitution of the Clergy, 69–70, 93
civil justice, 67, 85, 88, 90, 91
civil war, 2, 80n, 110, 160, 166, 171, 200
Claristes, 94
clergy, 24, 37, 41–42, 44, 55, 69
   constitutional, 54, 69–70, 92, 93, 203
   refractory or non-juring, 70, 85, 93, 107, 115, 198
Club(s), 44, 50, 83, 84, 94, 96, 118, 131, 162, 164
   de Bonnes, 96
   de Concert, 75
   Jacobin, 50, 83, 89, 118
   patriot, 50

popular, 50, 84, 97
political, 52
quartier, 84, 122, 132, 140, 145, 152, 144n, 160, 164
revolutionary, 58
sectional, 50, 52, 78, 109, 140–41, 151, 160, 162, 163, 165, 168, 176
See also Central Club
Code Pénal, 77, 85–86, 97, 100, 111, 117, 130, 147, 182–83, 198–9
Coindre, Jean-Jacques, 168, 175, 183
Collège de la Trinité, 16, 33, 53–54
Comité(s)
de surveillance (anti-Jacobin), 171, 175, 178
de surveillance (républicaine), 194
Jacobin, 137–9, 148, 152–4, 156n, 160, 162–64, 166, 168, 182, 185, 187n, 194, 195
de sûreté Générale, 148
du salut public, 156n, 191
Commercial Tribunal, 96
Commissaire National, 110, 132, 133, 141, 147, 178, 199, 206
Commissaires, 72, 81n, 131, 145, 150, 152, 153–54, 159–62, 164, 184, 203
Commission Populaire, 169, 176
Jacobin, 191
Committee of Twelve, 3
Compagnon, 15
Concours (competitions), 17
Condorcet, Marquis de, 129, 130
conspiracy, 4, 5, 105, 109, 114, 120, 139, 146, 181, 192, 193, 200
aristocratic, 56, 57
Jacobin, 181–82, 192, 199
royalist, 70, 94
conspirators, 145, 152, 153, 160, 179, 182, 191
consular
leaders, 93
officials, 42
consulate, 19, 42–43, 48, 20
consuls, 19, 38, 43, 48, 108, 203
contingency (laws), 4
Cordeliers (Church of), 20, 94
Monastery, 69

Couderc, 76
counter-revolutionaries, 58, 114–15, 137, 153, 158, 159, 160, 177, 179, 190, 193–94
Courrier de Lyon, 52–54
Couthon, Georges, 3, 5, 184, 187n, 188, 191, 200
Cozon, Jerôme, 85, 105, 123, 149, 150, 177–8
Croix-Rousse, 13, 164–65
Curé(s), 20, 26, 40, 54–55, 69–70, 86, 92, 145, 151, 203. See also clergy
Cusset, 119, 131, 206
Customs
barriers, 42, 49, 66, 204
duties, 18, 52

Declaration of the Rights of Man and the Citizen, 43, 65
Delandine, Antoine-François, 18
Département du Rhône (et Loire), (Department of the Rhone), 47, 107, 108
Departmental
authorities, 68, 78, 94, 96, 107, 108, 132, 138, 139, 163, 165, 166, 168, 177 (see also directory)
courts, 76, 105
Desmoulins, Camille, 108
Desutières-Sarcey, 14, 27
Dîme, 26, 29, 40, 54, 184
director of the jury, 76, 134, 136, 149, 154, 177, 178, 180
Directory (departmental), 81n, 93, 94
Dodieu, Antoine-Marie (Manlius), 109–110, 120, 121, 123, 131, 132, 134–7, 141, 146–50, 153–55, 156n, 157n, 161, 177–78, 198, 206
Doppet, General, 190–1
Dorfeuille, Philippe-Antoine, 191–92
Dubessey (Judge), 146–8, 156n, 161
Dubois, Louis, 180
Dubois-Crancé, 161, 164, 168, 173n, 177
Du Bouchet, 131
Dumontet, Guillin, 31, 57–58, 71, 74
Dumouriez (General) 159, 169, 195

Dumouriez, Les, 196
Duperret, 182
Duport, Adrien, 59
Dupuy, 131

Ecclesiastic(s), 70, 145, 162
Echerolles, Alexandrine des, 108, 116–17, 118, 144n, 158, 159, 190
Eden Treaty (1784), 15
émigrés, 85, 100, 106–7, 115, 139, 153, 159, 160, 162, 190, 198, 203
Émile, 25, 135
emotion(s), 4–5, 42, 43, 107, 158, 199
Encyclopaédie, 1, 16
enthusiasm(s), 1, 2, 4, 5, 38, 48, 50, 68, 107, 118, 182
en permanence, 140, 148, 163. *See also* in permanence
Estates-General, 39–41, 44n, 59, 203, 204, 205
Eustache (of Trévoux), 65, 75

Factionalism, 5, 107, 130, 199
Fain, 139, 140–1, 144n, 153, 154, 156n, 156n1, 169, 173n
Fanaticism, 2, 4–5, 139, 192, 198–200
fanatics, 94, 192, 195
Federalism, 2–3, 169–171
Federalist, 169
  cities, 170
  revolt, 3, 6n, 6n1, 169, 170–71
Fernex Judge, 123, 138, 147–8, 161
Feudal system, 43, 55, 57, 184
  abuses, 24, 40
  constraints, 25–6, 44, 71
  court, 31
  landlords, 26
  See also *seigneurs*
Feuillant(s), 75, 84, 106
  club, 75, 83
Feuille Villageoise, 54–5
Filiot, 117
Fillion, Pierre, 123, 135, 141, 150, 182, 188
Fillon, Didier, 181, 185
Fiscal
  crises, 37–38

Officers – *procureurs*, 26, 28, 204
  reforms, 44n, 66–68, 92
fixed prices, 40, 94, 109, 118, 120
food crisis, 37–38, 42, 52, 90, 122, 132, 191, 195
  riots, 93, 117
Foret, Jean-Baptiste, 181
Freemasonry (movement), 17, 56, 122
Freemasons, 44, 55
Fouché, Joseph, 194
fusillades, 202

Gaillard, Judge, 123, 133, 135, 150, 154, 156n, 161, 168, 177, 179, 185, 187n
Garin, Judge, 28
Gauthier, 161, 164–8
Germany, 13, 119
Gilibert, Jean-Emanuelle, 17, 152, 169, 171, 206
Girondin(s), 52, 129, 130, 140, 155, 169–71, 184
Goudard, Pierre, 75–76
Grandmaison, 110, 113n
Grand Théâtre, 95
Gravier, 135, 161, 185
Greffier, 90, 92, 148
Grenoble, 164, 165, 168
Grétry, André, 95, 96
grievances, 18, 20, 38, 40, 41, 66, 78, 203
Gruerie, 28, 31, 33, 58
Guillin. *See* Dumontet
guillotine, 1, 120, 129, 135, 138, 139, 144n, 181, 184, 185, 188, 194, 196, 200–202

Habermas, Jürgen, 16
habituation (to violence), 116
Halle aux Blés, 87, 88, 134, 186n
hanging, 131, 202
Harpics, 13
Herbois, Collot d', 96, 187n, 194
Hidins (Rousseau), 110, 112n, 121, 132–33, 137, 141, 143n1, 143n2, 147, 148, 153–54, 156n, 178, 198, 199, 206
  Veuve, 153, 154, 155
hoarders. *See* speculators

Hôtel de Fléchères, 16, 78
Hôtel de Ville, 13, 48, 88, 120, 139, 141, 148, 165, 166, 181, 182
Imbert-Colomès, Jacones, 19, 48, 56–58, 206
in permanence, 141, 151, 180, 185. See also *en permanence*
Jacob, Jean-Claude-Etienne, 123
Jacobin(s), 17, 44, 55, 96, 109, 110, 117, 122, 123, 132, 140, 154, 162, 165, 166, 177, 180, 184
   club, 49, 50, 75, 78, 83, 106, 111n, 118, 124n, 204
   charge of murder against, 181–82
Jesuit
   college, 54
   priests, 21, 31, 33
   teachers, 16, 21
Journal de Lyon, 53, 137, 139, 141, 142, 144n, 147, 152–54, 169, 181, 183
Jolyclerc, François, 86, 92, 145, 151, 168–69
Judicial
   feud, 198–99
   office, 2, 5, 14, 84, 101, 102, 121, 123, 134, 136, 147, 160
   officers, 2, 14, 24, 25, 68, 70, 73, 96, 103, 117, 133, 135, 149, 155, 166, 177, 199
   reform, 18, 40, 47, 50, 53, 54, 59, 65–68, 75, 76, 92–93, 97, 100, 101, 103
judges, 2–3, 5, 65–66, 73, 76–77, 78, 84, 85, 92, 97, 100–102, 105, 108, 109, 111, 117, 121–23, 129, 131–36, 140, 141, 142, 145–50, 153, 154, 155, 161, 162, 166, 177–79, 181, 182, 185, 191–93, 198–99, 200. See also magistrates
Juge(s) de paix (Justices of the Peace), 2, 3, 40, 53, 54, 67, 75, 76, 79n, 80n, 85, 86, 87–93, 97, 100, 102, 103, 105, 106–7, 117, 123, 133–35, 137, 142, 146–48, 149, 150–51, 153, 161, 166, 177–78, 182, 186n, 187n, 188, 190, 191, 194, 204
Julliard (Joseph), 95, 188

Jullien, Rosalie, 114, 116, 124n, 200
Juré
   d'accusation, 76, 87, 91, 178
   de jugement, 76, 91, 147
juries, 54, 59, 76, 85, 97, 147, 185
jury, 85, 86, 91, 92, 100, 134, 135, 136, 137, 146, 147, 154, 155, 157n, 178, 180, 188, 196n
justice, 2, 5, 14, 16, 24, 40, 53, 54, 59, 66, 67, 68, 73, 74, 76, 80n, 85, 88, 89, 91, 92, 97, 101, 102, 103, 105, 109, 116, 130, 135, 145, 148, 149, 150, 151, 161, 163, 166, 178, 179, 183, 185, 191, 196, 198, 200
   civil, 28, 40–41, 47, 67, 73, 75, 85
   criminal, 35n, 41, 49, 59, 66, 76–78, 85, 91, 134
   seigneurial, 28, 35n, 40–41, 58, 59, 66, 73, 85, 90
justices, 78, 97, 200

king(s), 12, 19, 26, 28, 37, 38–41, 42, 44, 56, 66, 70–71, 78, 84, 85, 89, 101, 102, 105, 106, 107, 109, 110, 13n, 129, 136, 176, 203, 204
   execution of, 134, 153
   flight of, 71, 75, 84–5
   trial of, 129–33, 142n, 199, 200
kingdom, 20, 37, 40, 42
Koi, Takashi, 132, 176

La Croisette, 133, 152, 162, 206
Lafayette (General)
   defection, 107
L'Ange, François-Joseph, 68, 90, 93, 123, 132, 150, 153, 178, 198, 206
La Fabrique, 11, 20, 42, 43, 50
Lager, Antoine, 49
La Grande Côte, 152, 168
Lamourette, Adrien, 70, 107, 119, 136
Lanthenas, Adrien, 119, 131
Laukhard, Frédéric, 1–2, 6
Launay, Etienne, 146
Laussel, François-Auguste, 79n, 120, 123, 125n, 138, 153–54, 156n, 157n1, 157n2, 178
Legendre (*commissaire*), 152

Legislative Assembly, 84, 100, 106, 107, 108, 119, 130, 136
Le Patriote française, 53, 75
Le Peletier (club), 161–62
Les Chaliers. See Chalier-Jacobins
Lescot, 137
Le Surveillant, 76
liberty, 84, 94, 119, 133, 145, 151, 154, 158, 159, 166, 179, 180, 181, 190, 191, 192, 200
  tree of, 133, 175
Limonest, 25
Lindet, Robert, 168, 173n1, 173n2, 184
Linsolas, Abbé de, 70, 152
lit de justice, 101
Longwy, 114

Maître-ouvrier, 15, 132
Marat, Jean-Paul, 106, 108, 131, 169, 177
Marbeuf (Monsignor), 43, 57, 70
Marie-Antoinette, 15, 106
massacres
  29 May 1793, 185
  September 1792, 116–118, 122
  Tuileries, 129
maximum (prices), 118
Menu peuple, 20, 40, 42, 48–50, 59, 117, 120–21, 132, 165, 167, 204
merchant(s), 13, 14, 16, 17, 19, 38, 40, 42–44, 56, 90, 121, 131, 140, 162
Millanois, Jacques, 17, 44, 55, 75, 83
Mitraillade, 195–96
Modérées (Moderates), 17, 56, 159, 204
Monnet, Denis, 38, 159–60
Montagnard(s), 52, 97, 102, 119, 130, 162, 169, 173n, 184, 196n, 199
Montesquieu, 103
Montesquiou (General), 107, 116
Montfalcon, Jacques, 138, 181
Morand bridge, 13, 138
Morand, Jean-Antoine, 16, 144n
Morand, Jean-François, 146–47
Mont d'Or, 25, 32, 36n
  Marquis de, 37, 39, 43

municipality, 31, 57, 58, 66, 68, 70, 75, 84, 89, 90, 92, 93, 94, 97, 99n, 105, 107, 108, 109, 115, 118, 119, 120–23, 125n, 133, 145, 161, 182, 191
  Jacobin, 132, 139, 140, 144, 148, 152, 154, 162, 164–65, 167, 176, 180–81, 188, 199
  provisional, 168–69, 176–77, 179, 182, 183–85, 189
  and violence against priests, 94
  and women's demands, 118

National Assembly, 41, 42, 44, 53, 57, 67, 71, 75
National Constituent Assembly (NCA), 43, 44, 47, 55, 59, 67, 68, 70, 75, 78, 84, 85, 87
National Convention, 5, 31, 118–120, 129, 130–31, 135, 148, 151, 152, 158–59, 161, 162, 166, 168–171, 176–77, 179, 188, 189, 191, 193, 194, 203
National Guard, 47, 48, 65, 68, 70, 94, 95, 107, 110, 11, 115, 116, 120, 151, 164, 188, 191
  and Poleymieux massacre, 71–72, 75, 78
  and uprising of 29 May, 165, 181, 182
Négociants, 13, 14–16, 17, 22n, 48, 132, 169, 204
Neuville-sur-Saône, 25, 28, 73
Nioche, 161, 164–166, 168
Nivière-Chol, Antoine, 66, 79n, 115, 19, 123, 133, 144n, 147, 148, 162, 165, 206
  and Mayoral election, 139–142, 152
nobility, 19, 37
nobles, 20, 24, 37, 39, 42, 44, 56, 57, 84, 176
notables, 19, 38, 43, 58, 65, 68, 84, 88, 138, 181

obsession, 2, 5, 160
Octrois
  barriers, 40, 49
  Roland and, 96, 121
  taxes, 52–3, 68, 80n, 204

Opéra-comique, 95
Oratorians, 31
outlaws, 85

Palerne de Savy, Fleury-Zacharie-Simon, 17, 48, 139
Parlements, 59, 204
patriot(s), 43, 48, 55, 56, 65–66, 75, 78, 85, 96, 132, 150, 158, 159, 164, 166, 188, 191, 193–94, 204
peasants, 26, 29, 33, 39, 41, 54, 71, 79n
Penal code, 198. See also *Code Pénal*
Perisse-Duluc, Jean-André, 36n, 44, 55, 75, 87, 98n, 206
Perret. Jean-François, 119
Perrin-Précy (Count), 176, 191
Perris, Françoise, 185
Piedmont-Sardinia, 13, 119
Pierre-Scize, 48, 60n, 115, 139
Pillnitz Declaration, 106
Plain (*plaine*), 130, 184
Plumtre, Anne, 11, 21n
Pointe, Noel, 119, 131
Poivre, Pierre, 25
Poleymieux, 6n, 21, 24–8, 32–3, 38, 47, 55, 57, 58, 65, 69, 71, 73, 75, 78, 87, 88, 90, 98n, 102, 103, 116
 castle, 3–2, 58
 Church of, 32, 55–6, 71–72
Poleymoriots, 33, 57, 71, 78
Police Correctionelle, 76, 92, 147, 151, 177, 176, 183, 184. See also *Tribunal correctionnel*
political power, 3, 117
 of people, 42
 of sections, 164
Pressavin, Jean-Baptiste, 31, 65, 68–69, 76, 79n, 80n, 85, 110, 119, 131, 178, 207
Primary assemblies, 47, 168, 176, 203
Procureur
 fiscal, 24, 28, 31–2
 Lyon, 58, 65, 79n, 85, 90, 105, 110, 119, 123, 148, 151, 154, 157n, 204
 syndic, 57
Provincial assemblies, 38

Prussia, 106, 114
Prussian(s), 1, 83, 114
 army, 118–119
public
 agitation, 134
 education, 40
 interest, 66, 76, 161
 life, 68
 man, 102, 154
 office, 84, 182
 opinion, 16, 152
 roles, 134
 spaces, 16–17, 53, 95
 sphere, 16, 39, 147

quartiers, 19, 88, 140, 165, 176, 204
queen. See *Marie-Antoinette*

Raynal, Guillaume, 18
refractories, 70, 94, 97, 106–107, 137, 160
refractory (clergy, priests), 70, 92–94, 100, 106–108, 114, 115, 137, 139, 152, 198, 204
regeneration, 47, 50, 55, 103
regenerate(d), 55, 65, 76, 85, 100, 159, 192
Renard, Louis, 178, 180
Rentes (dues), 24
Représentants en mission (representatives-on-mission), 112n, 159, 188, 191, 194, 203. See also *commissaires*
Republic, 5, 75, 84, 118, 119, 130, 137, 153, 160, 166, 169, 170, 176, 178, 191, 198, 204
 Dutch, 159
 Jacobin, 3, 154
Revol, 138, 150, 155
Revolt (29 May 1793), 165–68, 170–71, 178, 188, 194
revolts (popular), 42. See also *federalist*
Revolutionary Tribunal, 132, 138, 161, 164, 185, 191, 198, 204. See also *Tribunal révolutionnaire*
Revoux, Jean-Pierre, 181
Riard-Beauvernais, 188

Rhône-et-Loire (*département*), 47, 106–107, 108, 119, 175, 185
Rhône river, 13, 25, 38, 61n, 88, 139, 189, 191
Roanne (prison of – *palais de*), 101, 115, 120, 146, 148, 191
Robespierre, Maximilien, 3, 106, 108, 116, 130, 155
Roch, Gilbert, 180, 193
Rogues, 134, 137, 184
Roland de la Platière, Jean-Marie, 17, 49–53, 58, 66, 68, 75, 84, 90, 96–97, 99n, 103, 105, 109, 110, 112n, 116, 119, 120–21, 125n1, 125n2, 133, 134
  Manon, 19, 53
Rolandin-Feuillantin, 110, 133
Rolandin(s), 52, 54, 66, 68, 83, 84, 89–90, 93, 108–110, 117, 119, 120, 121–23, 131, 133–36, 139, 145–46, 152, 155, 159–60, 164–65, 169, 182, 198–200, 204
Rousseau, Jean-Jacques, 25, 29–31, 39, 50, 103, 132
Roux, Claude, 33
Rovère, 152
Royalists, 115, 159, 160, 177, 189, 190
rule of law, 2–3, 77, 78, 93, 97, 103, 116, 134–36, 145, 146, 155, 166, 169, 182, 193, 198, 199–200
Russia, 13

Saint-Fargeau, Lepeletier de, 133
Saint-Joseph
  Church of, 94
  prison, 183
Saint Just, 129, 130
Saint-Nizier (Church of), 20, 70, 86, 88, 145, 151, 168
Saint-Vincent (*section* of), 168
Sans-culottes, 1, 20, 107, 110, 114, 116–17, 119, 121, 133, 136, 140, 152, 156n, 159–61, 162, 164, 169, 178, 183, 185, 195, 205. See also *menu peuple*
Saône river, 13, 16, 21, 25, 48, 88, 101, 183, 189, 191
Saulnier, Denis, 49

Sautemouche, Otto, 123, 183, 193
  murder of, 183
Savoy, 159, 161, 119
School, 16, 21, 26, 31, 33
  Veterinary Science, of, 17
Sections, 19, 47, 50, 133–34, 137, 140–41, 152, 160, 161, 163–5, 167–70, 172n, 173n, 176–78, 180, 183–84, 186n1, 186n2, 189, 192, 196n, 204, 205
Sectionnaires, 165–6, 170, 176, 180–81
Seigneurie (of Poleymieux), 31
Seigneurial
  domain, 24
  dues, 32
  system, 26
  See also justice
Seigneur(s), 29, 3–2, 55, 57, 66–67
  murder of, 71–6, 116–7
Sénéchaussée, 25, 37, 40–1, 67
sensibilité, 30, 96
Servan (*seigneur*), 28, 31
siege (of Lyon), 3, 156n, 173n, 186n1, 186n2, 187n, 189–194, 199
silk, 11–14, 93
  industry, 13–15, 17, 19, 21, 25, 41, 68, 75, 92, 93, 104, 132, 200
  merchants, 14
  weavers, 13, 52
  workers, 14–15, 19, 20, 38, 42, 43, 84, 88, 93, 109, 119, 121, 140, 159, 164, 178, 181
slavery, 18, 184
trade, 18, 32
social
  activists, 48, 89, 164, 205
  agitation, 38
Société d' agriculture, 50
Société des Amis de la Constitution (Friends of the Constitution), 49, 65
Société Philosophiques des sciences, 17
Soufflot, 13, 14, 207
Sourd, Charles, 155
sovereignty
  political, 43, 170
  popular, 129, 145, 180

speculators, 90, 132, 135
subsistence foods, 20, 40–42, 45n, 94, 118, 120, 122, 162
substitute(s), 67–8, 148, 151, 207
Sutières-Sarcey, Claude, 14
  family, 27
Swiss
  guards, 107, 114
  regiments, 48, 49
Switzerland, 119, 161

Tableaux de réforme, 150
taverns, 18, 21, 56, 122, 179
tax (barriers), 40, 42. See also *octrois*
taxation
  Populaire, 109, 1119, 120, 122, 134, 205
  reform, 39, 40
terror, 2–6, 116, 142, 144n, 171, 200, 202, 202n
  reign of, 3
theatre, 2, 11, 30, 33, 38, 54, 83, 95, 96, 97
Théâtre des Célestines, 86, 95–96, 115
Théâtre des Variétés, 95
Third Estate, 17, 18, 37, 39–43, 49, 50, 67, 205
Toulon, 171
Traboules, 14, 205
Tragédie patriotique, 95
Trévoux, 65, 75, 81n
Tribunal Correctionnel, 76, 78, 91, 92, 103, 117, 119, 123, 148, 150, 155, 182, 193, 194, 206
Tribunal Criminel, 76, 85, 91, 105, 111, 112n, 117, 120, 123, 135, 136, 146, 147, 153, 161, 182, 185, 188
Tribunal de conservation, 103, 206

Tribunal de district, 76, 77, 78, 103, 105, 108, 134, 136, 142, 146, 147, 155, 156n, 161, 177, 179, 182, 185
Tribunal révolutionnaire, 156n, 179, 181, 186n, 187n, 193, 194. *See also* Revolutionary Tribunal
Troncey, Benôite, 110
Turin, 56
  Charles, 180
Tyrant Capet, 133
tyrant(s), 133, 165

Valmy, 118, 159
Varennes, 71, 84
Vendée, 159–60, 162, 171, 192
Vienne, 135–36
Vieux Lyon, 13, 20
Ville Affranchie (Liberated City), 194
violence, 5, 30, 43, 52, 58, 75, 103, 111, 116, 133–34, 136, 151, 158, 159, 181, 183, 198
  anti-clerical, 93–94, 115
  popular, 2, 43, 50, 68, 78, 97, 116–17, 118, 123, 132, 183
Vingtrinier, Antoine, 66
Virtue, 95, 102, 103, 105, 129, 154–55, 159, 171, 182, 199, 200, 202n
Vitet, Louis, 17, 65, 83–84, 89, 109, 110, 115, 116, 119, 120, 122, 125n, 131, 136, 162, 165, 207
Voltaire, 5, 17, 31, 39, 66

Wheat, 26, 28, 34, 88, 94, 118, 120, 125n, 161
Willermoz, Jean-Baptiste, 17, 55
women, 13, 15, 18, 110, 117, 118, 123, 184, 185
  and the Church, 70
  and food riots, 118, 164
  market, 44, 118, 121